$\mathcal{EARLY}$
$\mathcal{JUDAISM}$

MARTIN S. JAFFEE
University of Washington

Prentice Hall, Upper Saddle River, New Jersey 07458

Library of Congress Cataloging-in-Publication Data

Jaffee, Martin S.
   Early Judaism : religious worlds of the first Judaic millennium /
Martin S. Jaffee.
     p.   cm.
   Includes index
   ISBN 0-13-519323-0
   1. Judaism—History—Post-exilic period, 586 B.C.–210 A.D.
2. Judaism—History—Talmudic period, 10–425. 3. Bible. O.T.—
Cannon. 4. Rabbinical literature—History and criticism.
5. Judaism—Doctrine.   I. Title.
BM176.J34   1997   96-12394
296'.09'01—dc20   CIP

Acquisitions editor: Angela Stone
Editorial assistant: Meg McGuane
Editorial/production supervision: Linda Pawelchak
Copyediting: Marlys Lehmann
Proofreading: Barbara Danzinger
Cover design: Jayne Conte
Photo editor: Lori Morris-Nantz
Photo research: Joelle Burrows
Manufacturing buyer: Lynn Pearlman

*This book was set in 10/12 Palatino by Americomp, Inc.
and was printed and bound by Courier Companies, Inc.
The cover was printed by Phoenix Color Corp.*

 © 1997 by Prentice-Hall, Inc.
Simon & Schuster / A Viacom Company
Upper Saddle River, New Jersey 07458

Printed in the United States of America
10 9 8 7 6 5 4 3 2 1

ISBN 0-13-519323-0

Prentice-Hall International (UK) Limited, *London*
Prentice-Hall of Australia Pty. Limited, *Sydney*
Prentice-Hall Canada Inc., *Toronto*
Prentice-Hall Hispanoamericana, S.A., *Mexico*
Prentice-Hall of India Private Limited, *New Delhi*
Prentice-Hall of Japan, Inc., *Tokyo*
Simon & Schuster Asia Pte. Ltd., *Singapore*
Editora Prentice-Hall do Brasil, Ltda., *Rio de Janeiro*

For

Leah bat Avraham Avinu

"Many are the heroic daughters,
but you surpass them all"
(Prov. 31:29)

Contents

_____Four_____
Social Foundations
of Early Judaic Worlds   125

Preface

This book introduces its readers to the complex reality of Judaism in ancient times, from roughly 450 BCE to 650 CE. The approach is, broadly speaking, historical and phenomenological. The historical approach means that every effort has been made to interpret all texts and ideas in terms of the social, cultural, or political factors that originally gave them meaning. The phenomenological approach represents a commitment to interpret texts, ideas, and social structures as expressions of total conceptions of reality—"worlds." The introduction to the book deals extensively with the reasons for using these approaches. Each chapter is an exercise in applying these approaches to the textual and archeological material surviving from the cultures of Judaic antiquity.

Unlike many introductory texts, this book does not take an "objectivist" approach to its subject. That is, the voice of the narrator does not encourage the pretense of omniscient impartiality. Rather, the style of the book is participatory. It invites the reader into the problems and processes of interpretation. It attempts to make the reader a partner in the interpretive process. This is, in my view, part of the book's mission as a contribution to teaching the comparative study of religions.

It is not possible to study religions without knowing large numbers of historical and textual facts. This book supplies them as needed. But the actual study is not a simple mastery of facts. Scholars of religion use facts as ways to pose and solve interpretive problems. Every page of this book seeks to embody this aspect of the comparative study of religions. The facts and interpretive problems regarding the first thousand years of the history of Judaism are here an occasion for learning the tools of the religionist's trade.

In light of its pedagogical goals, this book is directed primarily at students whose interest in Judaism is shaped within the context of broader training in historical and comparative study of religions. Advanced undergraduate students of any literate religious tradition of Asia or Europe will discover in this book multiple analogies to interpretive problems confronting them in the areas with which they are familiar. Students focusing on the history of Judaism in particular will find an approach that will serve them well as their curriculum takes them to the comparative study of other traditions. Finally, the book should prove useful as an orientation for beginning graduate students in the history of Judaism. It will exemplify one way of turning the information available in the scholarly literature into food for thought about Judaism as an embodied religious world.

Acknowledgments

This book emerges from some fifteen years of teaching its subject to both undergraduate and graduate students in two fine state universities, the University of Virginia and the University of Washington. It has been nourished by innumerable conversations with students and colleagues at both institutions, as well as with colleagues in North America and Israel. Over the course of its composition, I have benefited immensely by eavesdropping on *Ioudaios,* the finest electronic network of scholarly exchange in the study of Judaism. If I have been spared many gross errors of facts and judgment, it is largely due to all these conversations. I accept, of course, total responsibility for whatever remains uninformed or inaccurate.

Two colleagues in particular deserve special mention here, Michael Williams and Hillel Kieval. Both teach brilliantly in the Comparative Religion Program at the University of Washington. Both are fine scholars who have made important contributions to their respective fields: the history of early Christianity and the history of modern Jewry. They have made themselves constantly available to me for conversation and reflection about the interpretive puzzles posed by Judaism in millennium of its infancy and early maturity. This book has been enriched in countless ways by their willingness to listen to my ideas and to criticize the pages on which they were expressed. I must also thank my graduate student, Ms. Frances Wood, for many incisive comments of an earlier version of the manuscript.

I also wish to thank the following reviewers: Gary Alexander, University of Wisconsin-Stevens Point; William E. Paden, University of Vermont; and Benjamin G. Wright, Lehigh University.

As the Sages of the Talmud say, *akharon akharon khaviv*—last but not least: this book could never have been conceived and written without the support and encouragement of my partner in life, Leah Lucrisia Jaffee. Through her I have come to know in experience what were formerly ideas in musty books. By creating for me a Judaic world in my own home, she has helped me to imagine my way sympathetically into the worlds of other Judaisms in times long ago and places far off. She has patiently probed me to explain how what I have learned about Judaism in antiquity corresponds to our own efforts to live in the light of the Torah of Moses. She has been patient with me despite disappointing answers.

This book, therefore, is dedicated to her and to everything she holds sacred.

Martin S. Jaffee
Seattle, WA
Erev Yom haKippurim, 5756

Introduction

This book, as its title announces, is about early Judaism. You may know of other books that use terms such as "ancient Judaism," "late Judaism," or even "middle Judaism" to describe forms of Judaism prior to the European Middle Ages. Later on, I try to explain the reasons for this dispute about adjectives. But for now it is enough to say that our subject is the various forms of religious expression that thrived among Jewish communities on the Mediterranean coasts of Europe and Africa, in the Land of Israel, and as far eastward as the Tigris-Euphrates valley from roughly 450 BCE through 650 CE. Most historians recognize that forms of Judaism that thrived during this period were rather distinct from the Hebrew or Israelite religion that preceded them by many centuries. They also acknowledge that the religious and cultural patterns of early Judaism differ in crucial ways from those that thrived among Jews within the medieval civilizations of Christianity and Islam. Needless to say, all forms of early Judaism are very remote in cultural style from modern European, North American, and Israeli versions of Judaism.

Although historians commonly agree about the uniqueness of this period of the history of Judaism, they disagree about many details, such as when, for example, the period can be said to have begun and when it ended. They also disagree on precisely how Judaism during this period differed from earlier and later forms of Judaism as well as how it was connected to

A Word About Dates

The religious worlds of Christianity have perceived the birth of Jesus as inaugurating a fundamental break in the history of the universe. Since the early Middle Ages, a conventional way of expressing this judgment about time has been to identify all years since the Messiah's birth as the "Year of Our Lord" (Latin: *Anno Domini* or "AD"). In modern times, the entire era of history prior to the birth of the Christian Savior has come to be designated the era "Before Christ" (BC).

This book avoids the Christian convention, replacing it with a compromise that has become widely accepted in religious studies and related fields. The initials BCE, standing for "Before the Common Era," designate any date usually labeled "BC" in the Christian reckoning. CE, "Common Era," designates any date usually labeled "AD" in Christian reckoning. "Common Era" refers to the historical epoch in which Judaism and Christianity have coexisted.

This cosmetic change does little to alter the ethnocentricity of the Christian schema. Rabbinic Judaism, for its part, has for over a millennium calculated the years on the basis of the supposed date for the creation of the world. It knows nothing of BCE or CE, not to mention BC and AD. By its calculation, for example, September 25, 1995, CE inaugurated the year 5756 since Creation.

Moreover, imagining all of history to be shaped by the mutual relationship of Judaism and Christianity ignores the temporal sensibilities of Muslims, Buddhists, and Hindus, among others. For an enormous segment of humanity, the relationship of Jews and Christians is scarcely so significant as to shape the very contour of time!

Despite these flaws, however, we shall be content with the BCE/CE schema. The Christian reckoning of dates, along with the Gregorian calendar that undergirds it, has become second nature in all industrialized cultures and is readily recognizable. The BCE/CE system will, at the very least, remind us of the way that all temporal schemas represent an index of cultural values.

early Christianity. These differences influence their choice of the terms "ancient," "late," "middle," or "early" to describe the Judaism they find. We will reflect upon these questions before the end of this Introduction. For now, it is enough to offer some generalizations about the significance of this period in the history of Judaism.

During this epoch of just over 1000 years, Jews from the North African and southern European coasts of the Mediterranean all the way to the Persian Gulf of Mesopotamia enjoyed a remarkably diverse cultural life. They pursued that life by drawing upon their own ancestral culture, as well as those of the surrounding Persian, Hellenistic-Roman, and Sasanian empires that dominated them politically. In addition to a vast literature—the writings compiled into the Hebrew Bible are only the tip of the iceberg—they developed a wide range of political, cultural, and religious institutions, all of them in close communication with the surrounding environment. Many of these flourished for a time and later disappeared. Others would shape the character of Judaism for the rest of its history until the present. To grasp what Judaism became in the second millennium of its history (from 650 to 1650), or in our own portion of its third millennium, we must first come to terms with the material that engages our attention here.

Moreover, religious developments among the Jews of this time and place eventually made a profound impact beyond the confines of the history of Judaism. It was in the middle of this millennium, from roughly 30 to 100 CE, that what would become Christianity emerged as a form of Judaic religion. By the end of it, Christianity had succeeded in encouraging enormous numbers of human beings in Europe, North Africa, and the Middle East to think of themselves as spiritual heirs of the patriarchs, matriarchs, and prophets depicted in the Jewish writings that formed the first part of the Christian Bible (the Old Testament). Those writings were compiled and edited during the first half of the millennium we shall study. Thus, wherever in today's world the Old Testament is read as a divine address to the Church, there the cultural creation of early Judaism continues to inform contemporary Christian religion.

Islam as well, emerging in Arabia in the last half-century of this period, was shaped in important ways by religious traditions that Jews had brought with them into the Arabian peninsula. Within a few centuries, Islam would spread well beyond the Mesopotamian and North African areas of the old Christian Byzantine empire. It reached eastward, as well, into Zoroastrian Persia and into India and the Buddhist lands of China and southeast Asia. Wherever Islam took root, it brought its own sacred scripture, the Quran. A collection of inspired, highly poetic utterances of the visionary Muhammad, the Quran draws in part upon Jewish traditions regarding key events in the lives of biblical heroes such as Noah (Arabic: Nuh), Abraham (Ibrahim), and Moses (Musa), among others. Thus, wherever the Quran became part of Islamic historical imagination, the religious traditions of early Judaism contributed to the remarkably rich cultures of the Islamic peoples.

Through Christianity and Islam, then, early Judaism's cultural heritage has entered the religious traditions of most of humanity. This book defines a number of different routes into the historical interpretation of early Judaism. Its primary concern, as the subtitle announces, is to describe the religious worlds inhabited by diverse Jewish communities during Judaism's crucial first millennium. These worlds often overlapped and recapitulated each other; but just as surely, they usually offered quite distinct conceptions of the cosmos and how to live within it. Indeed, no single religious world seems ever to have incorporated all Jews of this period into a uniform tradition of thought, a common set of social patterns, or a universally shared cultural idiom. Our study, therefore, is really a survey of the impressive variety of Jewish religious life in this period and an attempt to discern patterns that might lend some coherence to that variety.

This is a complicated interpretive task, and each chapter guides you in examining the evidence of Judaic religious worlds and interpreting the meaning of that evidence. But before we get down to the actual business of interpretation, there are some important preliminary matters to clarify. This book employs the terms "religion" and "world" in specific and, perhaps, unfamiliar senses. Therefore, our first business is to clarify what the term "religious world" sets out to describe. Second, as this book is about the religious worlds of Judaism, we ought to be clear about how we come to regard some religious worlds as examples of Judaism and others not. Only after we have done so will it be possible to clarify the matter alluded to in the first paragraph: precisely why we insist upon defining the Judaic worlds of 450 BCE–650 CE as forms of "early" Judaism, distinct in important ways from what preceded and what came after.

Religion and Religious Worlds

Writers on religion—at least the professional students of the subject—normally take pains to clarify exactly what they mean by the term "religion." This is because, having studied it for the better portion of their adult lives, they find commonsense meanings increasingly unhelpful in enabling them to understand what they study.[1]

Take, for example, the self-evident proposition that religion is a collection of beliefs about divine beings expressed in moral behavior, prayers, and various forms of communal celebration. This notion that religion is a personal "creed" expressed in public "worship" has, in fact, a history. It emerged in European culture between the sixteenth and the nineteenth centuries, as philosophers, politicians, and theologians struggled valiantly to define a role for the Christian churches (Catholic and Protestant) in the emerging national states of Europe. By defining religion as a combination of creed and worship, European thinkers achieved something important. They were able to distinguish political loyalties to a state or nation from religious loyalties to a particular historical church. Religious faith, as expressed through the institution of the Church, can be understood as a private, personal, essentially moral dimension of life. As such, it serves, but should not interfere with, the economic, cultural, and political affairs of the State. Because Church and State address separate spheres of life, citizens of many different religious beliefs may coexist as equals in a society that is offically neutral to a person's private religious faith.

This conception of religion as a set of deeply held personal beliefs distinct from political identity is a great cultural achievement of the Christian peoples of Western and Central Europe. It enabled centuries of religious warfare to be resolved. It lies at the heart of what modern states rightly celebrate as freedom of religion from governmental interference and regulation. The democracies of North America are unimaginable without such conceptions of religion. But they are also a radical departure from earlier European understandings of the role of the Church in the political and social order. Moreover, this European common sense about religion has little to do with the many ways in which non-European and non-Christian peoples have constructed their own conceptions of the role of holy communities and their institutions in the larger social and political order.

We must ask: shall a single, historically particular conception of religion define what counts as religion in a host of historically dissimilar and culturally diverse settings? Most professional students of religion, myself included, answer that question in the negative. But what then? How do we develop a conception of religion that is better than the one we have rejected? And what does "better" mean in this context? By way of answering these questions, let us hazard a definition of religion to guide us throughout our study of Judaism. It is crafted with two things in mind: it is narrow enough for use in understanding Judaism and broad enough for use in understanding other things that might qualify as religion.

Here it is:

> Religion is an intense and sustained cultivation of a style of life that heightens awareness of morally binding connections between the self, the human community, and the most essential structures of reality. Religions posit various orders of reality and help individuals and groups to negotiate their relations with those orders.

To grasp what is at stake in this definition—what it allows us to see and what it might obscure from our view—it is helpful to focus on some of the key terms. The most important thing to notice about this definition is that it does not focus on beliefs or rituals as the defining traits of religion. Rather, it focuses on life paths, comprehensive patterns of behavior that include but move far beyond dogmatically held beliefs or formal ritual actions. Religious patterns of behavior encourage human beings to interpret themselves as moral beings whose destiny is bound with others in a project that brings them into relationship with the fundamental reality of things.

So religions are certainly concerned with beliefs, but these beliefs are not confined to abstractly held propositions or creeds. Rather, they are part of the way humans experience themselves, subtle perceptions about their place in the overall structure of social and cosmic reality. Formal articles of belief may try to organize and clarify such perceptions, but the perceptions usually precede the creeds, even as the creeds then influence in turn the way people tend to interpret their own experience.

The good thing—and the bad thing—about this way of defining religion is that it permits us to consider all kinds of life paths that, according to our usual mental habits, are not religions. Revolutionary political movements (both fascist and socialist), for example, come very close to being religion on this definition. To some degree, the latter part of our definition, which focuses upon "various orders of reality," tends to exclude movements of a purely political focus. But, then again, do "national liberation" or "freedom"—the great symbolic visions of revolutions—constitute an "order of reality" distinct from the normal world of "oppression" or "alienation"? One would have to study such movements carefully in order to decide.

Whether this imprecision of definition is good or bad, of course, depends upon how firm you want to be about the uniqueness of religion among the forms of human culture. For better or worse, I'm not overly worried about protecting the boundaries of religion. I'd rather have to consider how certain things—such as, say, athletic tournaments—have religious dimensions than to define religion in terms dictated by a single type of religious tradition. The best test of the definition I've offered will be your own reading of this book. Does the definition help to focus on aspects of early Judaism that the creed and worship model might have led you to overlook? Does the definition's illumination of Judaism help you to see other religions, or other domains of human culture, with new appreciation? If the answer to either of these questions is mostly affirmative, this definition will have performed its task. Then you can create another definition for a different task. Theories are not holy. Rather, their holes are the things that make them interesting and useful.

So let's take a closer look at the precise language of our definition. It begins by asserting that "religion is an intense and sustained cultivation of a style of life." The point here is that our search for religion should, at least provisionally, direct our attention toward ways of life that are pursued in a disciplined manner and with a certain degree of emotional investment. How we measure such things is, of course, impossible to say at the outset. But we should want to admit that even though religion can be (and at times is *designed* to be) a matter of rote and habit, it is not normatively so. It is something that, at least in theory, should structure much of our activity and engage our emotional and intellectual capacities on a regular and involving basis. Perhaps some things called religion make fewer demands on all aspects of life, while others might make more such demands; or they focus intensity on different areas. This would not make one religion *less* religious than another but would simply tell us that traditions are variable in the way they stake out certain areas of life as central. Those differences are what make the study of religion so thoroughly fascinating.

Back to our definition. It continues by positing that the way of life mapped out by religion "heightens awareness of morally binding connections between the self, the human community, and the most essential structures of reality." This is the core of the matter. Religions are that domain of culture most preoccupied with driving home into personal consciousness an abiding sense of the comprehensive interrelatedness of all levels of experience. In religious systems, the self identified through personal, autobiographical memory tends to be enlarged or enriched as it is interpreted in contexts well beyond personal experience. Personal identity in a religious setting, in other words, includes far more than the web of relations containing the individual, the family, friends, or immediate social group of one's personal acquaintance. It normally includes a conception of how all these relationships are connected to generations of the distant past and the far-off future, as well to the forces and powers that are held to account for the world as it is.

In religions, the question of personal and social identity is routinely—one could say almost obsessively—linked to the question of the origins and destiny of things as well as to the subsisting powers that maintain all things as they are. Religions charge the processes of the natural order—weather patterns, celestial movements, seasonal changes—with moral as well as economic or intellectual significance. Convictions about the nature and quality of life, as well as the meaning or nonmeaning of death, are framed within the most comprehensive understandings of universal order and the limits of time. And these, in turn, structure one's concrete actions in the here and now, in relation to the natural order and one's human associates.

Here is an important limiting case that distinguishes religion from other patterns of culture. Where not only the social order, but the cosmos as a whole, is framed as a moral field in which one's life discipline is pursued, there we begin to distinguish religion from analogous cultural forms such as political, legal, or philosophical systems. However, the converse is also important. Where political, legal, or philosophical systems begin to draw intimate links between the visible and the invisible order of the universe and the moral order of self and society, they begin to look very much like religion.

This last point brings us to the final element of our definition, the one that clarifies the basic distinction between religion and other analogous things. This is its commitment to the proposition that human life takes place amidst "various orders of reality" with which humans must actively negotiate proper relationships. Unlike most modern political movements, philosophical systems, ethical systems, and the like, religions implicate human beings in relationships with normally unseen, usually personal forces that are regarded as in some sense more powerful or, at least, closer to the core of reality than are humans. That is, religions have gods. Gods usually have homes in other worlds and, occasionally, also have relations with humans in this one.

Some religions—certain types of Buddhism, for example—deny ultimacy to gods, promising rather a liberation from a false knowledge that ordinarily might lead one to fear gods or to seek their aid. One way or the other, therefore, religions take gods seriously as powers to be related to, reckoned with, or overcome. They also take seriously the conception of other domains of being, or worlds, that are either parallel to or intersecting with the human and cosmic orders. The substance of religious life—ritual activities, moral self-scrutiny, acts of communal solidarity, prayer, and so forth—are the complex ways in which religions enable human beings to communicate with and establish proper relations with those powers that are at the center of the cosmic process. One way of grasping the notion of religious world is to imagine it as a kind of conceptual map in which these various powers are located in space and time.

This desire to participate in the essential structures of the world lies behind the pervasive role of ritual in religious traditions. All religions have many different kinds of rituals. Some of these—associated, perhaps, with hygiene or hospitality—are performed routinely without even thinking about what they might mean. Unconscious mastery of such rituals is part of the cultural process of becoming a member of a specific religious tradition.

Other rituals, however, are explicitly mastered as a kind of technology by which humans can at times enter fully or partially into the diverse worlds posited by tradition. Those associated with worship, for example, often open communication with the gods in their world while worshippers remain in their own. By contrast, rituals associated with entering holy places are often means of transport into the world of the gods and dwelling there for a time. Yet others—the ritualized meditative practices of Buddhism, for example— lead the mind beyond the perception of all worlds and their gods to a place of undivided consciousness in which the truth of things is immediately apparent. The means of transport and the conceptualizations of alternate worlds will, of course, differ from religion to religion. But constant is the tendency of religion to puncture the apparent solidity of mundane experience and to privilege intimations of other worlds at profounder levels of being.

This final observation brings our definitional discussion of religion to a close. If religion is a way of sustaining the experienced coherence of various orders of reality, religious worlds are those comprehensive maps of reality in which specific forms of life discipline, moral imagination, and ritual practice make eminent good sense. This theory of religious worlds guides our study of early Judaism. We focus on the ways in which Jews living under Persian, Hellenistic-Roman, and Sasanian empires employed the cultural resources at their disposal to construct various intensely lived religious worlds. We track how the different sorts of collective awareness cultivated by the Jews in this period correlated with conceptions of the larger cosmic processes and forces that governed all reality. In sum, we try to discern how the many religious worlds of early Judaism routinely transformed human beings into Jews, to appreciate what kinds of human beings Jews became by living in such worlds.

Identifying Judaism

With our conception of religion firmly in hand, it should now be rather simple to define Judaism. Any dictionary you open offers such a definition in a few lines, at most. But, as with the term "religion," useful commonsense definitions of Judaism (or any other religious tradition, for that matter) cease to serve very long. They become less useful the more seriously we think about the various forms of religion, ancient and modern, that have claimed the name. Moreover, even though the term "Judaism" is quite ancient (as we shall see in a moment), not every religious world we might wish to call Judaism applied the term to itself. This is true not only in the time period of our own study, but especially so during that millennium of Judaism's history that overlapped with the European-Christian Middle Ages.

So let's try to clear some ground in order to establish what we mean by Judaism for the purpose of our work here by reflecting upon some crucial issues. The first is the origin of the word Judaism itself and how that origin can help us in appreciating its meaning. Second, we focus on how to decide when a religion that we might call Judaism first came into being. In connection with this question, we discuss how we might use our definition of Judaism to distinguish various sorts of Judaism from religions that are similar to Judaism, but are ultimately something else. Each of these issues is much more complex than it might appear on the surface. By working through them, however, we are able to approach our study with a disciplined understanding of what we are doing.

The Word "Judaism"

The oldest direct ancestor of the word "Judaism" first appears in the writings of Greek-speaking Jews sometime during the last few centuries before the appearance of Christianity. The word is *ioudaismos*. It identified the customs and folkways of the Israelite people of the province of Yehudah (*ioudaia*; Latin: *judea*). Yehudah is the Hebrew name of what was then, as it is today, a territory in the hill country just inland of the eastern Mediterranean coast. These Israelites, who already identified themselves to non-Israelites by the Hebrew term *yehudim* (Yehudahites), thus came to be called *ioudaioi* (Judeans; singular: *ioudaios*). These geographically linked terms are the ancestors of the words "Jew" and "Judaism" by which those claiming ancestry from these Judeans continue to be known.[2]

Whereas the term ioudaismos first appears in Jewish writings, we do not know whether Israelites invented the term or whether it was coined by their neighbors. The point is that these Israelites, both those living in the Land of Israel and those who found themselves in territorial dispersion (*diaspora*, in Greek), viewed themselves and were viewed by others as constituting a homogeneous ethnic group bound by a noticeable body of ethnic customs. Ioudaismos referred to the entire body of national custom that distinguished Jews from other peoples. Germans, for example, have for centuries spoken of *die Deutschtum* or "Germanness" in the same way.

Ioudaismos did not refer to religion alone, because in the Greek-speaking world of that time the very word "religion" (which comes from a Latin root) did not exist. Nor did the modern notion of religion as creed and worship. Every people of the ancient Greek-speaking world, rather, had its *eusebeia* (piety), its ancestral tradition of serving the gods of specific states, cities, or territories. The Jews had their eusebeia as well. It was well known that they pledged sole loyalty to a single God of Israel. He was believed to be present everywhere, and various Jewish customs reflected the conviction that he was intimately aware of his people's behavior. But his priesthood offered him sacrifice in only a single place—his House of Holiness, the Temple in the sacred city of Jerusalem. This piety of the Jews toward their unique god was part of the larger body of custom that constituted their distinctive ioudaismos. But it didn't exhaust it by any means. No more, at least, than celebrating the Mass of the Church of England exhausts what it means to be British or praying in a Mosque defines the entire cultural identity of an Egyptian.

The term "Judaism," then, got its start as a reference to what we might call the national culture of the Judeans and those descended from them. This is, broadly speaking, how we employ it as well. We explore the particularly religious dimension of that culture during a specified period of its history. But as soon as we announce such a program of study, a difficult question arises. Granting that the term "Judaism" has a certain history, is it plausible that the religious and cultural tradition defined by the term comes into being only with the term itself? After all, the existence of subatomic particles surely precedes their conceptualization among modern physicists. Furthermore, is it out of the question that communities that didn't apply the term "Judaism" to themselves may nevertheless be part of the evidence for the history of Judaism? These questions bring us beyond simple terminology. They involve the crucial question of how we identify the religious culture we wish to study.

The Things Called "Judaism"

One way to clarify our definition of Judaism as a historical religious culture is to consider its origins. How do we identify the *earliest* version of Judaism? By what historical point can we confidently assert that something called Judaism had come into being? Those who cherish a family tree, for example, link all members of an extended family to an original ancestral pair regarded as the founders of the family. But how, barring the admission of Adam and Eve into the family, do they decide where to locate those founders? The case of the history of a religious tradition is comparable. In this case, we want to know how to identify the ancestral form of Judaism that defines the family relations of all other Judaic religious worlds, despite the enormous differences that might distinguish them from one another.

A second and related historical problem emerges quite obviously from the first. It focuses on identifying diverse forms of Judaism beyond the earliest. How do we decide when a religious world is not an example of a Judaic world, but of some other? To continue our familial metaphor, how do we judge that an apparent member of the family tree is in fact a foundling of different lineage; part of the family, perhaps, through adoption and association, but not linked biologically to the founders? Or, to try the other possibility: on what grounds do we decide that a particular individual, regarded as a stranger by the family, is in fact a long lost and forgotten cousin?[3]

In order to answer these questions as historians of Judaism, it might first be helpful to explore how they have normally been answered within Judaic worlds. In such worlds, the *earliest* Judaism is identified by pointing to that portion of the Hebrew Bible often called by the Greek term "Pentateuch" (Five Books) or, in Hebrew, the Torah. As the Torah has been read in Judaic worlds, Judaism begins in one of two possible ways. In one version (condensed considerably here), the divine creator of heaven and earth calls out to a Mesopotamian peasant-herdsman named Abram to obey him (see Gen. 12:1 ff.). When Abram does obey, Judaism is born. In another, Judaism is born when Abram's descendants, the Children of Israel, receive from their leader Moses a constitution of revealed laws that binds them in obedience to that same creator who spoke to Abram (see Ex. 20:1 ff.). Insofar as the Torah links both of these events together (separated by about 500 years or so), they really can be seen as a series of revelational spawnings from which all the later versions of Judaism emerge. The point is that as most Judaic accounts of the origins of Judaism have understood the matter, Judaism begins with divine revelations to Abram and/or Moses. And all true Judaism continues to live in conversation with that revelation.

This helps to explain as well how various forms of Judaism have dealt with our second problem, that of diversity—who is in the Judaic family and who is not. For much of the known history of Judaism, the main way of determining Judaic authenticity has been by reference to patterns of behavior and social custom. Much of the Torah is occupied with lists of laws by which the Children of Israel are expected by Moses and God to conduct themselves. Important conflicts in the history of Judaism arose concerning the interpretation of the precise ways in which those laws are to be applied in various cultural and historical settings. Usually, where one group of Jews has decided that another group of Jews is not practicing Judaism, the reason has been a dispute in the interpretation of law. This is not to say that all Jews have ever interpreted the laws of the Torah identically—there is, in fact, enormous diversity of legal interpretation in historical Judaism. But the point is that if a group has been perceived to deviate too sharply from a broad consensus it has run the risk of being defined as deviant—no longer in genuine continuity with revelation.

Judaism, to conclude, seems to know well when it begins and how to determine who belongs to its family line. Why, then, should we not simply follow its own principles? Here's the problem: these ways in which Judaism has identified its earliest form and defined what constitutes its legitimate later forms are important information for our understanding of Judaism. But we are not permitted to use them as *our* points of historical or definitional reference. The reason is simple and requires us to remember our definition of religion.

Stories about a religion's origins, such as those in the Torah, are part of a complex web of stories by which religious communities locate themselves in the context of the cosmos, time, and the hidden worlds with which they communicate. Because such stories speak about the distant past, it is tempting to regard them as historical reports akin to books written by modern historians. But there is a key difference between these two ways of depicting the past. The intention of religious stories about origins—precisely because they are *religious*—is to explain why, in terms of the past, the community is what it is here and now in its experienced present. Their purpose is to orient people within a comprehensive world of personal, communal, and cosmic meaning.

The purposes of modern historical research to the contrary (at least in theory) are rather different. Historians are most often concerned to reconstruct events in the past on the basis of conflicting reports about what happened. They are interested in what all the "witnesses" say but want to interrogate all of them to discover which version of events is the most likely. The goal of this interrogation is, of course, to get at the causes, be they few or many, of what actually occurred. But, except in eccentric cases, no historian assumes that the results of her or his work will ever exhaust the entire range of causes or explanations for what happened in the past. Similarly, even though historians sometimes make pious bows to the notion that "those ignorant of history are condemned to repeat it," few expect that their books will guide people in reaching comprehensive understandings of their experience in society and the cosmos. Those with such expectations usually direct their writings for marketing next to the *National Enquirer* at the supermarket checkout.

Unlike the modern discipline of historical research, then, religious depictions of the past are not reconstructed by sifting carefully through all sorts of evidence ferreted out from the dark corners of moldy archives. They are not provisional reconstructions designed to serve until clearer images of the past become possible. Rather, these portrayals of the past are based upon a passionate embrace of received tradition or, as we shall see, attempts to harmonize different pictures of the past, all of which are regarded as having authoritative force. Images of the past found in religious memory, that is, are *claims* about the past but not eyewitness recordings of it. As interpreters of these claims, our task is not to embrace them religiously but to understand their meaning for the diverse communities that embraced them.[4]

What this means for students of religion is that such claims have to be weighed in light of other types of evidence supplied by the study of the past. The *earliest* historical expression of a given religious world, therefore, may turn out to be much more recent than the stories of the community's origins might affirm. In other words, we have the earliest version of a religion only when we can isolate, on the basis of all available evidence, the point at which the characteristic story of its origins *is first told and widely affirmed.*

In some religions, such as Islam or Christianity, the origins of the community can be identified to within a half-century or so of the events recorded in traditionally revered stories of Muhammad or Jesus. These religions originate, in other words, among groups who celebrate the story of the Messiah Jesus who conquered death, or of the Prophet Muhammad who brought the revelation of God to the Arabs. Historians have confidence in dating the origins of such religions because they can find evidence of identifiable communities of people who circulated versions of these stories at datable points in time.

By contrast, the origins of Judaism are considerably more obscure. Here's why. If the Torah's stories about Abram and Moses describe historical individuals, these individuals would have lived somewhere between the seventeenth and the thirteenth centuries before the emergence of Christianity, that is, between 1600 and 1200 BCE. But according to most biblical historians, the stories of the Torah that describe these individuals and the revelations they experienced do not seem to have originated much before 1000 to 600 BCE. In any case, they are found in a book, the Torah of Moses, which probably reached its present form sometime later.

As historians of Judaism, then, we will have to seek the earliest describable Judaism at that point at which we can firmly link the circulation of the Torah's version of the Israelite past to a concrete Jewish community. We will want evidence of when and where the Torah in its authoritative form first helped people to locate themselves in historical time and cosmic space and in relation to the world of the God who created everything that exists and called Israel to be his special partner. For reasons to be reviewed further on, our example of the earliest Judaism is not the Judaism of Abram or Moses. As historians, we can know next to nothing about such a Judaism. What we can know about, however, is the Judaism of a small Israelite community living in Jerusalem under Persian protection. Around 450 BCE, this community seems to have embraced the Torah as its official history book and legal charter.

For these reasons, this book, unlike many other texts for the study of Judaism, does not contain a lengthy section on the "Biblical Period" of Judaism—the period from roughly 1800 to 450 BCE in which most of the biblical stories are set. The idea of a Biblical Period is itself a remnant of a time when historians were quite confident that the Hebrew Bible accurately reflects the religious world of the patriarchs, matriarchs, priests, and prophets whose names dot the biblical narratives. It was once assumed that most of the Hebrew Bible was written down from roughly 1000 to 587 BCE, during which time literary traditions from various sectors of ancient Israelite society were shaped in Jerusalem, either by priestly scribes associated with the Temple or by other writers associated either with the court of the royal Davidic dynasty or with various nonroyalist groups.

Historians supposed, that is, that much of the biblical literature was based upon eyewitness sources transmitted accurately by tradition or was shaped by later writers who, much like modern historians, were interested in sifting through various types of historical evidence. In recent decades, however—largely because of an increased appreciation of how religious descriptions of the past are composed and transmitted—this confidence has been shaken. The relation of the religion of ancient Israelites to those who composed the Hebrew Bible, as well as to all forms of Judaism, must be more cautiously described.[5]

This is not to deny, however, that what used to be termed the "Biblical Period" is the seedbed of traditions that everywhere inform Judaism. We note in the following chapter that earlier forms of the stories and laws now found in the Torah of Moses circulated among some ancient Israelite priests and scribes well before the destruction of Israelite society in Yehudah in 587 BCE. Just as surely, Israelite patterns of sacrificial worship in Jerusalem's Temple or theological themes articulated by Israelite sages, priests, or religious visionaries exercised a powerful influence long after the destruction of the Israelite society and culture that nourished such religious forms. Nevertheless, the Israelite sources of Judaism must be distinguished from the later religious world in which those sources are venerated, interpreted, and transformed.

To get back to our family-tree metaphor: the religious worlds of the ancient Israelites surely have certain genetic links to Judaism in the same way that genetic links to the human species are shared in common by diverse ethnic groups. But the ethnic groups have their own distinctive points of temporal and geographic origin, which physical anthropologists try to determine. So, too, does Judaism. As a descendant of ancient Israelite religion, it is part of a single species of religion in which it shares lineage with such monotheistic traditions as Christianity and Islam. But Judaism's own family lineage must be sought independently of the common ancestor.

If you have followed the line of argument this far, you will be able to anticipate the next point. Just as Judaism's image of its origins cannot serve as our point of historical orientation, neither can we rely upon its general principle for defining what is and is not Judaism. That is, we cannot identify a single "correct" interpretation of biblical laws that can serve as a way of distinguishing authentic from inauthentic Judaisms. Moreover, we cannot even use legal criteria as our main way of deciding what will count as Judaism. We have to employ a different strategy to decide which religious worlds exemplify Judaism.

We have to rely again on our definition of religion. Let me recast that definition now by weaving into it the particulars of Judaism. Broadly speaking:

> Judaic worlds may be sought where communities construct disciplined ways of life that serve to heighten awareness of the personal, communal, and, indeed, the cosmic implications of constituting the direct physical descendants of God's people, Israel.

The stress on *physical* descent is crucial. It is possible, as in Christianity or Islam, to recognize a *spiritual* kinship with ancient Israel as worshippers of the same God or heirs to a continuous series of revelations. But part of what makes a religion Judaism is this stress on physical, ethnic continuity. This is not to say that Judaism is comprised solely of direct physical descendants of ancient Israelites. No existing community of Jews can verify such a claim. Rather, Judaism is comprised in part by people who insist on making it.

This brings us to another fundamental marker of Judaic worlds, particularly in ancient and medieval times. They all ground their claim to constitute the descendants of the people Israel on their possession of and loyalty to an authentic version of the Torah of Moses. All assume that this Torah is a direct disclosure or revelation of God's love and will for Israel and that the path to establish a proper relationship to the God of Israel is somehow to be discovered within the Torah or in correctly guided interpretations of it. When, therefore, we encounter in Persian, Hellenistic-Roman, and Sasanian cultures a community claiming ethnic *and* spiritual continuity with ancient Israel on the basis of some interpretation of the Torah, we have the right to say we are talking about Judaism. Where the physical claim is denied or the primacy of the Torah is radically displaced in favor of some other textual inheritance, we have to look more carefully to see if we have a Judaism or not. A good deal of gray appears in the history of early Judaic worlds. This book sorts out the various shades.

Why "Early" Judaism?

A word, at last, about why this book defines the period from 450 BCE to 650 CE as a unified epoch in which there existed something called early Judaism. We have already pointed out that historians remain committed to a number of different descriptive terms for this period and often divide it into further subdivisions. They usually have good reasons for their preferences. It is important to consider, however, that each way of defining this period serves some larger theory of what Judaism is and how to study its forms in antiquity. Once we are clear about our own program of study, we will also be clear about why early Judaism is the most appropriate definition of our subject for the purposes we have chosen. Let's first clarify the programs of study supported by the alternative terms.[6]

During the late nineteenth and much of the twentieth century, New Testament scholarship stemming from German and other European universities and theological seminaries commonly spoke of something called "late" Judaism. This term usually defined the period between the establishment of a Jewish settlement in Yehudah under Persian rule (roughly 539 BCE) and the destruction of Judaism's main religious shrine, the Jerusalem Temple, by the Romans in 70 CE. "Intertestamental Judaism" was another common designation, denoting Judaism as it existed between the end of one scriptural revelation (the Old Testament) and before the beginning of a second (the New Testament).[7]

Scholars using these terms normally viewed the Biblical Period (1200–587 BCE) as the truly creative period of Judaism, when it was the setting for divine communication. After 587 BCE, on this view, Israel lost its connection with living revelation. It fell into a religious decline, characterized by the rule of law under a priestly theocracy. Late Judaism was the result—Judaism at the end of its history. Indeed, for this tradition of scholarship, the advent of Christianity constituted a kind of renewal and perfection of the original impulse of "biblical faith" that late Judaism had smothered.

The flaws in this way of imagining Judaism are clear. Late Judaism is a way of naming a religion in the process of decay, a process redeemed only by a new religion, Christianity. To call the Judaism of our period "late," in other words, is to affirm traditional Christian claims to have displaced Judaism as the true covenantal community. Not all contemporary Christians— and, obviously, few Jews—wish to affirm this. But those who do must recognize that such judgments are grounded in theological judgments rather than in the interests of critical historical understanding. Indeed, the continued vitality of Judaic worlds for centuries after the emergence of Christianity as its own family of religious worlds reminds us that what is late Judaism for Christian theology is just the beginning for the history of Judaism.

Perhaps the most common term, "ancient" Judaism, resulted in part from attempts to avoid the negative evaluation of Judaism implied by the term "late." Scholars who speak of ancient Judaism have rarely offered a careful analysis of the term. Most have in mind forms of Judaism that thrived in the land of Israel and the Diaspora from about 520 BCE, when Judean Jews began to rebuild the Temple that the Babylonian invaders of 587 BCE had de-

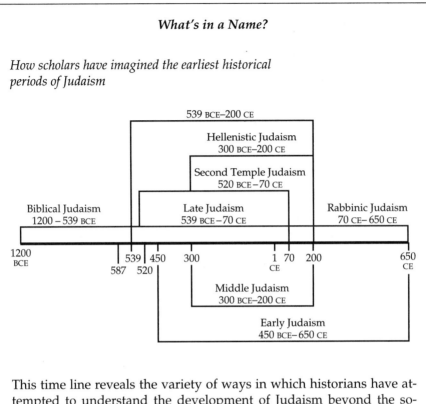

What's in a Name?

How scholars have imagined the earliest historical periods of Judaism

This time line reveals the variety of ways in which historians have attempted to understand the development of Judaism beyond the so-called "Biblical Period." Note that each name and chronological segmentation expresses a larger theory of the nature and history of Judaism.

stroyed, until 70 CE, when the most recent version of that structure was again razed.

Scholars who use ancient Judaism normally qualify it by other terms of a more precise range of meaning. "Second Temple Judaism," for example, is often used to describe the Judaism of the land of Israel in particular during the period 520 BCE–70 CE. Yet another term, "Hellenistic Judaism," has often been used to describe the religion of Greek-speaking Jews outside the homeland, specifically during the period from 300 BCE to 200 CE. Thus, Hellenistic Judaism emerges within the chronological boundary of Second Temple Judaism and endures about a century or so beyond it.

From the perspective of those who think of ancient Judaism in its Second Temple and Hellenistic forms, the centuries from 70 to 650 are usually characterized as the age of "rabbinic" Judaism. This is because the great literary traditions of rabbinic Sages, reaching classical form in the Babylonian Talmud of the fifth to seventh centuries, appear to originate in the decades after the Second Temple's destruction in 70 CE. Thus, rabbinic Judaism develops in the interval between the end of Second Temple Judaism and the disappearance of Hellenistic Judaism and carries the history of Judaism forward until the time of the Islamic conquests of the mid-seventh century CE.[8]

The merit of this division between ancient and rabbinic Judaism is that it clearly uses developments internal to Judaism, rather than Christian theological models of history, as ways of guiding our studies. The problem is that the division between ancient and rabbinic Judaism is itself somewhat artificial. As we shall see further on, many of the Judaic worlds of Second Temple Judea and the Hellenistic Diaspora persisted for quite some time into the post–70 CE period and influenced rabbinic Judaism dramatically. Finally, and perhaps more to the point, rabbinic Judaism did not even begin to dominate the religious imagination and life patterns of large groups of Jews until the third century CE at the earliest. And it did not finally succeed until well after 650 CE.

The term "middle" Judaism is the most recent attempt to apply a theologically neutral, genuinely descriptive label to the Judaic worlds we study. It was coined in 1991 by the Italian scholar Gabriele Boccaccini to designate in particular the period from 300 BCE to 200 CE.[9] Boccaccini sees this period as distinct from early (or ancient) Judaism, which he locates in the period from the sixth century to the fourth century BCE. Middle Judaism, in his view, serves as the springboard for two competing forms of later Judaic religion, rabbinic Judaism and Christianity. Their histories begin toward the end of this period and develop well beyond its scope. The great merit of Boccaccini's proposal is that it self-consciously attempts to avoid theological judgments of history, be they Christian or Judaic. It also highlights the well-appreciated fact that the entry of the Jews into Hellenistic culture, which began shortly before 300 BCE, served to define much of the religious thought found in Jewish writings from 300 BCE to 200 CE. It is beyond question that the intellectual expressions of Judaism during this period are all deeply indebted to forms of thought stemming from Hellenism.

I find the term "middle" Judaism ultimately unsatisfactory, however, for two reasons. One has to do with the definition of "religion" offered earlier, the other with the definition of "Judaism." Let's start with the former. Recall that religious worlds include not only intellectual constructions, but comprehensive patterns of life linked to fundamental pictures of the world. From this perspective, it is a serious limitation to define an entire epoch of Judaism on the basis of theological thought alone. As we see, the relevance of intellectual Hellenism to the interpretation of concrete Judaic worlds (as opposed to specifically theological systems) throughout the period from 450 BCE to 650 CE is varied. For this reason, we use a chronological scheme that permits us to track various patterns of Judaic expression beyond the strict boundaries of the Hellenistic period—within the Persian culture that yielded to Hellenism and within the late Roman and Sasanian cultures that bequeathed various styles of Hellenism to the bearers of Islam.

A second problem with the conception of middle Judaism is more important. Boccaccini is clear that the point of identifying a middle Judaism is to enable historians to conceive both rabbinic Judaism and Christianity as competing models of later (to use his term "modern") Judaism. In his view, rabbinic Judaism and Christianity are Judaic religions rooted in middle Judaism. The only issue for historians is to identify the historical moment at which these two Judaisms were no longer capable of grasping themselves as bearers of the same tradition. The date 200 CE represents this point of no return.

The date 200 CE is certainly a convenient point to locate an irreversible split between Judaic and Christian religious communities. And it is a fascinating experiment to imagine the history of Christianity as one way of continuing the history of middle Judaism. Nevertheless, this experiment imagines Judaism too broadly to be useful for the study of religious worlds. Our own study, as seen earlier, is grounded on a model of Judaism that takes seriously (if not always definitively) the ways in which communities imagine their own boundaries. On this view, Judaism is, at the least, a religious world inhabited by people who regard themselves as physical descendants of the Israelites.

The description of Christianity as a form of Judaism has merit, therefore, primarily for the earliest phase of the movement among first-century CE Palestinian Jews. In Chapter Four, we consider the Judaism of Christian Jews in the second and third centuries as well. But on the whole, historians of religion are bound to acknowledge most of historical Christianity as a set of religious worlds related to but distinct from Judaism. Both traditions come into conflict over their claims to be the authentic bearers of the covenant of ancient Israel. This is what links them into a single family of religious tradition. But the cousins no longer dwell together—and, from a historical perspective, neither lives in the religious world each imagines as biblical Israel.

This leaves us with early Judaism as our term of choice. Scholars began to use this term largely out of the motives that led to experiments with ancient and middle Judaism.[10] Our use of the term here differs from conventional usage in an important respect. Most references to early Judaism cover roughly the period that Boccaccini claims for middle Judaism. To this degree, they reproduce the tendency, noted earlier, of employing Hellenistic culture as the basic prism through which to refract various forms of Judaism. The present account of early Judaism, by contrast, is far more broad. We apply it to an entire millennium, attempting to see the *plurality* of the Judaic worlds in Persian, Hellenistic-Roman, and Sasanian civilizations as precisely what defines them as a coherent whole. We might call this "the millennium of Judaic diversity."[11] By doing so, we intend to say that the most radical departure in the history of Judaism did not occur *within* this period. It was not the advent of Hellenism or the destruction of the Jerusalem Temple in 70 that radically altered the forms of Judaic religious worlds. Rather, this came only after the conquests of Islam, when the traditions of rabbinic Judaism first became universal among Jews of the Middle East and began a steady penetration of Christian Europe. Hence, the year 650 CE serves as the concluding date in our epoch. It is in the mid-seventh century that the truly profound transformation of early Judaism really began. What had been for a millennium a plurality of contiguous but independent religious worlds began to reconfigure itself into an international rabbinic culture. But the study of the religious worlds of rabbinic Judaism under medieval Christianity and Islam is a task we cannot begin here.

The Plan of This Book

The theoretical questions we have just entertained will remain utterly meaningless unless they are embodied in the actual study of Judaism. The structure of this book is designed to highlight their significance. As you incrementally master more and more information about the various Judaic worlds in their historical settings, you should grow increasingly confident in your grasp of the general character of early Judaism as a distinctive formation of religious meaning.

Our discussion unfolds through six chapters. The first chapter, by way of orientation, sketches the geographical, social, and political settings of the various Judaic worlds of our period. Here we explain as well why the date 450 BCE looms so large in our estimate of the origins of Judaism and why 650 CE serves as a convenient conclusion. This chapter also serves as a source of historical and cultural reference points to help you contextualize the many details that require sorting and interpretation in the chapters to follow.

The second chapter, entitled "Dynamics of Texts and Traditions," traces the origins of the literary traditions, written and oral, that emerged out of and reflected the Judaic worlds we discuss. The Hebrew Bible—and other literature intimately in conversation with it—serves as important evidence for the ways in which Jews imagined the world they inhabited. As we have pointed out, a key marker of Judaism is a claim to communal identity grounded in at least some of these writings. This chapter, therefore, exposes the remarkably diverse manner of Judaism's engagement with its sacred writings and the traditions of interpretation that continually enlivened and renewed them.

The chapter entitled "Symbolic Vocabularies and Cosmic Structures" is really about what people usually call "theology" or, if they are sceptics, "ideology." What it in fact focuses upon is the way certain symbols—"God," "Torah," "Israel," and "Messiah," among others—underwent continuous redefinition and restatement as Jews' conceptions of the physical and temporal dimensions of their world changed as well. So we study the interaction between Judaic religious symbols and the way Jews imagined their situation in time and space. We give our attention to ways of thinking that were rather influential, as well as those that didn't quite work out.

A fourth chapter, "Social Foundations of Early Judaic Worlds," confronts an important fact about both religion and Judaism—radically different societies can be constructed out of the same scriptural heritage and dominant symbolic structures. A "religion," in other words, is not found primarily in the world of books and ideas, but in the concrete societies of people who know these books and think with these ideas. This chapter focuses on the various sorts of communities Jews formed within the general community of Judaism. We try to understand how Jews, with tools offered by Judaism, made important social distinctions of all sorts. These include, among others, distinctions between real Jews and false Jews, between Jews and Gentiles, and between male Jews and female Jews.

In Chapters Five and Six, finally, we confront that dimension of early Judaism that made it a genuinely religious rather than a cultural, national, or ethnic tradition. How did different forms of early Judaism regulate the passage of Jews between the various orders of reality and the power that sustains them?

To this end, the chapter on "Ritual Space and Performance in Early Judaism" focuses on the areas of life that presented opportunities for opening up passage to or communication with the heavenly world of the God of Israel. By exploring different patterns of formal worship in such diverse spaces as the Jerusalem Temple, the Byzantine synagogue, and the home, we will see how the worlds of early Judaism were permeable at different points to the penetration of extramundane presences.

The concluding chapter, "Transformative Knowledge," focuses on groups in early Judaism that made the cultivation of extra mundane knowledge a special preoccupation. We study specific rituals that helped their practitioners to penetrate worlds beyond the everyday and ask about the *results* of that penetration. What did Jews bring back with them from their communication with the most powerful and overwhelming presences that structured their conceptions of reality? How did they share their knowledge? What did they hope to become by knowing what they knew?

The scope of our study, then, is very broad. Many details cannot be filled in here. You will want and will need to read other books to fill in these details. The notes to each chapter supply a start at what I think are the most helpful sources for the next stage of study. But you will certainly learn enough here to help you interpret whatever your curiosity leads you to discover on your own.

Notes

1. The discussion in this section draws on the work of many theorists of religion. An excellent place to trace the development of modern European ideas of religion is J. Samuel Preus, *Explaining Religion: Criticism and Theory from Bodin to Freud* (New Haven and London: Yale University Press, 1987).

   The background of the definition of religion that follows can be traced in the essays of Clifford Geertz, "Religion as a Cultural System," in C. Geertz, *The Interpretation of Cultures* (New York: Basic Books, 1973), pp. 87–125 and Talal Asad, "The Construction of Religion as an Anthropological Category," in T. Asad, *Genealogies of Religion: Discipline and Reasons of Power in Christianity and Islam* (Baltimore: Johns Hopkins University Press, 1993), pp. 27–54.

   The concept of "religious world" is spelled out in the work of William E. Paden, *Religious Worlds: The Comparative Study of Religion. With a New Preface* (Boston: Beacon Press, 1994), pp. 51–65.

2. James D.G. Dunn offers a good summary of the earliest terms for Judaism in "Judaism in the Land of Israel in the First Century," in Jacob Neusner, ed., *Judaism in Late Antiquity. Part Two: Historical Syntheses* (Leiden, The Netherlands: E.J. Brill, 1995), pp. 232–236.

3. The following account of the nature of Judaism as a historical religious tradition has been shaped by the many writings of my teacher, Jacob Neusner. His views on the definition of Judaism and its historical development can be consulted most conveniently in Jacob Neusner, *The Way of Torah: An Introduction to Judaism,* 5th ed. (Belmont, CA: Wadsworth, 1993), pp. 3–24. For a fuller discussion, consult Jacob Neusner, *Self-Fulfilling Prophecy: Exile and Return in the History of Judaism* (Atlanta: Scholars Press, 1990).

4. One of the best discussions of the difference between religious traditions about the past and reconstructions of the past by historians happens to have been written by a historian of the Jews, Yosef H. Yerushalmi, *Zakhor: Jewish Memory and Jewish History* (Seattle: University of Washington Press, 1982).

5. Among academic historians of Judaism, Jacob Neusner is one of the few to write introductory texts that draw a sharp distinction between Judaism and ancient Israelite religion. His *The Way of Torah,* cited earlier, is an example. Most contemporary historians recognize the distinction; the debate is how sharply to draw it.

   Many, such as Shaye J.D. Cohen, *From the Maccabees to the Mishnah* (Philadelphia: Westminster Press, 1987), pp. 13–26, discern continuities of ideas and institutions that suggest a rather close relationship between what is often called "Israelite Religion" and later "Judaism." A few, such as Philip R. Davies, *In Search of "Ancient Israel"* (Sheffield, England: JSOT Press, 1992), question whether there was ever in historical actuality an ancient Israel or an ancient Israelite religion. Most students of the matter take a position somewhere between these two. You may sense the heated character of the debate by consulting the articles of Iain W. Provan, Thomas L. Thompson, and Philip R. Davies in the *Journal of Biblical Literature,* 114 (1995), pp. 585–606, 683–698, and 699–705.

6. For another way of approaching the issue of names, see the recent essay by Gabriele Boccaccini, "History of Judaism: Its Periods in Antiquity," in J. Neusner, ed., *Judaism in Late Antiquity. Part Two: Historical Syntheses,* pp. 285–308. We discuss Boccaccini's own contribution to the debate in a few paragraphs.

7. The term "late" Judaism was probably coined in 1903 by the German scholar Wilhelm Bousset, in his widely read *Die Religion des Judentums im neutestamentlichen Zeitalter* (Berlin: W. Peisser, 1903). This work was never translated

into English, but its impact on English-language scholarship is evident, for example, in an influential book by the great scholar R.H. Charles: *Religious Developments Between the Old and the New Testament* (New York and London: Holt & Co., 1914).

8. A sample introduction is that of F.C. Grant, *Ancient Judaism and the New Testament* (Edinburgh: TET Clark, 1960). The term is still in wide use among scholars.

    A useful example of a historical account of the Second Temple Period is that of Menahem Stern, "The Period of the Second Temple," in H.H. Ben-Sasson, ed., *A History of the Jewish People* (Cambridge, MA: Harvard University Press, 1969), pp. 185–303.

    The concept of Hellenistic Judaism as a particular product of the Jewish Diaspora has been often used to explain the rapid spread of Christianity beyond Palestine. A classic of this genre is W.O.E. Oesterley, *The Jews and Judaism during the Greek Period: The Background of Christianity* (London and New York: Macmillan, 1941).

    The most succinct definition of the rabbinic period as a new departure inaugurating an "age of definition" is offered by Jacob Neusner in *The Way of Torah*, pp. 18–19. He often subdivides the period into two, 70–200 and 200–650, to distinguish between the period of rabbinic origins and its classical form. See *Self-Fulfilling Prophecy*, pp. 62–150.

9. Gabriele Boccaccini, *Middle Judaism: Jewish Thought 300 BCE to 200 CE* (Minneapolis: Fortress Press, 1991). His discussion of the term "middle Judaism" is on pp. 7–25.

10. Boccaccini shows that F.C. Grant coined the term "early" Judaism in the 1930s (ibid., p. 56). But it did not come into vogue until much later. See, for example, Robert A. Kraft and George W.E. Nickelsburg, eds., *Early Judaism and Its Modern Interpreters* (Atlanta: Scholars Press, 1986), pp. 1–30, and George W.E. Nickelsburg and Michael E. Stone, *Faith and Piety in Early Judaism: Texts and Documents* (Philadelphia: Fortress Press, 1983).

11. For a recent reflection of this point of view in what will surely become a standard reference work, consult the excellent series of seven articles under the general heading "Judaism" in David Noel Freedman, ed., *The Anchor Bible Dictionary*, Vol. III (New York: Doubleday, 1992), pp. 1037–1089. These articles approach the problem of describing Judaism through a combination of chronological ("Greco-Roman Period," "Mishnaic Period") and geographical ("Palestinian," "Egypt," "North Africa," "Rome," "Babylonia") terms. Although they take no stand on a comprehensive title for our epoch, these entries constitute a small introductory guide to responsible judgments on most matters touching on the history of what we call early Judaism.

One

Social and Political Settings of Early Judaism

Introduction

Few human institutions of any complexity—least of all religions—really begin at a specific moment. Accounts of the pristine origins of a unique community responding as one to the direct utterance of a god or to the inspired preachings of a charismatic prophet belong to the realm of religious story. They express a community's sense of participating in a radical new beginning or a transformative moment of revelation. What is recalled by the faithful as a sudden reorientation toward reality usually appears to the historian of religion as the result of much prior historical preparation. Like most cultural traditions, religions normally emerge from a peculiar mixture of plan and accident, conditions imposed by the cultural-historical environment and by creative (and often unorchestrated) human responses.

As historians of religion, therefore, we cannot be satisfied with Judaism's claim to have originated in revelations to Abraham or Moses. It would be no less misleading, however, to state without qualification that Judaism began on some particular day in 450 BCE (or in 449 or 451) in the territory of Yehudah. To the contrary, the origins of the religious worlds we call Judaism are diffuse. The date we have chosen is a conventional reference marker rather than an absolute point separating the past of Israelite religion from the future of Judaism.

Think about the matter of Judaic origins with the help of a metaphor drawn from the textile craft. Early Judaism can be imagined as a cloth woven by many hands over a period of centuries within a broad geographical and cultural landscape. Some of the oldest fibers that dominate the patterns of the earliest identifiable Judaic cloth were surely contributed to the weave by the vanished Israelite civilization that had once thrived in the Land of Israel. But the design into which these fibers were woven comes from other hands. Basic motifs were contributed in Persian Yehudah. Yet others seem to have entered the weave through the labors of Israelites outside the ancestral territory, particularly in Mesopotamia. To the dominant patterns set on the loom by the mid-fifth century BCE were added later elements of coloring and different sorts of yarn, randomly contributed by a variety of hands, in and beyond the Land of Israel, for a millennium thereafter.

The result, of course, is a rather unruly and rough weave reflecting generations of artisans employing a wide variety of styles, without a single overseer to coordinate all the weaving. To complicate matters, if this cloth was ever sewn into a completed garment, it is surely lost to us by now. What has survived, rather, are unmatched swatches of the fabric itself, their colors faded by time and their edges torn and frayed. Subsequent chapters of our book explore some of the patterns and colors of this poorly preserved fabric in great detail. For the present, it helps to identify the main artisans.

Which communities of ancient Israelites seem to have been key participants in the cultural labor that produced the fabric of the earliest Judaic worlds? Where and when did they live? Is it possible to identify the circumstances under which they worked or their specific contributions to the common (if largely uncoordinated) labor they shared with others across large stretches of time, space, and culture?

The Israelite Inheritance of Early Judaism

The geographical and cultural context of Judaic origins extends from the coastal cities of the Nile River delta in North Africa to the rich Mesopotamian urban and agricultural heartland between the Tigris and the Euphrates rivers near the Persian Gulf. Flanked by an ancient Egyptian civilization on the west and those of Assyria and Babylonia on the east, the center stage is occupied by the Land of Israel. On this land, often the object of political designs and military invasions by the successive empires surrounding it, there arose between 1000 and 587 BCE the Hebrew-speaking civilization of which all forms of Judaism claim to be the successor.[1]

The heartland of the Land of Israel is the territory on either side of a spine of hills running north and south through the land between the Mediter-

The Ancient Near East

The dotted area is usually called "The Fertile Crescent." The fertile lands watered by the Nile in Egypt and the Tigris and Euphrates in Mesopotamia enabled the development of the great civilizations that preceded by two millennia the earliest emergence of Hebrew civilization in the Land of Israel.

ranean coast on the west and the Jordan River on the east. On this territory, the ancient Hebrews—whom the Hebrew Bible calls "Israelites" (Hebrew: *b'nei yisrael*)—pursued some 400 years of fractious political life. Early on, an Israelite empire established by a king named David (ruled ca. 1000–961 BCE) became a major Middle Eastern political player. David appears to have extended his dominion to parts of what are now southern Lebanon, southwestern Syria, and western Jordan, threatening powerful neighbors on either side of his borders. But the experience of Israel as an international superpower was short-lived. The later history of the empire under David's dynastic heirs included a divisive civil war and the creation, by 922, of two contending kingdoms, frequently boxed in by superior surrounding empires.

The southern kingdom, called Yehudah, remained under the control of a Davidic dynasty; the northern kingdom, called Yisrael (Israel), suffered a series of dynastic struggles throughout its history. Both kingdoms were eventually conquered by foreign invaders. The northern kingdom of Yisrael fell to Assyrian armies in 722 BCE. Many refugees streamed southward into Yehudah and became absorbed into the closely related cultural life of the Davidic kingdom. Others, deported to various areas of the Assyrian lands, disappeared from the stream of Israelite civilization. The southern kingdom of Yehudah, for its part, wobbled on as a rather weak state for more than a century after the destruction of its northern neighbor. It collapsed after a series of invasions from an expanding Babylonian Empire between 597 and 587 BCE. With the banishment of the last king of Yehudah, Zedekiah, to Babylonian imprisonment, the history of ancient Israelite civilization as a political and social entity confined to a single territory comes to an end.

Judaism did not yet exist at the destruction of the Davidic state in 587 BCE. Yet nearly every aspect of Judaism resonates in some fashion with the civilization created during the life of that state. Here we can briefly point to some themes that play an important role in future chapters.

Like all civilizations of the ancient Middle East, that of Yehudah was permeated by a sense that its land was the central point at which the heavenly world, with its divine beings, came into contact with the world of human activity. In most Middle Eastern cultures, the precise point of intersection could be located. It was on the altar of the national shrine. There priests offered regular gifts of slaughtered animals and other agricultural goods to the divinities of heaven, particularly the divine protector of the state. In Yehudah, the most important shrine was the Temple in the capital city of Jerusalem. Built by David's son and heir, Solomon, it was believed to shelter the Glory (Hebrew: *kavod*) of God, that element of the divine reality that could be manifested in the human world. In the Temple, the Glory was served in a daily routine of sacrificial rites offered by priests descended from Aaron, the brother of Moses, who was celebrated as the founder of the Israelite priesthood. When Judaism would finally emerge among the fifth-century BCE community of Yehudah, memories of that Temple and all it

United Israelite Kingdom Under David and Solomon

The kingdom bequeathed by David to his son Solomon lasted a mere forty years. But memories of its glory nourished the theological imagination of ancient Israelite prophets and, in later centuries, the messianic visions of Judaism.

represented would play an important role. Indeed, the second Temple was built upon the spot occupied by the first. And Aaronide priests were restored to its service.

The Solomonic Temple, in addition to its function as the intersection of heaven and earth, was also a center of what might be called the national memory. Its priestly scribes kept economic records, cultivated empirical knowledge about the movements of heavenly bodies, and chronicled events in human history and the national life. They also preserved a variety of ritual and legal traditions relevant to their own priestly roles as well as to the conduct of society at large. As preservers of memory, however, the Aaronide priests of Jerusalem enjoyed no monopoly. Priests out of favor with the monarchy, stemming from non-Aaronide lineages, had been exiled, at times, to less central shrines or had been deprived entirely of cultic responsibilities. They, too, preserved their own accounts of the past. Needless to say, these did not coincide in all aspects with those of the royally empowered Aaronide priests.

The royal dynasty also preserved historical records and narratives. Quite naturally, these often identified the royal Palace, rather than the official priesthood, as the key factors in the dynasty's success. Although royal house and priesthood enjoyed a convergence of interests, they could nevertheless compete for primacy in the life of the state. Like the Temple, moreover, the Palace was also an important intellectual center. As in other Middle Eastern kingdoms, scribes, sages, and poets served as appointees at the royal court. There they cultivated and preserved their own traditions of theology, cosmology, and worldly wisdom. Thus, both Temple and Palace collected, generated, and preserved much of the intellectual and religious culture of Yehudah. All these diverse sources of cultural tradition—and, doubtless, many others that can no longer be traced by literary historians—would, in the centuries after 587 BCE, nourish the formation of Judaism. In much revised form, many of these sources would find their way into the official communal literature that would take shape among the Persian Israelites of fifth-century Yehudah.

But the lines of cultural continuity were seriously interrupted by the events of 587. The Babylonian conquerors of Yehudah dealt with its inhabitants much as they, and the Assyrians before them, had defused the political will to resistance of other conquered peoples. They depopulated Yehudah of its political, cultural, and economic leaders—those, in other words, who preserved the intellectual culture and owned the wealth of the national group—and transferred them to the Babylonian urban centers. Many of those escaping deportation eastward to Babylonia sought refuge in Egyptian territories to the west, securing their lives in the one empire that seemed able to withstand the Babylonian expansions. The Israelite small landholders, artisans, and herders remaining in their land were soon joined by other foreign deportees, themselves the victims of similar Babylonian depopulations of their own native territories.

In later Judaic tradition, this experience of political defeat and territorial dislocation was captured in the image of the "Exile" (Hebrew: *galut*) to Babylonia. As we shall see, the theological interpretation of the causes of this event is among the crucial markers of any religious world called Judaism. For now, however, it is enough to point out a principal social consequence of Yehudah's fall. After nearly half a millennium of continuous political life in a relatively bounded territory, the group calling itself Israel was dispersed both within and outside its ancestral land. Beyond Yehudah—in Babylonia or Egypt—they were defeated exiles, dislocated refugees, and, at times, slaves; within it they shared pasturage and villages with strangers under the domination of a conquering empire.

Living a national life on the Land of Israel had once been a defining aspect of what it meant to be the People Israel. With Yehudah under foreign control, its official political and religious institutions shattered, and the cultural elite scattered far and wide, it was hardly clear in the decades after 587 where a new organizing center of Israel's collective life might be found.

The Emergence of Judaism in Persian "Yehud"

No solutions seem to have emerged immediately. But political events did begin to create opportunities. The Babylonian Empire itself fell, in about 540 BCE, to the invading Achemenid armies under King Cyrus the Great of Persia. Unlike his predecessors, Cyrus pursued a rather benign policy regarding his subject populations, designed to curry loyalty to the Achemenid regime. Where possible, he repatriated deportees and appointed local ethnic administrations to govern ancestral lands. Such administrations, with Persian approval and enforcement, developed legal charters grounded in local traditions. This permitted the governed to see local ethnic leaders applying local laws, while the presence of the Empire, at least in everyday matters, receded into the background.[2]

Throughout the sixth to the fourth centuries BCE, a series of Persian rulers encouraged the descendants of deported Israelite political and cultural leaders to engage in the repopulation and reconstruction of Israelite communal life in the district now known, in the Aramaic language of the Persian Empire, as Yehud. Centered on the ancient Davidic capital of Jerusalem, Yehud slowly became a principal center of economic and cultural life. With the help of Persian financing and military supervision, key elements of urban life in Jerusalem were restored. By around 515 BCE, the central shrine of Israelite sacrificial worship had been rebuilt and rededicated. Priests claiming descent from Zadok, an Aaronid priest whose family served in the Temple during the Davidic dynasty, were placed in prominent positions of Temple and civil administration.

The enhancement of Jerusalem as a provincial capital had important

The Persian Empire of Cyrus the Great

The shaded area indicates the extent of the Achemenid Dynasty's power under Cyrus and his successors.

consequences beyond its walls as well. On the one hand, much of the peasantry of the countryside enjoyed physical protection and economic benefit from its allegiance to the new order forming in Jerusalem. On the other hand, the Babylonian-born Israelites in control of that order were not natives of the land. They often had to struggle with an indigenous population that saw itself, with some justification, as the authentic preserver of Israel's traditional ways.

So, from the late sixth century until well into the fourth BCE, Yehud was the site of a tense and—from hindsight—immensely productive cultural struggle. The struggle occurred at various points of social tension: between the laws of the new state and the venerable customs of the land; between the culture of the city and that of the countryside; between native Israelite and Babylonian-born Israelite. A key conflict, alluded to clearly in the biblical books of Ezra and Nehemiah, concerned the definition of who was actually an Israelite. Here those whom the priestly administrators of the state defined as full-blooded Israelites were privileged in relation to those regarded as being of mixed lineage (see Ezra 10:1–44 and Neh. 13:23–28). Much of the struggle resolved itself to a single crucial matter: who truly really belonged to the Land of Israel and how should those who truly belonged to it live upon it?

Those contending over a period of centuries to define the course of the

The Persian Province of Yehud

The shaded area represents the range of Jewish settlement permitted by the Persians after 539 BCE. Jerusalem was the center of the small colony, which occupied only a small portion of the former Kingdom of Yehudah. (Based on T. Eskenazi and K. Richards, *Second Temple Studies, 2: The Temple Community in the Persian Period* [Sheffield, England: Sheffield Academic Press, 1992], p. 142.)

successor civilization to Davidic Yehudah are, from our present perspective, the first weavers of the fabric of Judaism. The narrative threads of that fabric were gathered from diverse memories of the glory of Israel's national past and the tragedy of its collective degradation in exile. Other threads were supplied from preserved records of priestly ritual, traditions of scribal wisdom, and documents of royal legislation. The loom was built of opportunities provided by Persian foreign policy. With these materials, the earliest generations of the Jews of Yehud wove a patterned cloth that would be added to by others in many places and times. Unfortunately, historical sources are so scarce for the earliest period that it is difficult to reconstruct much of what actually happened, either in the homeland or in Egypt and Babylonia. As we see in Chapter Two, most of what we can say must be grounded in inferences drawn from a single piece of cloth—some of the surviving texts of the Hebrew Bible.

Homeland and Diaspora Under Hellenistic Empires

The haze covering the origins of the earliest Judaic religious world doesn't really lift until the late fourth century BCE and later. And by then, Israel found itself in a rather different cultural milieu. In 332 BCE, the Persian Empire had fallen to a new world power, that of Greece, whose conquests under Alexander the Great had extended Greek control from southern Europe and North Africa all the way to India. When Alexander died in 323, his successors divided his vast empire into more manageable spheres of influence. Under this division, the territories of the ancient Land of Israel fell between the spheres of two competing dynasties, the Egyptian Ptolemies and the Seleucids of Syria. The Ptolemies retained firm control of the area from 301 to about 201 BCE, until it was seized by the Seleucids under the Emperor Antiochus III the Great. Seleucid rule was, in turn, finally overthrown by the Jews themselves in 152. But let's not get ahead of ourselves just yet.

Unlike their Persian predecessor, the empires that succeeded Alexander saw themselves as more than the bringers of political and social stability. Although often competing among themselves for political and military primacy, they nevertheless regarded themselves as the bearers of a civilization that constituted a kind of universal norm of culture. Grounded in Greek language, political traditions, artistic forms, and intellectual life, this cultural complex came to be called "Hellenism" after the country Hellas (Greece), from whence it spread.

Each of the Hellenistic Empires developed its own particular cultural style indelibly colored by the North African or Middle Eastern political, artistic, and intellectual traditions that had preceded the Alexandrian conquests. Even within the same empire, the nature of the Hellenistic cultural world was modulated by many local influences. Urban cultures, for example, dif-

---

Tracking Hellenism in the Land of Israel:
Some Key Dates

323 BCE: Death of Alexander the Great
301: Land of Israel absorbed into Egyptian Ptolemaic Empire
201: Syrian Seleucids establish authority in Land of Israel
175: Onias III replaced by Jason as High Priest in Jerusalem
168: Maccabees begin "anti-Hellenistic" resistance
167: Antiochus IV Epiphanes intervenes against Maccabees
164: Jerusalem placed under Maccabean authority
152: Jonathan appointed as first Hasmonean High Priest
152–63: Succession of Hasmonean High Priests/Kings

---

fered from one another in important ways. Consider how the contemporary urban cultures of Montreal and Los Angeles—for all they share in common, from McDonalds to universities to professional sports—are deeply marked by regional cultures. And everywhere in the Hellenistic world, as in our own, the urban centers were more cosmopolitan and "international" than were the cultures of the countrysides.

So cultural Hellenism was a highly diverse blend of Greek tradition shaped and interpreted by specific non-Greek peoples. Each hellenized region shaped Hellenism to its own distinctive pattern; each hellenized people created its own Hellenism. This is the case with the Israelites as well. Our introductory chapter has already observed that both native and diaspora Israelites were identified by the geographical/ethnic term *ioudaioi*, which we have rendered as "Judeans" or "Jews." By all accounts, the Jews were widely recognized as a distinctive people. For example, the major cultural center of Ptolemaic Egypt, the coastal city of Alexandria, had an enormous Jewish population that may have reached into the hundreds of thousands. From the third century BCE until well into the second century CE, Alexandrian Jews produced a prolific literature in Greek. Including such Hellenistic genres as drama, poetry, philosophy, and history, these writings demonstrate the degree to which the Jews of this Egyptian oasis of Hellenistic culture absorbed it as their preferred form of creative expression.[3]

It was once assumed by historians of Judaism that the hellenization of the Jewish Diaspora could be contrasted to the relatively pure, uncontaminated Judaic culture of the Land of Israel. That opinion is no longer tenable. The main reason is that archeological studies show that Jews living in their ancestral land possessed more than a passing knowledge of Greek language,

The Ptolemaic and Seleucid Empires

For over a century after the death of Alexander, the Ptolemies of Egypt and the Seleucids of Syria contested for control of the Land of Israel. This map shows the land under Seleucid control prior to 201 BCE.

---

architectural styles, theories of urban planning, and other markers of Hellenistic culture. Jewish archeological remains in the land, that is, are rather similar to Jewish and non-Jewish archeological remains throughout Hellenistic North Africa, Italy, and Asia Minor. So the hellenization of the Jews must be imagined as a matter of various degrees and styles.

In both the Diaspora and in the homeland, Judaism functioned in two ways: it served to distinguish the Jews from their cultural surroundings; but it also helped them to make an identity for themselves within that multiethnic environment as part of it. So various diaspora *styles* of Judaism might certainly differ from those of the homeland (as they might differ from one another), but all bore significant traits of Hellenistic culture.[4]

In the Diaspora, as we have already pointed out, the Jews seem eagerly to have absorbed the literary and intellectual traditions of the Greeks and made them their own. But in the course of doing so, they preserved their ethnic cohesiveness. Reports about the Jews of Hellenistic Alexandria, for example, dwell on the propensity of these Jews to live in their own parts of the city, to preserve customs and laws regarded by non-Jews as either noble and wise or parochial and irrational, and—notably—to insist upon exemptions from certain acts of citizenship that involved sacrifice to local deities. Apparently, Jews used the forms of Egyptian Hellenistic culture to create their distinctive Judaic style within that culture. They defined themselves—and others recognized them—as a distinctive people within the larger collection of groups making up the various subcultures of Egypt.

This type of self-definition within the setting of a larger cultural tradition occurred among Jews throughout the hellenized Diaspora, in such centers as Rome and Sardis. It is nothing more than what the Jews of the homeland were doing as well. Throughout the third and second centuries BCE, the face of Coele-Syria (as the Greeks called Yehudah and its environs west of the Jordan River) had been transformed by trade and immigration. Both stimulated the establishment of the characteristic form of hellenized urban life, the city composed of free citizens (Greek: *polis*). As a result of such demographic and social changes, Aramaic-speaking Judean Jews routinely rubbed shoulders with Greek-speaking foreigners, both Jews and non-Jews. They learned to speak their language and grasp their particular ways of understanding the world. Political leaders of native Jewry—appointed by imperial decree from among the hereditary Aaronide priesthood of Jerusalem—became familiar with the court styles and diplomatic protocols of the Ptolemaic or Seleucid powers and moved easily within them. In general, Jews in positions of social and economic power reproduced in their own country patterns of social, economic, and political life that were the acknowledged norm throughout the civilized world.

But for all that, the hellenization of important groups within native Jewry took a different form from that common in the Diaspora. In the homeland, Judaism carried with it almost necessarily a political meaning that was implicit only in the Diaspora. Language was an important factor here. Jews living in their land knew Greek, which they used in the hellenized cities, but they spoke in their homes and towns a Jewish dialect of Aramaic acquired during the Persian era. Greek-speaking Jews of the Diaspora defined their distinctiveness *within* the sphere of Greek language. Judeans, by contrast, did so with an ancestral language that preceded the Greek experience. No longer associated with Persian domination, it came to seem quintessentially Jewish—no less so than the ancient Hebrew to which it was closely related.

Even though they moved rather comfortably in the hellenized environment of their country, Jews nevertheless retained awareness of being natives in a land under foreign, imperial domination. One of the most important political events of this period involved a powerful conflict among Yehudah's priestly elites over the meaning of Hellenism and of the place of Judaism within the larger Hellenistic world. The event started as a civil war among Jews and turned into a Jewish war of liberation against the Seleucid Empire. It resulted in the creation of a Jewish kingdom under the Hasmonean family. That kingdom was to be the last independent Jewish state in the Land of Israel until the founding of the State of Israel in 1948.[5]

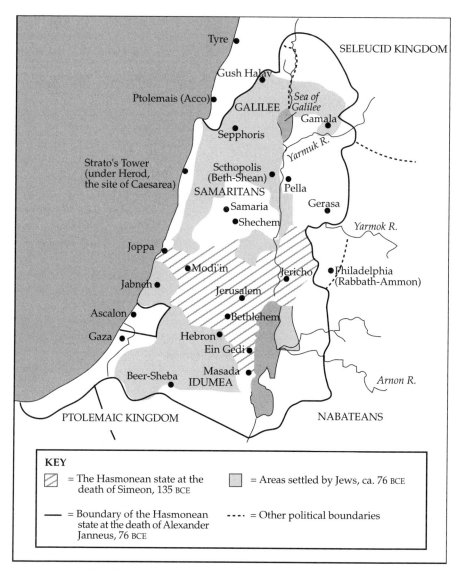

The Hasmonean State, Second–First Century BCE

The boundaries of the Hasmonean Kingdom fluctuated in relation to the state's need to accommodate the dictates of powerful imperial neighbors. The Roman conquest of 63 BCE removed any pretense regarding the actual control of the country.

The terms of the struggle that helped to create the Hasmonean kingdom deserve our attention, for they highlight the way in which terms such as "Hellenism" and "Judaism" took on political as well as cultural meanings. Throughout the period of Ptolemaic rule, the Jews of Coele-Syria had been governed from Jerusalem by Aaronide High Priests who served as provincial administrators responsible to the emperor. These High Priests served a dual role. Wearing the priestly robes, they were representatives of public religious tradition, responsible for supervising the sacrificial rites of the Jerusalem Temple. But they were also political figures, charged with supervising the routine affairs of government through a bureacracy of professional civil servants or scribes.

As in other territories, this upper level of local leadership grew increasingly at home in the international cultural scene and looked to the imperial government to preserve its standing and privilege. It also represented to the peasantry, urban artisans, and tradespeople a prestigious local power charged with protecting their interests. This apparently peaceful local situation began to suffer disruption after the Seleucid conquest of the land in 201 BCE. Circles associated with the High Priest continued to remain loyal to the Egyptian Ptolemaic dynasty. By 175, the reigning High Priest, Onias III, was removed from office by the Seleucids. The new emperor, Antiochus IV Epiphanes, sold the office to Onias' brother Jason. In return for this gift of power, Jason expressed his loyalty to the new emperor by embarking upon an ambitious campaign to reform the official culture of Jewish Coele-Syria along more internationalist lines.

Jason's policies included the transformation of Jerusalem into a polis. By granting the rights of citizenship to selected Jewish aristocrats and property holders, the Greek constitution of the polis enabled them to become full citizens of the empire and significantly enhance their social and economic horizons. Jerusalem's new status transformed as well the status of distinctively Greek institutions, such as athletic contests, public baths, and so forth. They were no longer private activities but took on the character of public works, official institutions of the city. Jason's policy of reform drew attention to an issue that had until then been only implicitly addressed. It was one thing for Hellenistic culture to informally take root almost imperceptibly in the folkways and economic life of the country. But to make such acculturation an official policy of the local Jewish government and afford it ideological primacy in the official life of the community was another matter entirely.

Jason's policies, and the more extreme measures proposed by his successor, Menelaus (ruled 171–167), drew a sharp response among Jews in the countryside in particular. Hellenism came to be identified by many opponents of the priestly Jerusalem elites as the cultural weapon of Greek political domination, wielded in this case by Jewish turncoats. Judaism, by contrast, was now represented as a pristine tradition wholly alien to the international culture of the time, a banner around which to organize political resistance to

Hellenism. From the perspective of hindsight, however, it is clear that the debate was not between Judaism and Hellenism as opposed forces, but really over the degree to which an already hellenized Judaism would self-consciously conform even further to international cultural norms. But hindsight is the luxury of historians, not of historical actors. The fact is that the ideological struggle created a climate of opinion in which it was possible to imagine Judaism and Hellenism as radically opposed spiritual entities. The forces of tradition, standing for Judaism, found themselves in pitched battle against the Hellenizers, who represented irreverence and innovation.

By 168 BCE, a full-scale civil war had broken out between the supporters of the High Priestly administration and various opposition groups, led by Judah the Maccabee ("the Hammerer"), of the Hasmonean family. The goal of the Maccabean forces was to depose the sitting High Priesthood and to reverse its policies of official hellenization. Naturally, the civil war required Antiochus to intervene on behalf of his Jewish loyalists. Thus, a civil war became an international incident; a war against Jewish reformers became a war against a foreign oppressor. This war against the Seleucids ground on for years until 152, when internal affairs among the Seleucids convinced them to abandon the fight and concede political independence to the Jewish rebels. In that year, Jonathan, brother of Judah the Hammerer, officially accepted the title of High Priest. He inaugurated the Hasmonean dynasty that, within a half century, would style its priestly leader as both "King" and "Priest of the Most High God." This dynasty of non-Aaronide priests with royal titles ruled Judea as an independent kingdom until the Roman conquest of 63 BCE.

The Hasmonean experience was to have a profound impact upon Judaism in Judea and its environs. The bitterness spawned in the battle against Hellenism did not dissipate with the Hasmonean victory. To the contrary, as the Hasmonean dynasty wore on, it was routinely accused by outsiders to power of betraying the original ideals of the anti-Hellenistic revolution, of outdistancing even the ancient Hellenizers in diluting the pure essence of Judaism. Opponents could easily question the legitimacy of Hasmonean political leadership from two perspectives: as Kings, the leaders were not Davidic; as High Priests, they were not descended from Aaron through Zadok.

From the mid-second century BCE and after, native Jewry gave birth to a variety of groups calling for one or another form of religious revitalization or political reform. The Temple and its priesthood became a source of conflict and controversy rather than a factor promoting political unity and ideological uniformity. Some of the groups involved in this controversy, such as the Samaritans and the Dead Sea community, will figure prominently in Chapter Four in our description of early Judaism.[6]

We can now sum up the situation of the Jews in the Hellenistic world. Nearly *all* Jews came into contact with Hellenistic culture and shaped it in ways distinctive to their own situations. The hellenized Judaism of the Diaspora retained a rich sense of its ethnic distinctiveness and traditions within a comprehensive mastery of all aspects of Greek cultural expression. Jews of the homeland adapted to the Hellenistic environment on rather different terms, conditioned by the particular political pressures of living in their ancestral country. Defining themselves in opposition to what they identified as Hellenism, they cultivated literary and cultural traditions that they perceived as more ancient than those of Greece. To put it in other terms, the most articulate diaspora Jews—and many in the homeland as well—tended to see their Judaism as an expression of all that was best in Hellenism. Other native Jews, however, were inclined to view their Judaism as an antithesis of everything represented by Hellenism. But however Jews perceived their Judaism, none of them inhabited the insular Judaic world created in Persian Yehud centuries earlier. The Persian cloth had been taken up by a whole new team of weavers whose skills and tastes were profoundly shaped by the experience of living in cosmopolitan Hellenistic culture.

Political Experience Under Roman Domination

The Roman legions of General Pompey entered Jerusalem in 63 BCE to resolve a dynastic struggle between two Hasmonean brothers, Hyrcanus II and Aristobulus II. Hyrcanus was appointed High Priest and executor of Roman political power, so the dynastic question was resolved. But the Romans—except for a brief period of rule by Parthian invaders from 40 to 37 BCE—never left. Their conquest of the land they later called "Palestine" was part of a larger expansion of Roman control throughout the territories of Alexander's heirs, an expansion that gave birth to the Roman Empire. The cultural consequences of Roman domination of diaspora and Palestinian Jewry were relatively minor, for Roman civilization was itself a thoroughly hellenized cultural tradition. Diaspora and Palestinian Jews continued to develop longstanding patterns of culture. But the political consequences of Roman domination proved enormous.[7]

Rome thoroughly reorganized the administration of Palestine into various districts, installing the Hasmonean heir Hyrcanus as a High Priest without any effective political power. The regime remained unstable. Within a short time, an Idumean nobleman named Antipater, whose Jewish ethnicity has often been questioned, had insinuated himself into effective administrative control. With Roman support, he appointed his sons, Herod and Phasael, as district governors. Antipater was poisoned in 43 BCE, preparing the path for the Parthian invasion of 40. Antipater's son Herod was instrumental in leading a force that repelled the Parthians in 37. As a reward, Herod was appointed King of Judea with the full support of Roman military might. For perhaps the first time since the restoration of Persian Yehud, Jews were governed in their own country by a nonpriestly royal administration.

Herod was, by all accounts of the period, a vicious and despotic ruler.

The Roman Presence in Palestine, ca. 30 CE

This map of Palestine under the procuratorship of Pontius Pilate discloses how ancestral territories were divided by the Romans into administrative areas in accordance with imperial needs.

He routinely ordered the murders of political enemies and even family members in order to consolidate his power. But he was also a man who liked a fine marble building and was willing to pay for it out of his public works budget. His reign was distinguished by the inauguration of impressive construction projects throughout the country. A special beneficiary of his attention was

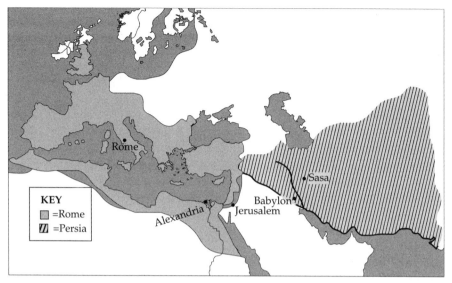

Roman and Persian Empires

The great Mesopotamian empires of the Parthians and, from 224 CE, the Sasanians constituted a powerful threat to Rome's Middle Eastern holdings, including Palestine. The dark area to the right contained heavy pockets of Jewish population, particularly in the areas between the Tigris and Euphrates.

Jerusalem. He built aqueducts, stadiums, and an elegant race track in downtown Jerusalem. He presided over a lavish overhaul of the Temple, transforming it into an enormous and exquisite compound. In short, he made Jerusalem an international city on a scale it had never enjoyed—the pride of Jews throughout the Roman Empire and a symbol of their "arrival" as integral members of world civilization.

With Herod's death in 4 BCE (only a few days after he had had his son Antipater executed), the Romans once again reorganized the administration of Palestine. Archeleus, one of Herod's surviving sons, was named successor over the largest part of Herod's territory, the districts of Judea, Samaria, and Idumea. More despotic than his father, Archeleus' appointment caused great unrest among the Jews, leading to his removal by Roman authorities in 6 CE. Thereafter, Rome dispensed with any pretense to autonomous Jewish rule. It placed the entire territory under the control of a series of Roman procurators, or governors. Each had to deal with an increasingly restive and resentful Jewish population longing to rid itself of the domination of foreigners and their despotic local puppets.

Roman Presence in the Land of Israel:
Some Key Dates

63 BCE: Pompey invited into Jerusalem to resolve Hasmonean dynastic struggle in favor of Hyrcanus II

40–37: Parthian occupation

37: Herod appointed King of Judea by Romans in reward for anti-Parthian activities

20: Work begins on Herodian Temple renovations

4: Death of Herod

6 CE: Herod's successor, Archeleus, deposed; Coponius appointed first Roman procurator

26: Pontius Pilate appointed procurator

30: Crucifixion of Jesus of Nazareth

66: Palestinian Jews revolt against Roman occupation

70: Herodian Temple destroyed by Romans

73: Fall of Judean resistance at Massada

ca. 95: Rabban Gamaliel II appointed Patriarch by Romans under Emperor Domitian

115–117: Anti-Roman diaspora rebellions; decimation of Alexandrian Jewish community by Emperor Trajan

132: Bar Kosiba leads rebellion against Rome; takes title of Patriarch

135: Emperor Hadrian suppresses Bar Kosiba's revolt

138: Hadrian's death ends measures to suppress Judaism

140: Rabban Shimon b. Gamaliel II appointed Patriarch under Emperor Antoninus Pius

170: Rabbi Judah b. Shimon b. Gamaliel appointed Patriarch under Emperor Marcus Aurelius

212: Edict of Emperor Caracalla confers Roman citizenship on all Empire's residents, including Jews

313: Emperor Constantine's Edict of Milan establishes Christianity as a legal religion in Roman Empire

361–363: Emperor Julian initiates attempts to rebuild Jerusalem Temple; his death signals end of project

425: Emperor Theodosius declines to appoint successor to Gamaliel VI as Patriarch; Patriarchate ends

The most famous of these procurators, of course, was Pontius Pilate (ruled 26–36 CE). His execution of Jesus of Nazareth on charges of political agitation had consequences for Rome that Pilate (and, probably, Jesus himself) could never have imagined. The last of the procurators was Gessius Florus (ruled 64–66). His particularly stupid blunder—unlike Pilate, he should have foreseen the consequences—was to forcibly expropriate from the Temple treasury a rather large sum of gold in compensation for back taxes. Since Temple funds were considered sanctified and could be put only to the purposes of the Temple itself, the act was seized upon by the Jews as an idolatrous desecration. Anti-Roman riots naturally ensued. The riots turned into a full-scale war to expel Rome from the Land of Israel. The war, from the Jewish point of view, was a disaster. It dragged on, with much loss of life and property, until 73, with the fall of the last Judean fortress, Masada. But the fatal wound had already occurred in 70, with the Roman destruction of Jerusalem and the burning of Herod's magnificent Temple.

For diaspora and Judean Jews, the pillage of Jerusalem and the burning of the Temple recalled the horrors of half a millennium earlier. The religious consequences of these events will occupy us in detail in Chapter Two in particular. But for now, the political and economic dimensions of the catastrophe are worthy of note. The Temple served, even under Roman domination, as a potent international symbol of Jewish political identity. Its violation was not only a sacrilege, but a statement of utter contempt for the Jewish nation. It was a political as well as a religious humiliation. Morever, the Temple—like other Middle Eastern religious centers—functioned as a financial hub of the country's economic life, a center for banking and the exchange of currencies. Its destruction, along with the mass burning of productive agricultural lands, threw the peasantry, artisans, and merchants of the country into desperate financial straits.

It appears that Judean as well as diaspora Jews could not reconcile themselves to what had occurred. After a generation of relative calm and regrouping, Jewish political unrest once again emerged, this time in the traditionally pacifist Diaspora. From 115 to 117 CE, under the reigns of the Emperors Trajan and Hadrian, diaspora Jews from North Africa to Mesopotamia took up arms in what appeared to be a coordinated series of riotous outbreaks. Very little is known of the motives of these disturbances; but they were severe enough to engage Rome's best military tacticians in their suppression.

Palestinian Jewry seems to have sat out this period of unrest, but it reentered the anti-Roman battle in 132. Sparked by a charismatic guerilla leader, Shimon bar Kosiba, this war clearly had as its object the expulsion of Rome from Palestine and the re-creation of an independent Jewish kingdom in the Land of Israel. Bar Kosiba called himself by a title, "Prince" (Hebrew: *nasi*), that had clear royalist implications. He also was given the punning nickname "bar Kokhba" (Son of the Star). This recalled the prophecy from

the Torah about a star that would "proceed from Jacob" to establish dominion (Num. 24:17). All this suggests that he and his followers viewed their rebellion as the political stage of a larger world drama that would culminate
with divine intervention on behalf of Israel. For a short time, at any rate, bar
Kosiba's forces managed to regain Jerusalem and restore sacrificial services
in the Temple ruins. A government was formed, coins dated "Year One of the
Liberation of Israel" were struck, and taxes were collected. Despite the ex-
citement, an exhausted Diaspora seems to have been unable to muster much
enthusiasm for bar Kosiba's war and did little to detract Rome's military attention from Palestine. Eventually, superior Roman military power and economic resources prevailed. By 135, the last of bar Kosiba's forces fell at the
battle of Betar.

The victorious Emperor Hadrian punished Jewish survivors of the rebellion with massive punitive measures. These included deportations from
Judea, mass executions, and the prohibition of Jewish customs regarded as
politically subversive. By 135, the face of Judea had been transformed.
Nearly all the Jewish population was gone, being deported into the northern
province of the Galilee or finding a haven as refugees in the Parthian
provinces of Mesopotamia. Jerusalem had become the site of a new Roman
city, Aelia Capitolina. And what remained of Herod's Temple housed an altar dedicated to Jupiter, the chief god of the Roman imperial religion. With
Jewry's political and economic center destroyed, its diaspora populations in
disarray, and its homeland depopulated, there is every reason for Rome to
have been confident that the Jews would soon cease to be a significant factor
in the life of the empire.[8]

Reconstituting Jewish Society in Palestine and Babylonia

Rome was correct in its political judgment. Neither Palestinian nor diaspora
Jewry would ever again become a political flashpoint. But Rome did not anticipate that its own policies toward the Jews would encourage a dramatic restructuring of Judaism. Two factors were at work here. The first was
indigenous to Palestinian Jewish culture—the postwar rise to prominence of
a community of Torah scholars who called themselves "Sages" (Hebrew:
hakhamim) and often bore the title "Rabbi" (Master). We discuss these rabbis
in great detail in later chapters. For now, we simply observe that their distinctive interpretations of Jewish history and law proved immensely influential among Palestinian and Babylonian Jews in particular. Taking up the
charred fabric of Hellenistic Jewish culture in Palestine and the Diaspora, the
Sages preserved what they could of the inherited weave and added to it patterns of their own strikingly original design.

The rabbis' new cloth, however, would have found few Jewish buyers without their corresponding success in establishing a market for its display. This brings us to the second crucial factor in the post-70 survival of Judaism— Roman policy regarding Jewish political expression. As important as the emergence of the Sages as teachers was their ability to convince first Roman and, later, Babylonian imperial authorities that they could be effective in governing a numerous and politically volatile Jewish population in both empires. Our survey of the social and cultural setting of early Judaic worlds concludes, therefore, by tracing the role of rabbinic figures in shaping Jewish political life in the later Roman Empire and in the Sasanian Empire of Babylonia.

The fundamental patterns of Rome's policy regarding Jewish self-government in Palestine were sketched within a generation after Rome's suppression of the war of 66–70. The bar Kosiba episode constituted only a brief interruption of a process that had gotten underway sometime during the reign of the Emperor Domitian (81–96). Rome's administration of Jewish Palestine was calculated to pacify the Jews, not by persecution and humiliation, but rather by offering them significant privileges of self-government in return for political quiescence. Jews in Palestine could preserve their ancestral customs, as long as these were compatible with Roman law and did not lead to social unrest. As Persian policy had done centuries earlier in Yehud, Rome's intentions in Palestine were to cultivate local leaders who could directly administer Jewish affairs and distance the imperial hand from everyday life.

Rome pursued this policy by placing Palestinian Jewry under the authority of a Jewish appointee who bore the official Greek title of Ethnarch (Leader of the People) or Patriarch (Leader of the Fatherland). The Hebrew title by which the office was known, *nasi* (Prince), drew upon biblical memories of great tribal leadership and, especially, the prophet Ezekiel's vision of a future leader of restored Israel (Ezek. 46:1–18). From the last decade of the first century until the first quarter of the fifth, Palestinian Jewry was organized under the Patriarchate. The title was deemed so important that even the rebel bar Kosiba claimed it as his own in his bid for political independence from Rome.[9]

The role of the Patriarch as a Roman official was a complex one with international significance. For Jews outside Palestine—in Egypt, Asia Minor, or Italy—the office eventually became an important symbol of Jewish ethnic autonomy within the polyglot environment of the empire's diverse peoples. What the Temple and its High Priest had represented before 70—the national dignity of the Diaspora's Jews—the Patriarchate stood for by 200. In the homeland, of course, the holder of the office embodied the last vestiges of Jewish political independence, administering a delicate balance of political submission and cultural autonomy. By 200, the holders of the office claimed matrilineal descent from the ancient Davidic royal family. Once and for all, Jewish self-government in the Jewish homeland had passed from the hands of High Priests who ruled as non-Davidic Kings to a leader who claimed the prestige of Davidic origins without the advantage of priestly lineage.

From its inception in the nineties, the patriarchal office seems to have been a hereditary one. The first holder of the title was a rabbinic master named Gamaliel b. Shimon b. Gamaliel. The office remained in the Gamaliel family throughout its entire history in an unbroken chain of fathers, sons, and grandsons. It remains unclear why Rome chose a rabbinic family for this powerful position. Nor is it certain why, among rabbinic families, that of Gamiliel was selected. Nevertheless, the results of placing a rabbinic Sage in charge of administering Jewish affairs in the homeland were largely foreseeable. Wherever patriarchal influence extended in Palestine or the Diaspora, rabbinic interpretations of Jewish traditions came effectively to enjoy the status of Jewish civil law and ritual custom. The Judaic world in which the rabbis lived came increasingly to dominate other patterns of Judaism that had survived the wars. Rabbinic custom was slowly transformed from the communal tradition of the Sages into Jewish law per se.

The principal architect of this transformation was the most famous Patriarch, Judah b. Shimon b. Gamaliel, who ruled in the late second and early third centuries. He loomed so massively in later rabbinic memory that he remained the only rabbinic authority referred to simply as "Rabbi," without a proper name to identify him. Rabbi ensured that rabbinic legal tradition would become the main source of law in Jewish courts under patriarchal jurisdiction. It was under his reign, and those of his successors, that a compilation of rabbinic traditions called the Mishnah (Hebrew: Repeated Tradition) became the central nourishment of rabbinic intellectual life, spawning the tradition that would eventually issue into the vast talmudic literature of later centuries. We discuss this literature at length in the next chapter.[10]

The Palestinian Patriarch, as the sole legal representation of the Jewish polity in the Roman Empire, enjoyed enormous influence and prestige. But from the early fourth century and on, the Patriarchate became somewhat problematic. The principal reason was the sudden rise to political prominence of Christianity. Beginning as a Jewish messianic movement focused on the first-century CE teacher Jesus of Nazareth, Christian communities had by the end of that century begun to move beyond Jewish communal boundaries. Focusing now on the vast missionary possibilities of the non-Jewish peoples of the Roman Empire, Christianity had become by the third century a successful—but controversial—religion. As monotheists, Christians refused to participate in Roman imperial religious rituals, which included offerings to the emperor as a divinity. Jews had long been exempted from such rites. But Christians—who took pains to explain that they were not Jews—were suspected of harboring seditious political views. The second and third centuries saw frequent and vicious Roman persecution of Christianity.

Things changed, however, in the fourth century. In 313, the Emperor Constantine, who had strong sympathies with Christianity, issued the Edict of Milan, which established Christianity as one of the tolerated religions of the Roman state. After Constantine, with the exception of the brief reign of

Julian (361–363), the emperor himself was a Christian. Especially in the eastern territories of the Byzantine Empire, this had important consequences for the Jewish political prominence represented by the Palestinian Patriarch. It had been one thing for Imperial Rome, the persecutor of the Church, to acknowledge the political and cultural integrity of a subdued Jewish ethnic minority. It was quite another for Christian Byzantium to tolerate expressions of Jewish royal nostalgia among the people who had rejected the Kingship of Christ. The Patriarchate survived the transition of the Roman Empire to Christianity for about a century. By 425, with the death of the incumbent, Gamaliel VI, the Emperor Theodosius allowed the office to lapse. An unseemly expression of pride among a people who were privileged to survive in Christendom only on conditions of subordination, the Patriarchate was an office whose time had passed.[11]

During the centuries of the Patriarchate, a parallel institution—the Exilarchate—was developing in Mesopotamia, under the Parthian and, from 226, the Sasanian Empires. Called in Aramaic the *resh galuta* (Head of the Exiles), the Exilarchate had its roots in the mid-second century under the Parthians. It appears to have been born from that empire's calculations regarding the possible role of the Jews as allies in its foreign policy relating to Rome, its chief rival for control of the Middle East.

The Parthians had never forgotten their nearly successful conquest of Palestine in 40–37 BCE and hoped to regain the country. Accordingly, they carefully cultivated the loyalties of the substantial Jewish communities within their own borders. These communities had grown, by the mid-second century, through significant migrations of Jews from war-ravaged Palestine, among whom were numbered many rabbinic disciples. Such refugees were hardly supporters of Rome. The Parthian appointment of a prominent figure Huna as Exilarch in 170 was at least in part an effort to demonstrate to Palestinian Jews the sympathies of Persia for their plight. If anti-Roman Jewish unrest could be fomented in Rome's Palestinian eastern frontier, this might serve as a pretext for a Persian invasion and a restoration of Palestine (with its fertile fields, rich cities, and valuable coastal ports) to its ancestral Persian political constellation.

The Parthian goals ultimately went unfulfilled, and even the Sasanian successors to the Parthian territories were frustrated in their own designs against Rome. Nevertheless, the Exilarchate proved to be an institution of crucial importance for Mesopotamian Jewry. The great Sasanian emperor, Shapur I, significantly enhanced the authority and standing of the Exilarchate after 242. Although never, like its Palestinian counterpart, the familial perquisite of a prominent rabbinic house, the exilarchal families nevertheless claimed even stronger connections to the Davidic House than did the Palestinian Gamalians. The Patriarchate claimed matrilineal descent from David, whereas the Exilarchate claimed a more prestigious patrilineal relationship.

A series of Exilarchs, relatively poor in rabbinic learning but rich in

---

Babylonian Jewry Under Achemenids, Seleucids, Parthians, and Sasanians: Some Key Dates

597–587 BCE: Successive waves of Jewish deportees transported from land of Israel to Babylonia

540: Babylonian Empire under Nabonidus falls to Cyrus the Great of Persia, first major ruler in the Achemenid Dynasty

539: Cyrus permits repatriation of Jewish exiles

ca. 450–398: Emperor Artaxerxes I or Artaxerxes II encourages restoration of Yehud under guidance of Babylonian Jews, Ezra and Nehemiah

331: Alexander the Great conquers Persian Achemenid Empire and establishes control in Babylonia

323: Babylonia claimed for Seleucid Empire

ca. 240: Arsaces I founds Arsacid Dynasty in Parthia

120: Parthian Arsacids establish control of Babylonia

ca. 135 CE: Rabbinic refugees from Palestine establish a center in Huzal

ca. 170: Huna I appointed Exilarch under Parthian Emperor Vologases III

226: Sasanian Dynasty establishes control in Babylonia

242: Sasanian Emperor Shapur I enhances Exilarchate of Mar Ukba I

455: Zoroastrian persecutions of Jews and Christians under Sasanian Emperor Yezdegerd I

ca. 470: Execution of Exilarch Huna V under Sasanian Emperior Firuz

520: Execution of Exilarch Mar Zutra II under Sasanian Emperor Kovad I

634: Sasanian Empire falls to Islam during Exilarchate of Bustenai

---

power conferred by the Sasanian state, tried to work with the increasingly influential rabbinic masters then establishing centers of learning in the empire. Requiring rabbinic legal expertise for their own operations, and seeking scholarly confirmation of their Davidic legitimacy, the Exilarchs were crucial in establishing rabbinic legal and ritual custom as the binding traditions in Mesopotamia's Jewish courts and schools. Thus, Palestinian rabbinic contributions to the fabric of Judaism were taken up and enhanced among the rabbinic circles of Babylonia.

As long as the Palestinian Patriarchate remained in existence, the Exilarch cultivated a posture of submission to the prestigious institution emanating from the Land of Israel. Patriarchal prerogatives in such crucial matters as establishing the religious calendar in accord with calculations of the phases of the moon, the ordination of rabbinic disciples as teachers, and other issues were readily acknowledged. After 425, however, the vacuum in Palestinian leadership enabled the Exilarch to emerge for a time as the premier political figure in the Jewish world. In the late fifth century, however, the existence of the Exilarchate was threatened by governmental policies against Judaism and Christianity. The Exilarch Huna V was executed in 470, and the office lapsed temporarily, until it was restored early in the sixth century. Thereafter it remained tightly controlled by imperial policies.

Rabbinic attitudes toward the Exilarch, recorded in the talmudic literature, were complex. During the existence of the Patriarchate, which joined an impeccable rabbinic family to the prestige of Davidic lineage, Mesopotamian sages owed their primary allegiance to the Patriarch. Yet in order to pursue rabbinic religious goals in Mesopotamia, it was necessary to work with the Exilarch. Thus, while rabbinic Sages lampooned his relative ignorance of their traditions, or otherwise questioned his competence to rule, they were bound to the Exilarch in a marriage of political convenience. The heads of the great rabbinic academies (Hebrew: *yeshivot*) of the cities of Sura and Pumbedita were cultivated by the Exilarch, and they in turn enhanced their prestige by their relationship to him.[12]

Unlike the Palestinian Patriarchate, the Exilarchate received enough support from its imperial sponsors to survive radical political and cultural changes in the empire. When Muslim armies gained final political control of the Byzantine and Sasanian lands by the mid-seventh century, the Exilarchate appeared an eminently useful tool for governing the Jewish masses under Islamic social policies. The office thrived, especially after 661 under the Umayyad dynasty. But the history of the Exilarchate in the Islamic world takes us far beyond the scope of this book.

Conclusion

Our social and political survey of the first Judaic millennium has focused upon the attempts of Jews to secure their social and political interests under the domination of Persian, Hellenistic, Roman, and Sasanian empires. We have seen that the continuous Jewish habitation of the Land of Israel (under various names), and of important diaspora centers such as Egypt and Babylonia, served as the setting for major developments in the way Jews defined themselves as a group and expressed that collective self-understanding.

In the homeland—from the earliest expression of Judaism in Persian Yehud to the last years of the Palestinian Patriarchate under Rome—Judaism continuously reshaped itself in conversation with the occupiers of the land and the cultures they brought to it. So, too, in the Diaspora, a continuous communication between the surrounding cultures and the Jewry of the homeland fostered important modulations of what could be meant by the term "Judaism" at any particular time. Ioudaismos might have seemed rather uniform to outsiders; but among the Jews it took many forms.

We have, then, pointed out some of the key weavers of the cloth that became Judaism, identified some of the materials they used in their work, and described the cultural settings in which they labored. But what did they make? We begin now to look more closely at the threads themselves and the larger patterns into which they were woven.

Notes

1. The historical scholarship on the history of ancient Israel is enormous, complex, and filled with controversy. A highly respected collection of scholarly essays on various aspects of ancient Israelite history is provided by John H. Hayes and J. Maxwell Miller, eds., *Israelite and Judean History* (Philadelphia: Westminster Press, 1977). A similar collection of excellent essays on the diverse religious life of ancient Israel is that of Patrick D. Miller Jr., Paul D. Hanson, and S. Dean McBride, eds., *Ancient Israelite Religion* (Philadelphia: Fortress Press, 1987).

   Archeologists debate rather sharply the degree to which archeological discoveries confirm the biblical accounts of Israel's history on its land. A comprehensive account from one who sees biblical sources as rather reliable records is that of Amihai Mazar, *Archaeology of the Land of the Bible: 10,000–586 BCE* (New York: Doubleday, 1990). This should be supplemented by an account that sees less convergence of biblical and archeological information: Robert B. Coote and Keith W. Whitelam, eds., *The Emergence of Early Israel in Historical Perspective* (Sheffield, England: The Almond Press, 1987).

   A rapid survey of Israelite history by careful scholars for nonprofessional readers can be consulted in Hershel Shanks, ed., *Ancient Israel: A Short History from Abraham to the Roman Destruction of the Temple* (Englewood Cliffs, NJ: Prentice Hall, 1988), pp. 1–149.

2. The best introduction to what is known about the Persian Period can be found in Lester L. Grabbe, *Judaism from Cyrus to Hadrian. Volume One: The Persian and Greek Periods* (Minneapolis: Fortress Press, 1992), pp. 27–145. For in-depth discussions of specific questions, the following two volumes are indispensable. Philip R. Davies, ed., *Second Temple Studies: 1. Persian Period* (Sheffield, England: Sheffield Academic Press, 1991), and Tamara C. Eskenazi and Kent H. Richards, eds., *Second Temple Studies: 2. Temple Community in the Persian Period* (Sheffield, England: Sheffield Academic Press, 1994).

3. A reliable and interesting survey of the nature of Jewish cultural identity in the Hellenistic Diaspora is provided by John J. Collins, *Between Athens and Jerusalem: Jewish Identity in the Hellenistic Diaspora* (New York: Crossroad, 1983).

4. Readable summaries of how Hellenism affected different types of Jewish populations in different ways may be consulted in Alan F. Segal, *Rebecca's Children: Judaism and Christianity in the Roman World* (Cambridge, MA, and London: Harvard University Press, 1986), pp. 13–37, and Shaye J.D. Cohen, *From the Maccabees to the Mishnah* (Philadelphia: The Westminster Press, 1987), pp. 34–45. For greater depth, see Grabbe, *Judaism from Cyrus to Hadrian: Volume One*, pp. 147–170.

5. For guidance in interpreting the complex sources of information regarding the origins of the Hasmonean state, see Daniel J. Harrington, *The Maccabean Revolt: Anatomy of a Revolution* (Wilmington: Michael Glazer Press, 1988). A handier discussion may be consulted in Grabbe, *Judaism from Cyrus to Hadrian: Volume One*, pp. 246–268.

6. Good initial orientations to the nature of Jewish political and religious controversies during the Hasmonean dynasty can be found in two articles: J. Andrew Overman and William Scott Green, "Judaism (Greco-Roman Period)" in David Noel Freedman, ed., *The Anchor Bible Dictionary, Volume III* (New York: Doubleday, 1992), pp. 1037–1054 and Steven D. Fraade, "Palestinian Judaism," *Anchor Bible Dictionary, 3* pp. 1054–1061.

   An excellent but demanding account of the tensions aroused by the Hasmonean attempt to unite the role of King and High Priest is offered by David Goodblatt, *The Monarchic Principle: Studies in Jewish Self-Government in Antiquity* (Tuebingen, Germany: J.C.B. Mohr [Paul Siebeck], 1994), pp. 15–29.

7. Summaries of events in Jewish Palestine from 63 BCE to 70 CE are conveniently available in Grabbe, *Judaism From Cyrus to Hadrian: Volume Two: The Roman Period* (Minneapolis: Fortress Press, 1992), pp. 313–554.

8. A comprehensive scholarly treatment of the period from the destruction of Jerusalem in 70 through the third century is offered by Mary E. Smallwood, *The Jews Under Roman Rule from Pompey to Diocletian* (Leiden, The Netherlands: E.J. Brill, 1976), pp. 293–506. See Schiffman, *From Text to Tradition*, pp. 171–176 for the quick tour.

9. My understanding of the origins of the Patriarchate closely follows the most recent discussion of the complex rabbinic and nonrabbinic evidence offered by Goodblatt, *The Monarchic Priniciple*, pp. 131–231.

10. The later history of the Palestinian Patriarchate is summarized in Lee I. Levine, *The Rabbinic Class of Roman Palestine in Late Antiquity* (Jerusalem and New York: Yad Izhak Ben-Zvi and Jewish Theological Seminary of America, 1989), pp. 134–191.

11. For the history of the Patriarchate during the Byzantine period, see Michael Avi-Yonah, *The Jews of Palestine: A Political History from the Bar Kochba War to the Arab Conquest* (Oxford: Basil Blackwell, 1976), pp. 208–231.

12. Jacob Neusner, *Israel's Politics in Sasanian Iran: Jewish Self-Government in Talmudic Times* (Lanham, MD: University Press of America, 1986), is the handiest discussion of the history of the Babylonian Exilarchate and its relations with the main rabbinic schools.

_____ *Two* _____

Dynamics
of Texts
and Traditions

Introduction

The Umayyad Muslims established their dynasty in the Syrian city of Damascus in 661, commanding many of the former territories of the Christian Byzantine and Zoroastrian Sasanian Empires. Those territories, of course, encompassed the large Jewish populations of Egypt, Palestine, and Babylonia. It was a population that had become, over the past centuries, increasingly familiar with the religious world taking shape among the rabbinic Sages and their growing numbers of disciples.

This is not to say that the majority of Jews in the Umayyad lands would have considered themselves disciples of the Sages. To the contrary, rabbinic writings are quite clear that the Sages often met resistance to their authority over the private lives of Jewish townspeople. But whatever Jews might have thought of the Sages' teachings, they had little choice but to abide by the rabbinic laws applied in the Jewish courts of the empire or to recognize the authority of the rabbinic appointees in the Exilarch's administration. Whether Jews encountered a rabbinic Sage as a neighbor, a fellow worshipper, a business partner, a preacher, or a local official, it would have been impossible to miss a striking fact. Whatever the Sage did—how he ate, dressed, prayed, sold his goods, or tried cases—he was guided by rather distinctive understandings of the Torah of Moses, understandings he regarded as ancient traditions of all Israel.

Central to the training of rabbinic disciples was a peculiar discipline of memory, particularly in the memorization of literary texts. Some of these texts, such as those recorded in the Hebrew Bible, had existed long before the rise of the rabbinic movement and formed a crucial imaginative resource for numerous worlds of Judaism. Sages knew them by the particular name "Written Torah." In addition, a disciple would also have mastered a complementary body of rabbinic teachings called "Oral Torah." He proved his worthiness as a scholar by holding forth upon this entire textual tradition of Written and Oral Torah in extended public disquisitions on legal and theological topics.

This explicit theory of a dual Torah as written scripture and oral tradition was unique to rabbinic Judaism. For the half millennium prior to the emergence of rabbinic Judaism, the demarcation between scriptural writings and nonscriptural traditions had been far less clear-cut. Much of the present chapter, accordingly, is devoted to the problem of scripture and tradition in nonrabbinic Judaic worlds. We begin with an account of the origins of the Hebrew Bible itself, the collection of writings that Jews throughout our period referred to as "Scripture." Then we explore some of the ways in which different Judaic communities interpreted the relation of these writings to other authoritative literary works in their tradition. By the end of this chapter, it will be possible to appreciate what was at stake in the rabbinic division of all sacred learning—"Torah"—into Written and Oral sources.

Our story, then, is largely about the sacred writings of early Judaism and their echoes in Judaic tradition. It is important, therefore, as a kind of prelude, to discuss one of the central problems that all students of the history of religions must confront sooner or later. What are "sacred scriptures," and how do they differ from other sorts of writings that also enjoy authority in religious communities? Working through this question will prepare us to discuss the nature of the scriptural collection of early Judaism and the interpretive traditions that transmitted its meaning.

The Hebrew Bible as a Scripture

The Hebrew Bible has been known by many names. Among the Jews of our period and the earliest generations of Christians, "Scripture" was perhaps the most common designation. Jews since the Middle Ages have commonly referred to it as the "Tanakh." Christians, of course, have known it as their "Old Testament" since the late second century CE. The term "Bible" is an inheritance from Greek-speaking Jews who referred to their scriptures as *ta biblia ta hagia*, "the holy books." Just about every name for this book, it seems, testifies to a particular religious community's reverence for it. In order to speak about it as a historical object, we shall use the neutral term "Hebrew Bible." The noun "Bible" allows us to acknowledge this work's authoritative status in diverse religious groups; the adjective "Hebrew" identifies the ancient language in which most of it (but for some Aramaic sections) was originally written.

By whatever name it is called, however, today it looks like a modern book. The appearance is deceptive. Most modern books are written by authors who are proud to identify themselves with their work, regard it as their personal creative statement, and want to protect their writing from being used by others without due credit. Authors (or publishers) choose the titles, the author's name is emblazoned on the cover, and the finished product is marketed by advertising. So a modern book, such as the one you are holding at this moment, represents a specific kind of a cultural object. Publishers call it "intellectual property."

The Hebrew Bible originated as a very different kind of object. In the first place, although it has composers, none of them took responsibility for their work. Biblical writings came into being in a culture that did not regard authorship as a creative activity. Rather, many whom we might regard as "authors" regarded themselves as mere "arrangers" or "retellers" who organized and recounted what they had received as ancient tradition. If, in preserving for the future the wisdom of the past, writers changed what they received, they did so—in their view—in order to enhance it, not necessarily to falsify it.

Authorship was not viewed as self-expression. Therefore, when ancient books were linked to authors, these were rarely the actual composers of the book. More commonly, the "author" was the ancient figure of the past—Moses, or some other figure deemed close to God—whose inspired communications were believed to have been preserved in tradition long enough to be recorded by later writers in the book bearing his name. This is why ancient scribes could, quite honestly, claim an inspired or revealed status for a book of their own composition. They viewed themselves as mere vehicles through which the truths given to the inspired ancient author spoke to the present and the future.

Throughout the history of Persian Yehud and well into the Hellenistic period, Jews composed many such books. The Hebrew Bible is a collection of only twenty-four of them. These books have many different authors (none of them known for certain). Until well into the early centuries CE, most Jews would never have seen all of these books gathered together in a single place. The entire collection of writings would be found only in particularly sacred settings, such as the archive of the Jerusalem Temple. And few people outside the priesthood or trained scribes would have had occasion to consult all of them. It was, in fact, early Christian missionaries who, in the late first century CE, first brought Greek translations of these books together into a single volume between covers. For centuries, Judaism resisted the Christian innovation of the bound book (Latin: *codex*) as a form for preserving scriptural texts.

Jews knew these writings primarily as separate, rather unwieldy, scrolls. Written on papyrus or treated hides, some could be dozens of feet long. For centuries, there was little universal agreement about precisely how many such scrolls were included in the scriptural collection, which writings should enjoy scriptural status, or which versions of the texts were the authentic versions. Very few people would have owned the entire collection or would ever have studied it all on their own. Most people would have learned to read and write by copying out crucial passages of some of the scriptures. More commonly, they would have known many of the writings only as something heard in the course of public addresses of a religious, educational, or political nature. Even for the thoroughly literate, scripture was primarily something *heard* in the exposition of a teacher much more than something read by oneself.

In all, for most of the history of early Judaism, scripture was a rather more fluid reality than the solid, printed modern version in your hands might suggest. In its cultural origins, it was not a "book" at all, but a rather diverse library. As a medium of knowledge, it was mostly heard in public as an evocative utterance from a teacher rather than read in private as a source of personal instruction.[1]

Scripture, Tradition, and Canon

This last point about the communal setting for communicating knowledge of the Hebrew Bible gets us into the heart of our discussion. Throughout this chapter you will meet familiar concepts such as "scripture," "tradition," and "canon." But we will use them in a rather specialized sense developed by recent historians of religion. As in our introductory reflections on common terms such as "religion" and "Judaism," the point is not to develop an esoteric language for the sake of sounding educated. Rather, we attempt to clarify just what is at stake when venerable writings, such as the Hebrew Bible, are found at the center of a community's collective life.[2]

Let's begin with "scripture": *a scripture is a writing preserved by a religious community as an authoritative source of teaching, reflection, or worship.* The great attention devoted to scriptures derives in part from conceptions of their origins. Scriptures are not understood to be authored. Rather they are "received." Although the texts are preserved by human memory and inscribed on permanent surfaces in human languages, they are believed to have originally been delivered to the communal ancestors complete and perfect. Very commonly, they are believed to originate as communications from a god or a heavenly messenger.

The matter of origins is crucial. There is an important difference between a writing received by a particular composer as an inspired revelation

Reading from a Scriptural Scroll

Until well into the Common Era, Jews preserved their most important literary texts on scrolls of animal skin or papyrus. Illustrated here is a fresco representing a Jew reading from such a scroll. The fresco was found in the remains of a third-century CE synagogue in the Syrian archeological site of Dura-Europos. It is possible that the painter intended this to be a portrait of the prophet Moses or of the post-exilic leader Ezra.

Source: Goodenough, E.R., *Jewish Symbols in the Greco-Roman Period*. Copyright © 1988 by Princeton University Press. Reprinted/reproduced by permission of Princeton University Press.

and a writing received by a religious community as its scripture. The former need not necessarily attain the recognition of the latter. Texts normally do not become scriptures simply because the latest composer claims to have received it. Rather, writings become scriptures only because human communities have at some point agreed to place them at the center of the common life. Any text regarded as scripture came to be so because a community, formally or informally, gave it a central place in the pattern of communal life. Often, the precise role of a given text in the common life is a source of conflict. Different segments of a larger community might dispute whether this or that writing is truly authoritative for all members. Thus, it often happens that a text that is "scripture" in one community is simply a "writing" in another. Disputes within religious communities over what is and what is not scripture are a common theme in the history of religions.

The communal consensus that regards a text as scripture brings into play the second term we have introduced, "tradition": *tradition is simply that which has been handed down from the past for preservation in the present.* This can include writings. In the history of religions, it is tradition that sustains writings in the life of a community long enough for them to acquire the exalted status of scripture. There are relatively few examples of writings penned by a single known author who intended to write a scripture and saw his intentions realized. The works of the Hellenistic teacher Mani and of the nineteenth-century founder of Mormonism Joseph Smith are rare exceptions. Even the Quran of Islam, which was received by the prophet Mohammad from the angel Jibril over a period of decades, was not received by the Islamic community as its sole and complete scripture until a generation after Mohammad's death. This is a remarkably swift transition. Usually, a writing has been transmitted for some generations—or even centuries—before achieving its scriptural place in a community's life.

In this sense, scripture and tradition are mutually intertwined realities. A particular writing must have first become a tradition before it could have become a scripture. Once a traditional literary work becomes scripture, it is usually preserved in a fixed text that cannot be changed or emended. When scriptures are preserved in oral form, they are usually preserved by professional memorizers trained in sophisticated memorization techniques. In the more common case of written scriptures, great effort is invested in ensuring that copies of the text are reproduced word for word and letter for letter, for nothing in the holy writing can be lost or altered.

In the long ages prior to the printing press, scribes were entrusted with the crucial mission of producing letter-perfect copies of scriptural texts. But even the most careful scribe is capable of error. Especially when a community might have only one manuscript of its scripture, even the occasional errors of scribes can be copied and recopied as part of the sacred scripture. Ancient scribes and other authorities were aware of this possibility and took measures to determine which version of their scripture was the authentic received version. Often drawing upon the literary science of Hellenistic scholarship, Judaism, Christianity, and Islam all developed very sophisticated critical standards for determining the correct versions of their scriptural texts.

This is where the term "canon" enters the picture. In one sense, *a canon is a norm by which a community determines which version of a scriptural text is authentic or authoritative.* That is, the canonical version of the text is the one used as the standard for making copies. Thanks to the discovery of the Dead Sea Scrolls, which we shall discuss from a variety of perspectives, historians are able to demonstrate significant variety in the texts of ancient versions of the Hebrew Bible. Apparently, prior to the canonization of the present received text of the Hebrew Bible, there were other versions of the text in circulation. Which, if any, were canonical beyond the boundaries of the communities that preserved them is difficult to say. Most probably, different Jewish communities preserved their own traditions of the canonical text.

The term "canon" also has a second meaning: *a canon is a collection of scriptures.* The norms for determining whether a given writing is canonical or not vary. Some communities test the content of a writing in light of doctrinal or legal content, others in terms of its antiquity or supposed authorship. The canon of any community's scripture is that collection that passes the scrutiny of these various norms.

The canon of the Hebrew Bible, for example, shifts in different communal settings. Some early Jewish—and most Christian communities until the sixteenth century—had a canon of writings rather larger than the canon accepted within rabbinic Judaism since the early centuries CE. The Greek translation of the Hebrew Bible, known as the Septuagint, is an important example, for it became the foundation for the Old Testament of Christianity. But even today there is no universal Christian agreement upon the precise content of the Old Testament canon. The point to grasp now is that the canon of scripture is the product of various communal negotiations.

It is helpful to view scripture, tradition, and canon as complex processes that represent the results of interpretive reflection within historically specific communities. Only rarely, as in the Indian Vedic tradition, is the sacredness of a scripture bound up with its preservation in a dead language understood by few. In Judaism, Christianity, and Islam, in particular, interpretation is the very life of the scriptural process. As scriptures are handed on from generation to generation in canonical versions, they must be *interpreted* so that the unchangeable text continues meaningfully to penetrate the lives of those who revere it.

The question of the text's meaning becomes central. Unfamiliar words cannot be replaced with more up-to-date terms; rather, they must be defined. Obscure concepts or perplexing episodes cannot be ignored; rather, they must be explained. In many cases, translations must be made for those who are unfamiliar with the original language of the scriptural texts. All of this work of transmitting the meaning of scriptures is another kind of tradition— *the tradition of interpretation.* In many cases, differences of opinion about the meaning of a shared scripture can become controversial. If such differences of tradition are not reconciled, they can justify religious divisions, the birth of competing communities or sects, and, even, religiously motivated violence.

We can summarize this discussion of scripture, tradition, and canon by resorting once again to metaphor. Think of canonization as a snapshot of a sweeping motion, say, that of a dancer's leap. That leap is the historical transmission and growth of literary tradition. Like a photograph, the canon represents a momentary freezing of a continuous process that began before the snapshot was taken and that continues long afterwards. This frozen image—the dancer suspended in the air—becomes the offical portrait of a community's tradition, its scripture.

Note that the canonical freezing of scripture is accurate and false at once. It is accurate in that it captures perfectly a single moment. It is false in that it separates that moment from all that preceded and followed it in time. The dancer is always in mid-motion. Earlier forms of the tradition are no longer visible to the community as part of the canonical scripture. They drop from memory, or they can survive as embellishments of the canonical scripture. Similarly, the subsequent life of tradition—the next step of the dance—is also lost. Or it is preserved beyond the borders of the canonical portrait of scripture and begins to frame it. Knowing the dancer's entire performance, however, can enhance one's appreciation of the photograph of part of it.

This is our task here. Let's try to put some flesh on the bones of this rather puzzling metaphor.

The Emergence of Scripture in Persian Yehud

To be candid, historians of Judaism are not in total agreement about when the first canonical snapshot was taken. No single historical reconstruction of the origins of Judaic scripture commands universal acceptance. This, however, is to be expected. Historians reach their opinions on the basis of their interpretations of evidence. And in the present case, not everyone agrees about what counts as evidence. Moreover, the evidence agreed upon is slender, and its interpretation is difficult. The issue, to oversimplify a bit, is one of literary history.

Few historians of Judaism doubt that Israelites living in Yisrael and Yehudah prior to the Babylonian deportations of 597–587 BCE possessed well-developed literary traditions, in both written and oral form. We have already surveyed some of these in the previous chapter. The disputed historical question, rather, has to do with the relationship of the contents of the Hebrew Bible to those traditions, on the one hand, and to the religion of ancient Israel, on the other. Two issues are involved. One is to what extent the present writings gathered in the Hebrew Bible are an accurate representation of Israelite traditions as they existed prior to the destruction of Yehudah in 587. The second is whether the present writings (or the traditions that preceded them) ever represented and shaped the religious world of Israelite civilization *as a whole* prior to 587.

Each of these questions is hotly debated.[3] We cannot enter too deeply into that debate here, although the note to the preceding sentence will give you some guidance to further reading. Our own discussion follows the views of many contemporary historians of Judaism who regard the writings of the Hebrew Bible *in their scriptural form* as a literary tradition originating primarily with the Jews of Persian Yehud. Accordingly, the Hebrew Bible testifies first of all to the religious world of those Jews, rather than to that of the ancient Israelite civilization whose traditions they selectively retrieved, composed, and interpreted.

To recall our textile metaphor of Chapter One (if it is not too threadbare)—the literary strands of the Hebrew Bible were contributed in large measure by ancient Israel, but the weaving was done on a Persian loom. For this reason, our point of view is that the scriptural form of the writings in the Hebrew Bible represents the religious world of Jews who lived from the Persian through the early Hellenistic periods. Biblical Judaism, paradoxically, comes into existence in the Persian period.

The Canonical Shape of the Hebrew Bible

But even an answer to the question of the origins of the Hebrew Bible does not explain its present form. Here the snapshot metaphor we used a moment ago to understand the idea of canon is helpful. The Hebrew Bible is a snapshot of Jewish scriptural tradition. That snapshot was taken in the early centuries CE, probably by rabbinic photographers.

In order to understand the picture they composed for us, we might best attend to the key parts of the composition. We have already mentioned that a common Jewish term for the Hebrew Bible is "*TaNaKh*." This is an acrostic that refers to the three major divisions in which the collection is preserved: *Torah* ("Teaching"), *Nevi'im* ("Prophets") and *Ketuvim* (Writings). Each of these canons is a kind of peg upon which hang the narrative strands of the biblical story. This story will occupy us for the next few pages, because it contains the primary clues that will guide us to Persian Yehud as the point of its earliest circulation as scripture.

The Torah describes the origins of the world and the history of the Israelite nation from its beginnings with Abram to the death of its great leader Moses. The central focus of the Torah is the description of a series of covenants, or contracts, sealed between God and Israel. Abram (soon renamed Abraham) and his descendants, Isaac and Jacob (also known as Israel), receive the earliest of these. The culmination of these covenants, however, comes centuries after Jacob's death, in a collective covenant agreement between God and all Israel at Sinai. Moses plays the key role in mediating the covenantal terms between God and Israel. In return for Israel's obedience, God promises to grant it a rich land and protection from its enemies.

The narrative continues in Nevi'im, particularly the books of Joshua-

---

The Literary Coherence of the Scriptural Canon

In the form transmitted in Judaic tradition, the scriptural canon is a carefully structured whole containing a narrative and various works that comment on or otherwise amplify the narrative.

The narrative is organized into three thematic sections as follows:

TORAH	NEVI'IM	KETUVIM
Covenant Making	*Covenant Breaking*	*Covenant Renewal*
Genesis-Deuteronomy	Joshua-Kings	Chronicles and Ezra-Nehemiah
	Isaiah	Psalms
	Jeremiah	Proverbs
	Ezekiel	Job
	The Twelve	Song of Songs
		Ruth
		Lamentations
		Ecclesiastes
		Esther
		Daniel

In this context, the books of Isaiah, Jeremiah, Ezekiel, and the Twelve Minor Prophets interpret the Covenant Breaking narrative of Joshua-Kings and predict the Covenant Renewal narrative of Chronicles and Ezra-Nehemiah. In the same way, the books of Psalms through Daniel look backward toward the tragedies of the past and define the sorts of covenantal loyalty that will lead to the renewal of the covenant.

Kings. These describe the history of Israel's life in the land chosen for it by God and the events surrounding its loss of that land at the hands of Assyrian and Babylonian invaders. The major thesis of Nevi'im is that the land was lost because of Israel's repeated violations of its covenant agreement with God. With few exceptions, the kings of Yisrael and Yehudah led the people away from the teachings of God's prophets. Exile was the result.

The story concludes in the books of Chronicles and Ezra-Nehemiah, the last books of Ketuvim. They depict the eventual resettlement of the land by a remnant of the original people, under the guidance of a priest named Ezra and of Nehemiah, a provincial governor appointed by the Persian emperor. In the Bible's interpretation, that Persian emperor—scholars debate whether it was Artaxerxes I or his son, Artaxerxes II—was a mere vehicle of God. The return to the land was made possible only by Israel's sincere repentance of its earlier disobedience and its commitment to comply with all aspects of the original covenant set forth in the Torah.

The basic plot of the Tanakh, then, is quite simple: it narrates the history of a covenant. That covenant is made between God and Israel in the Torah, broken by Israel in Nevi'im, and restored by God in Ketuvim. In addition to this basic narrative line, the Bible contains as well a wide variety of writings that, in one way or another, supplement or amplify the plot. These are distributed throughout Nevi'im and Ketuvim, in particular. The former supplements the sad history of Israel's loss of its land with a series of books of poetic visions about the faithlessness of Israel and the covenantal loyalty of God, ascribed to ancient seers known as prophets. Ketuvim, for its part, introduces its optimistic image of Israel's return to its land with a diverse collection of writings. These include prayers and religious meditations (the book of Psalms), reflections on the meaning of suffering and happiness (Job and Ecclesiastes), and stories about ancient heroes and heroines (Daniel, Ruth, and Esther).

In its canonical form, then, the Hebrew Bible is essentially a three-act drama containing its own commentary—a very sophisticated piece of literary work. The Torah sets the fundamental theme, which is then amplified in exquisite detail in Nevi'im and Ketuvim. In order to see how this dramatic structure of the canon took shape, we must first ask when its basic story line might have originated.

We begin with a simple observation. The Hebrew Bible ends its story with the return of small groups of Jews to the Land of Israel from exile in Babylonia. If, like all stories, this one begins with the end already in mind, we may conclude that much of its depiction of early Israelite history is told from the perspective of those who are seeing the story whole from the perspective of their own day. Accordingly, the core narrative of the Hebrew Bible in its canonical form was conceived sometime after the return, in 539 BCE, of Israelite exiles to their ancestral territory under Cyrus.

The plot of the Hebrew Bible, after all, raises and answers questions that were fundamental to those who had resettled the Land of Israel and wished now to abide safely upon it. The story they told was essentially a confession of guilt and a resolution to atone for it. It explained how God's special people was descended from a great hero of absolute obedience, Abraham, born in the Babylonian city of Ur. The Torah's first introduction of Abraham is telling. Without any forewarning at all, God begins speaking to Abraham, ordering him to leave his family, birthplace, and everything familiar to him "for the land that I will show you." There, God promises, "I will make you a great nation, and I will bless you. I will make your name great, and you shall be a blessing . . . and all the families of the earth shall bless themselves by you" (Gen. 12:2–3). And Abraham follows. Abraham's obedience is his dominant trait. A few chapters later (Gen. 22:1–19), God tells Abraham to offer his favorite son, Isaac, as a sacrifice. Abraham wordlessly obeys, sparing Isaac only after a heavenly voice orders him to desist.

In many ways, the Torah's Abraham is both a model of what Israel ought to be and a confession of what it had failed to become. Through persistent violation of Abraham's example, Israel came to suffer the loss of its political independence and homeland. What would it mean in the setting of Persian Yehud to begin the history of Israel with the now famous stories of Abraham's obedience and end it with the return of the exiles? Quite simply, Israel's origins and destiny are bound up with each other.

The image of Abraham's silent submission to God's will in leaving his native Babylonia for an unknown land implies that the restoration of Jews from Babylonian captivity is more than an arbitrary action governed by the Persian emperor. Rather, it is under the control of the God whom Abraham obeyed. The descendants of the exiles, most of whom had known no other home than Babylonia, modeled their own repopulation of the land of Israel after that of Abraham and saw in Abraham's obedience to the divine call a way of expressing their own. The present generation sought to secure the promise to Abraham—of progeny, land, and blessing—by reenacting his obedience and perfecting the life of obedience once and for all.

It is in this sense that the origins of the biblical narrative and those of Judaism are closely bound together. The basic story of the Hebrew Bible emerged in the century following 539. Exactly who the storytellers were is almost impossible to say. But what they did is clear. They reshaped the diverse narrative and legal traditions of ancient Yehudah into a carefully plotted literary epic. Through the figures of ancient Israelite heroes, that epic told the tale of its tellers.

As they saw things, the history of the world provided the setting of Israelite history in the past and the future. Yehud's program for national survival was given thereby a cosmic significance. The daily confirmation of Israel's setting in cosmic history was the ancient sacrificial center of the Davidic dynasty, the Jerusalem Temple. Restored in successive building projects from about 520, its sacrificial service was reconstituted in line with traditions preserved by the surviving priesthoods of Persian Yehud. Now the Creator of the World could be served as he desired, conferring his blessing upon his people.

All the elements of a coherent religious world—the placing of self and community in a relationship to the fundamental structures of reality—were fully in place. These elements, in various combinations and emphases, would be carried forward by all versions of Judaism for the next millennium.

The Torah of Moses

The charter for Yehud's reconstruction—its epic of Israelite origins and compendium of national law—was a collection of five scrolls called the Torah of

Moses. A document with this title is mentioned many times in the book of Deuteronomy, where it is associated with a collection of laws. In its canonical version, however, the Torah is much more than a legal collection. It is, in fact, a history of the universe from the moment of its creation by the God of Israel down to the death of the people's greatest prophet and leader Moses.

The one clear reference in the Hebrew Bible to a Torah of Moses that contains just such a historical vision is not, however, in Deuteronomy. Rather, it is found in the account of the postexilic restoration recorded in Ezra-Nehemiah. The composer of this work describes the efforts of Persian-Jewish repatriates, sometime between 450 and 380 BCE, to rebuild Jerusalem's walls and restore proper observance of God's covenant among the population of Yehud.

A central figure in his account is the priest and scribe Ezra. He is portrayed (Neh. 8–9) as reading the Torah of Moses to an assembly of Jerusalemites in the restored Temple and guiding them in their early attempts to repent for their sins and to reconstitute a proper covenantal relationship with the God of Israel. Ezra's summary of the Torah of Moses in these chapters agrees with the scope of the canonical Torah.

Accounts of Ezra's activity may be almost as legendary as those of Moses. In many ways, as a mixture of lawgiver and priest, he is portrayed as a more perfect leader than Moses, whom God made to concede priestly duties to his brother, Aaron. Nevertheless, the description of the Torah read by Ezra establishes that by the fourth century BCE, a book like the present Torah in overall scope and argument was used as the basis of historical thought, religious teaching, civil administration, and sacrificial ritual in restored Jerusalem.

Some historians have suggested that it was drawn up in Babylonia precisely for this purpose. Given the opportunity to restore limited Jewish self-rule in Yehud, Babylonian Jewish leaders such as Ezra and Nehemiah compiled the Torah of Moses as their charter. This is a possible, but as yet unproven, scenario. At the very least, however, the Ezra-Nehemiah scroll shows that this Torah of Moses soon passed beyond the purely political status of being a charter of Babylonian-born Israelite expatriates. It became a public tradition sustaining the social and religious institutions of Yehud. It rooted in the distant past the new community governed by it. It also linked that community's destiny to the Creator of Heaven and Earth. By the end of the Persian period, the Torah of Moses had become a Judaic scripture.[4]

The main concerns of Persian Yehud's Judaism can be surmised from the single-mindedness of the Torah's retelling of the past. No matter what sort of ancient Israelite traditions it gathers together, it makes sure to structure the narration around a single theme: God's overpowering love for his creation is constantly rebuffed by the rebellious desires of humanity. Thus, for example, legends about pre-Israelite human history are told in such a way as to foreshadow and predict the later rebellious behavior of Israel under its covenant with God.

The well-known story of the first man and woman in the Garden of Eden is a case in point (Gen. 2:4–3:24). Given by God everything they could possibly require by way of material comforts, Adam and Eve are commanded only to refrain from certain forbidden fruits in the center of the Garden. This they prove unable to do; neither do they show any genuine remorse when God discovers their act. As punishment, God expels the humans from his Garden, making it impossible for them ever to return. As the story tells it, this is the moment that pain, suffering, and death enter the world. At the very origin of human history, then, the Torah finds a spirit of human rebellion that incurs the divine punishment of exile.

The Torah, moreover, sees Israel's history as a reenactment of human history within the confines of a single people. The covenant-making event at Mt. Sinai is described in the scroll of Exodus (18–25) as a moment of close bonding between God and Israel, with Israel eagerly entering into agreement to observe all the laws of God. Yet forty days later, with Moses still on the mountain communing with God, Israel begins to pine for a substitute deity and pressures Aaron into molding a golden calf to worship.

As the Torah describes it, only Moses' active intervention on behalf of his people prevents God from destroying them in punishment (Ex. 32). Then God permits the Israelites to build a wilderness Tent of Meeting in which God promises to make his presence available among the people. From that Tent, he reveals all the laws by which he is to be worshipped and through which Israel will express its love of him—Leviticus. Yet what is Israel's response? Much of the fourth scroll of the Torah, called Numbers, records stories in which Israel complains against the rigors of its desert wanderings, yearns longingly for its period of Egyptian servitude, and in other ways forgets or evades its responsibility to God.

The Torah ends, in Deuteronomy, with a long speech by Moses in which he predicts that if this spirit of disobedience continues after Israel is brought into its Land, the promise of the Land will indeed be revoked. The stark choice offered by Moses here is one of only many examples (Deut. 30:15–20):

> See, I set before you this day life and prosperity, death and adversity. For I command you this day, to love the LORD your God, to walk in his ways, and to keep his commandments, his laws and his rules, that you may thrive and increase, and that the LORD your God may bless you in the land that you are about to enter and possess. But if your heart turns away and you give no heed, and are lured into the worship and service of other gods, I declare to you this day that you shall certainly perish; you shall not long endure on the soil that you are crossing the Jordan to enter and possess. I call heaven and earth to witness against you this

day: I have put before you life and death, blessing and curse. Choose life—if you and your offspring would live—by loving the LORD your God, heeding his commands, and holding fast to him. For thereby you shall have life and shall long endure upon the soil that the LORD your God swore to your ancestors, Abraham, Isaac, and Jacob, to give to them.

The fifth scroll of the Torah ends with this choice ringing in the ears of its audience: obedience or rebellion; life or death? The history of early Judaic religious worlds is the history of those who defined that obedience and how life would reflect it.

Toward a Uniform Canon

The Torah of Moses received pride of place in the Judaism that developed around the Temple in Jerusalem. But it was still part of a larger national epic that included accounts of centuries of living under kings in the Land of Israel, of being swept off it and of returning to renew covenantal life upon it. This epic in its entirety—Genesis-Deuteronomy, Joshua-Kings, and Chronicles/Ezra-Nehemiah—existed by the fourth century BCE at the latest. Nevertheless, the present literary division of that story into three formal divisions—Torah, Nevi'im, and Ketuvim—and the inclusion of supplementary writings, did not become commonplace until the middle of the second century BCE.[5]

Indeed, it is remarkable that any uniform collection of Jewish scriptures emerged at all. As we have seen in detail in Chapter One, Judaic civilization after the fourth century BCE was anything but homogeneous. In addition to a small community centered in Jerusalem and other locations in the ancient homeland, most Jews of the Hellenistic period were scattered in lands as far apart as Egypt and Babylonia. Despite the superficial uniformity of a shared Hellenistic culture, Jews lived under competing and often warring political empires and spoke a variety of languages. The restored Temple in Jerusalem and its priesthood enjoyed high prestige among most of the dispersed Jewish world, but no authoritative religious or political institution extended from Jerusalem to legislate on such matters as the nature and content of scripture.

By the third century BCE, Greek-speaking Jews of Egypt began to translate the Torah and other Hebrew writings into Greek. Whether this was a sign of their fading grasp of Hebrew or an effort to promote the merits of their own ethnic literature in the circles of higher Egyptian culture—or a little of both—is not clear. This translation, the Septuagint mentioned earlier, eventually gathered together not only translated versions of Hebrew scriptures, but some works originally written in Greek, such as one called the Wisdom of Solomon. Alexandrian Jews in particular treasured this collection of writings as their own distinctive national "classic," analogous in prestige and in wisdom to the philosophical, dramatic, and poetic "classics" celebrated by Greek-speaking Egyptians.

An often-told Alexandrian story about the origins of the Septuagint reveals the high regard in which Jews held this scriptural translation. In its essential outlines, the story speaks of a powerful Ptolemaic king who, hearing of a book of philosophy preserved among the Jews of Jerusalem, resolved to have it translated for his famous library in Alexandria. The book is the Torah of Moses. The king sent for seventy Jewish scribes to produce the translation and sequestered them in seventy isolated rooms for seventy days. In the end, each emerged with the identical translation of the Torah. Clearly, the story's point is that the Greek rendering of the Torah, like the Hebrew original, is divinely inspired. The date of the completion of the translation was a widely celebrated holiday among Alexandrian Jewry. And the name "Septuagint," which means "Seventy," preserves the significance of the translation.[6]

Aramaic-speaking Jewish communities of Palestine preserved as well a wide variety of writings in Hebrew or Aramaic that seem to have enjoyed scriptural prestige, even though they are not found in the present canon. Some of these writings, such as the Wisdom of Joshua ben Sira, were eventually translated into Greek and preserved in versions of the Septuagint. Inherited by Greek-speaking Christians, they remain part of some collections of the Old Testament. Others, such as the Book of Jubilees (pages 74–78), a collection of visionary texts called the Book of Enoch, and the many Aramaic and Hebrew writings found in the Dead Sea Scrolls, also seem to have been frequently copied and circulated. But, however much these diverse writings might have been valued by some Jewish groups of this period or by later Christians, they did not find their way into the canon of scripture transmitted by rabbinic Jews in the era of Christianity.[7]

To conclude, the process by which certain books attained scriptural status while others enjoyed it for a time and then ultimately lost it is difficult to trace. It is clear, however, that the process of defining a scriptural canon extended over a period of centuries. For the first several centuries of its existence, that is, the Hebrew Bible was a scripture whose canonical boundaries remained open. Only in rabbinic sources from the third century and onward do we find the names and even the sequence of scriptural books corresponding to the present canon.

The rabbinic connection to the present canon cannot be overlooked, although its precise impact upon the canonical boundaries is difficult to define. Did the Sages merely tinker with the fine points of an inherited canon common to most Aramaic-speaking Jews (as some rabbinic traditions suggest)? Or did they, to the contrary, wield a ready scalpel in excising from their canon works highly regarded in the larger Palestinian setting? Scholars hold divergent views, and we cannot debate the matter here.[8]

It is clear, however, that any definition of the canon of scripture is part of the larger process of interpreting its meaning. As we shall now see, this

Tradition and the Shaping of Judaism's Scripture

The Hebrew Bible did not happen all at once. The chart that follows attempts to isolate key stages in the transformation of pre-scriptural traditions of ancient Israel into the canonical collection accepted by rabbinic Judaism.

Principal Sources of Ancient Israelite Tradition, ca. 1000–587 BCE

Primarily Oral Traditions

1. Heroic epics
2. Priestly ritual practices
3. Public oratory

Primarily Written Traditions

1. Civil and ritual law codes of royal scribes
2. Civil and ritual law codes of priestly scribes
3. Royal archives
4. Histories of royal deeds

Persian Period, ca. 539–323 BCE

1. 450–400: Selected oral and written traditions composed into the "Torah of Moses"
2. 450–400: Completion of written histories of pre-exilic monarchies (Joshua-Kings)
3. 450–350: Systematic compilation of prophetic oracles
4. 450–350: Early collections of psalms and proverbs
5. 400–350: Completion of written history of post-exilic restoration community (Chronicles and Ezra-Nehemiah)

Hellenistic Period ca. 323–63 BCE

1. 350–160: Composition of Esther, Ruth, Job, Ecclesiastes, Song of Songs, Daniel
2. 250–200: The Torah and other Hebrew writings are translated into Greek by Egyptian Jews
3. 200: Canon of Nevi'im circulates with Torah as a scriptural collection
4. 200–100 CE: Jubilees and other works compete with Torah and Nevi'im as authentic scriptures

---

Roman Period, ca. 63 BCE-320 CE

1. 100 CE: Rabbinic tradition defines the present boundaries of Jewish Canon
2. 200 CE: Rabbinic tradition begins to claim exclusive legitimacy as the true meaning of scriptures
3. 300 CE: Septuagint is abandoned by Jews and becomes basis of Christian Old Testament by 300 CE
4. 300 CE: Surviving nonrabbinic traditions of scriptural interpretation are absorbed into the interpretive traditions of rabbinic Judaism and Christianity

---

process of scriptural interpretation had been underway for centuries, even prior to the closing of the rabbinic canon itself.

The Problem of Scripture's Meaning

Our usual habit of thought is to imagine scriptures as writings that give rise to interpretations and commentaries. First there is the scripture, then there comes the explanation of its meaning. Things are not that simple. We have already observed that Judaism's earliest scriptural text, the Torah of Moses, is an interpretation of still earlier traditions of ancient Israel. We must now point out yet another important matter. Ancient Jews did not wait for the completion of their scriptural canon before beginning to interpret the books within it. Moreover, they did not always wait for the completion of the *books* before interpreting them. In more than a few cases, that is, books in the present scriptural canon contain within themselves *commentaries* on earlier versions of those same works. The commentary was included in the work before the text was "photographed" in its present canonical form. In such cases, we can try to reconstruct the dancer's earlier steps.

Interpretation Within the Canon of Scripture

A prime example, pointed out by many biblical scholars, can be found in the canonical book of Psalms. Psalms is a collection of poetry, usually in the form of prayers and songs. Historians regard some of these as versions of poetry sung during the sacrificial services of the first and second Temples; others are of uncertain origin. The canonical book has 150 of these poems. They include some of the most well-known passages of the Hebrew Bible, such as the famous Psalm 23: "The LORD is my shepherd, I shall not want . . ."

Of interest to us in the present context are the various introductory comments to individual psalms. These relate specific psalms to certain events in the life of David or other heroes. These events, invariably, are described at length in other portions of the scriptural canon. Consider the first stanza of Ps. 51:3–4:

> Have mercy upon me, O God, as befits Your faithfulness;
> in keeping with your abundant compassion,
> blot out my transgressions.
> Wash me thoroughly of my iniquity,
> and purify me of my sin;
> for I recognize my transgressions,
> and am ever conscious of my sin.

Consider now the way the following introductory lines illumine what you have just read (Ps. 51:1–2):

> For the Leader.
> A psalm of David.
> When Nathan the prophet came to him after his intimacy with
>   Bathsheba.

Without the introduction, the anonymous psalm is a prayer of contrition for an unspecified transgression against God. It proclaims the psalmist's trust in divine forgiveness (see verses 17–19).

The introduction, however, does three things. First, it provides a notation guiding the use of the psalm in communal worship ("For the Leader"). This is like the phrase "stage left" in the printed script of a play. It's not part of the performance. The second part of the introduction identifies the anonymous author as King David. Most important, for our purpose, is the third part, which relates the creation of the psalm to an event in David's life.

That event would be familiar to anyone who knew the history of David's early reign as described in the scriptural book of Samuel. Found in the canon of Nevi'im between the books of Judges and Kings, Samuel describes the events leading up to the coronation of David as king and the history of his reign. In its canonical form, it is divided into two scrolls, I and II Samuel. II Samuel 12 recounts how one Nathan, a court prophet of David, disclosed to the king his knowledge of a grotesque amorous plot.

The plot involved David's own scheme to possess a married woman named Bathsheba. The king had one day observed Bathsheba from his window bathing on the roof of a nearby house. Obsessed with her beauty, David had arranged for Bathsheba's husband, a soldier named Uriah, to be placed in the front line of battle. Upon Uriah's death, David married Bathsheba, who bore him a son. As the story is told in II Samuel, David now received a curse from Nathan for this behavior. The curse resulted in the death of the child born to Bathsheba. David is pictured as fasting and petitioning God all night long to avert the curse.

This is the background assumed by the introduction to Psalm 51. In light of II Samuel 12, the scribal commentator who introduced the psalm wants his readers to know two things. First, David's petition during that terrible night included more than a prayer to spare his son. It included as well a petition for forgiveness. More important, this psalm is that prayer.

The interpretive achievement of the few words of this introduction is remarkable. First of all, they have enriched an appreciation of II Samuel's picture of David. By reading the psalm into the story of II Samuel, we appreciate the depths of David's remorse for what he now recognizes as a horrible sin. So, by commenting on Psalm 51, the scribe has also commented on a story that he supposed would be in the minds of his audience.

The introduction also enables the psalm to have yet profounder significance. It can no longer be interpreted as an anonymous hymn. Rather, it now expresses a national hero's utterance of trust in the midst of profound emotional turmoil. The implication is that the reader can express his or her own response to similar life crises in the inspired words of David. Scripture is not only a record of past events, but a text that can be incorporated into life in its most intimate settings.

This sort of instructional introduction occurs frequently in the book of Psalms. They were added while the psalm texts were relatively unfixed in a canonical version. Their immediate purpose, apparently, was to link the psalm texts more closely to other works already regarded as scripture. But they also enhanced the power of the psalms to address the inner life of their audiences. As the psalm texts were received as canonically fixed writings, the interpretive introductions became part of scripture itself. Words that began their life as a commentary on scripture became, in the end, scripture.[9]

Interpretation Beyond the Scriptural Canon

The canonical "photograph" of the Hebrew Bible's scriptures, obviously, masks a good deal of interpretive "motion" in ancient Judaism's literary tradition. That motion is even livelier beyond the borders of the received canon.

Historians have long known of early Judaic writings that revise, retell, or otherwise offer interpretive renderings of passages now preserved in the Bible. Translations of some of these works into languages such as Amharic, Armenian, and Slavonic were for centuries preserved in ancient Christian monastic libraries, where they were revised in line with Christian ideas and treasured as prophetic testimonies to Christian belief. Others, preserved in Greek or Latin translations, were accorded a kind of quasi-scriptural status as "apocrypha" in the Old Testament canons of various Christian communities. The existence of yet others was entirely unsuspected until they were discovered, in 1947, in pottery jars secreted in caves in the Dead Sea wasteland of Qumran.

Each of these texts exhibits its own complex relationship to the scriptural works of the Tanakh's canon. Some are clearly dependent upon scriptural writings in nearly their present form. In not a few cases, however, it is difficult to be sure exactly how the composer or readers of the work understood its relationship to other writings presently part of the canon. These are the occasions that make life interesting for students of early Judaism. They allow us to see how writings, ignored by rabbinic Judaism for nearly 2000 years, once competed with the present works of scripture as authoritative expressions of the religious worlds of those who produced and preserved them.

Let's look at one such work, usually entitled the book of Jubilees. It presents itself as a record of what *really* happened when Moses spent forty days with God on Sinai. The book was probably composed in Hebrew in the middle of the second century BCE, during the early Hasmonean dynasty. Until the twentieth century, the only copies to survive the Roman destruction of Jewish Palestine were monastary translations in ancient Christian languages. But other Hebrew copies were recently found among the Dead Sea Scrolls. So before us is a work that apparently enjoyed rather wide ancient circulation among Palestinian Jews.

Jubilees' anonymous compiler lived some three centuries after the Torah of Moses had become the central scriptural text of Yehud. For at least a century, that Torah in Greek translation had dominated the scriptural canon of diaspora Jews. Against this background, Jubilees must make us wonder: if its compilers and audience regarded the Torah of Moses as a reliable historical account, how did they square it with the picture offered in Jubilees? And more curious still—if they regarded the picture offered in Jubilees as authoritative, how did they understand the authority of the Torah of Moses?[10]

Jubilees' distinctiveness can be appreciated only by first glancing at the Torah of Moses. There, the actual revelation of God's covenantal law at Sinai to Moses and Israel occurs in Exodus 19–24. The Ten Commandments are pronounced in Exodus 20. Then Exodus 21–24 presents a large compendium of rules and regulations for the conduct of society and the maintenance of proper relations with God. Finally, at the end of chapter 24, a thick cloud encasing the presence of God appears "as a consuming fire on the top of the mountain. Moses went inside the cloud and ascended the mountain; and Moses remained on the mountain forty days and forty nights" (Ex. 24:17–18). There he received the actual stone tablets of the covenant as well as explicit instructions for how to build a movable sacrificial Tabernacle (Ex. 25–31). The Tabernacle, also called the Tent of Meeting, is built (Ex. 34–40). It then serves, in the books of Leviticus and Numbers, as the site for further revelations of God to Moses and his priestly assistant, Aaron.

The composer of Jubilees depends upon the reader's knowledge of this scenario. But his independent point of view is forecast in the extended title that heads most copies of the text:

This is the account of the division of days of the Torah and the testimony for annual observance according to their weeks of years and their Jubilees throughout all the years of the world just as the LORD told it to Moses on Mount Sinai when he went up to receive the tablets of the Torah and the commandment by the word of the LORD, as he said to him [in Ex. 24:12], "Come up to the top of the mountain."

This heading's reference to "the division of days . . . for annual observance" signals the book's overall purpose. This is to establish a calendar for regulating the schedule of scripturally mandated Festivals. The Torah commands that these be celebrated in the Tent of Meeting with acts of sacrificial worship. For much of the history of Davidic Yehudah and early Judaism, however, the preferred site for these celebrations had been the Jerusalem Temple, where the Tent was stored in The Holy of Holies.

Only upon dipping into Jubilees, however, does its reader learn that the calendar of Festivals—indeed its entire way of marking each year's passage of time—differs rather dramatically from the one found in the Torah of Moses. The calendar of the Torah itself is based solely on lunar cycles. The twelve months of the year vary in length from twenty-nine to thirty days. This yields a lunar year somewhat shorter than a solar year. As a result, the months of the Torah's calendar can be out of synchronization with the solar seasons. Presumably, this had to be corrected by periodically adding a leap year. This would ensure, for example, that the Festival of Passover, which falls on the fifteenth day of the month of Aviv, would always be celebrated in the spring.

The composer of Jubilees had a different solution. He linked all Temple observances to a solar, rather than a lunar, calendar. In this scheme, each year has exactly 364 days and is divisible exactly into fifty-two weeks of seven days. Each of the year's twelve months has exactly thirty days and begins on a Wednesday. The four remaining days belong to no month at all. They serve as seasonal markers, dividing summer from fall and winter from spring. This regularity ensures that every Festival will fall on exactly the same day of the week each year rather than wandering unpredictably from one year to the next.

Jubilee's interest in organizing the solar year in terms of multiples of seven has implications beyond the creation of a regular Festival cycle. As the book unfolds, it becomes clear that the composer views all of history as a series of fifty immensely long epochs (Jubilees), each composed of seven weeks of seven lengthy years. Against this chronological system, he plots all the events of history from Creation until Israel's entry into the Land of Israel. He then links all the sacred seasons of the Temple calendar to events that occurred in that historically crucial period of wilderness wandering.

The mysterious language of "weeks of years" and "Jubilees" is part of the computational system he uses to determine the dates upon which those observances were established in the past. In such a meticulous work of historical scholarship, we should not be surprised that the scribes who copied the book of Jubilees divided it into fifty chapters. Why all this is so important to Jubilees will become clear momentarily.

The actual giving of the Torah to Moses, which Jubilees describes in detail, occurs nine years ("one week and two years") into the fiftieth and final Jubilee (Jub. 50:4). So presumably the composer of the work believed himself to be standing at some crucial turning of world history, the end of the fiftieth and final Jubilee. But that matter needn't concern us here, for he does not dwell upon it himself. The point for us is what the composer of Jubilees does with the Torah of Moses.

First, as we have seen, he proposes a significant practical improvement of the Torah's Festival calendar. Second, he situates the Torah's rather simple chronology within a vastly expanded temporal framework of eons. Most important, in order to fit the Torah's contents into his system, he offers his own conception of the origins of the Torah's various Festival laws. Many of the sacrificial and Festival laws in the canonical Torah are recorded in the book of Leviticus (e.g., Lev. 23:1–44). There the context of the revelation to Moses and Aaron is the Tent of Meeting—outside the explicit framework of the revelation at Sinai. In Jubilees, to the contrary, they are all revealed to Moses during his forty days on the mountain. In sum, Jubilees represents a view of the history of revelation that ignores the sequence chosen in the Torah of Moses.

And that's not all. Jubilees makes no effort to downplay its revisions of the canonical Torah's historical record. Rather, it challenges any possibility of viewing the canonical Torah of Moses as a complete and authoritative record of revelation. According to the composer of Jubilees, there was a witness on Sinai who saw what actually transpired between God and Moses. This witness, a mysterious figure called the "Angel of the Presence" is also a participant in the revelation. In fact, he appears to be the narrator of most of the book of Jubilees from the second chapter on.

Commissioned by God to "write for Moses from the first creation until my sanctuary is built in their midst forever and ever" (Jub. 1:28), the angel does so. Here is how Jubilees describes the beginning of the angel's commission:

> And the Angel of the Presence, who went before the camp of Israel, took the tablets of the division of years from the time of creation of the Torah and the testimony according to their weeks of years, according to the Jubilees, year by year throughout the full number of Jubilees, . . .

until the sanctuary of the LORD is created in Jerusalem upon Mount Zion . . . And the Angel of the Presence spoke to Moses by the word of the LORD, saying, "Write the whole account of creation, that in six days the LORD God completed all his work and all that he created. And he observed a Sabbath the seventh day, and he sanctified it for all ages. And he set it as a sign for all his works.

For on the first day he created the heavens, which are above, and the earth, and the waters and all of the spirits which minister before him: The angels of the presence, and the angels of sanctification, and the angels of fire, and the angels of the spirit of the winds, and the angels of the spirit of the clouds and darkness and snow and hail and frost, and the angels of resoundings and thunder and lightning, and the angels of the spirits of cold and heat and winter and springtime and harvest and summer, and all of the spirits of his creatures which are in heaven and on earth. . . . (Jub.1:29–2:2)

It seems that the Angel is reading to Moses from the "tablets" originally written by God. If so, Moses writes in his own hand what God wrote in his, mediated through the recitation of the angel. In any event, the Angel of the Presence narrates, and Moses records in writing, a rather different Torah from the one that circulated among most Jews as the canonical text of Mosaic teaching. The book of Jubilees is presented as the record of that Torah, the authentic one, to which angelic presence provides final testimony.

Let's consider what kind of statement Jubilees represented at the time of its composition, early in the Hasmonean period. Its main preoccupation is with structuring the sacrificial rites of the Jerusalem Temple so that the dates of all holidays fall in a regular sequence. It is unclear why this is so important. But one thing is clear—there is little reason to suppose that Hasmonean priests used Jubilees' calendar in their conduct of the Sabbaths and festivals. We must assume, therefore, that those who composed Jubilees or regarded it as persuasive were critical of the Hasmonean regime. Jubilees expresses that criticism through its account of revelation. Instead of confonting the Hasmonean regime explicitly, it undermines its religious legitimacy by presenting a new account of how Moses received the Torah and an alternate version of what that Torah contained. If Jubilees is an account of the revelation to Moses, then the Torah of Moses housed in the Hasmonean Temple is not.

We would, of course, love to be able to interview the composer or sympathetic readers of Jubilees to find out exactly how they understood the relation of this work to the Torah of Moses known to the Hasmoneans and others throughout the ancient Jewish world. Perhaps they would have said that Jubilees was an authoritative *explanation* of the Torah of Moses, verified by the angelic transmitter. So the mandate of the Torah of Moses could be best followed in accord with the instructions provided in Jubilees. Perhaps they would have gone further, claiming that Jubilees was the true Torah. But we can't interview them. And their conversations with their contemporaries about the matter are essentially lost. We know only that the proponents of Jubilees did not prevail in that conversation.

Jubilees failed to displace the Torah of Moses. The rabbinic canon, indeed, made no room for it. Although certain of its perspectives did indeed survive in later expressions of Jewish scriptural interpretation, the book as a whole disappeared from Jewish tradition. Perhaps the community that claimed Jubilees as Torah was supressed by the Hasmoneans and marginalized in the Palestinian community. The presence of Hebrew copies among the Dead Sea Scrolls may suggest as much, since (as we shall see in Chapter Four) the community at Qumran appears to have rejected the Hasmonean regime as corrupt. It also seems to have accepted a calendar much like that of Jubilees. Perhaps, then, in the religious world of Qumran, Jubilees was read as an amplification of the Torah of Moses and an authoritative statement of how its calendrical system should be applied.

But all explanations at this historical distance are speculative at best. The point for us is that in Jubilees we see the remarkable motion behind the picture-perfect canonical surface of the received biblical canon. Jubilees opens up to us a Judaic world that existed in close contact with the emerging scriptures of Judaism, competed with other visions of Judaism for primacy, but finally was not to survive. Ultimately, the arbiter of what could and could not survive as a Judaic world was the shifting character of Judaic interpretive tradition itself.[11] And this brings us, at last, to the rabbis.

The Sources of Rabbinic Tradition

As you'll recall from Chapter One, scholars with the title of "rabbi" played an important organizational role in Palestinian Jewry's recovery from the sacking of the Temple in 70 CE and the catastrophic consequences of Bar Kosiba's uprising in 132–135. Rabban Gamaliel, recalled in rabbinic memory as an important transmitter of rabbinic tradition, was probably the first Patriarch of Palestinian Jewry, appointed during the nineties. Within a generation after 135 the program of the post-70 generation of Sages was being vigorously pursued by the Patriarch Rabban Shimon ben Gamaliel with the help of a growing body of Sages and disciples. We have already noted that by the late second century, the Mishnah, the rabbinic movement's principal compilation of legal and religious tradition, had become the platform of Palestinian Jewish autonomy under the Patriarch Rabbi Judah ben Shimon ben Gamaliel.

One of the most perplexing historical questions of the post-70 period is how to account for this sudden rise of rabbinic Sages to political and religious prominence. Where were the rabbis before the war against Rome?

The Pharisees

It is not easy from our present standpoint to identify the social origins of these rabbis. But there are clues. For example, rabbinic texts from the third and fourth centuries CE record the names of Shemaiah, Avtalion, and an early-first-century Gamaliel as transmitters of teachings during the time of the second Temple. Greek forms of two of these names—Samaias and Polion—are mentioned in the writings of a late-first-century Jewish historian named Flavius Josephus. A teacher named Gamaliel, likewise, appears in the late-first-century Christian work, the Acts of the Apostles, now part of the New Testament canon. Samais, Polion, and Gamaliel are all identified with a group known as the *pharisaioi*—Pharisees. Later rabbinic sources refer to this group as *perushim*, a word that might mean "sectarians" or "interpreters." It's hard to tell.[12]

By all accounts, these Pharisees were rather important participants in the political and religious life of Jerusalem prior to the destruction of the Temple. Although rabbinic Judaism cannot be equated with the Judaism of the Pharisees, it is likely that at least some Pharisees were instrumental in the formation of the Judaic world transmitted within the later communities of rabbinic sages. This is, at least, the perspective of many passages of rabbinic literature. As we shall see, the earliest examples of rabbinic historical writing make a point of linking rabbinic traditions to the Pharisees and scribes (Hebrew: *sofrim*) who lived while the Temple still stood.

Just who the Pharisees were is not an easy question to answer. They have left no writings of their own, so there is no firsthand evidence from which to imagine the details of their religious world. We are entirely dependent upon what ancient writers, nearly all of whom wrote well after the heyday of Pharisees, chose to record about them. Readers of the Christian Gospels encounter the Pharisees as religious hypocrites who challenged Jesus' authority and who may have had a hand in his crucifixion. Fanatically loyal to what the Gospel of Mark calls "traditions of the elders" (e.g., Mk. 7:1 ff.), the Pharisees are said to have been more concerned with having clean hands and tithed food than with true love of God and humanity.

Other first-century CE writings, particularly those of Josephus, portray the Pharisees as a popular political party concerned with fostering deep loyalty to the Torah among the masses as well as to teaching certain ancestral traditions not included in the Torah itself. Whether the Pharisees were hypocrites, as the Gospels claim, or religious democrats, as Josephus holds, is not for us to determine, for we have no evidence other than these partisan depictions. But what does seem certain—because it is the only thing upon which our otherwise irreconcilable sources agree—is that the Pharisees placed a great premium on something called "ancestral tradition."

Even though such tradition was not written in the Mosaic Torah, it does seem to have governed pharisaic understandings of how to live in light of the Torah's requirements. We know very little of what this pharisaic interpretive tradition might have contained. All we have is the testimony of later rabbinic Judaism, which claimed the teachings of at least some Pharisees as its own. In the rabbinic versions of these teachings, however, the term "tradition" is not particularly prominent. Instead, the term "Torah" appears repeatedly as something far richer than the physical scroll of Mosaic writings; richer even than the entire collection of scripture itself. In the Judaism of rabbinic Sages, Torah comes to stand for the entire body of Jewish religious tradition, both what is written in the Torah of Moses as well as the interpretations needed to embody it in life.

Pharisaic Tradition and Rabbinic Torah

History has not preserved any firsthand writings from pharisaic sources. Therefore, any attempt to draw lines of continuity between the pharisaic "ancestral tradition" and the sense that Torah conveys in the later rabbinic world must be speculative. That being said, let us attempt one disciplined speculation.

The Gospels' Pharisees, you'll recall, are accused of always washing their hands and tithing their food. Jesus is said to have complained that the food they put into their mouths was more important to them than were the words that came out of them (Mk. 7:14–15; Mat. 15:10–11, 23:23–29). Josephus, our other main source of information about Pharisees, doesn't mention this aspect of their tradition. But early rabbinic literature is also deeply concerned with laws governing the purity of foods and their proper tithing. It devotes as well much attention to the conduct of the meals in which food is eaten and drink consumed. Perhaps this common interest in rituals surrounding food can help us think about the connection between pharisaic "ancestral tradition" and rabbinic Torah.

The Gospels have little interest in generous interpretations of the Pharisees' dietary compulsions. Rabbinic literature, by contrast, develops a rather full theory of what is at stake in such dietary laws. The purity of food, its proper tithing, and the specific decorum of the meal itself were believed to contribute to a most remarkable transformation of the dining table. Under the appropriate circumstances, common food could serve as a vehicle for invoking a sanctifying divine presence upon the dinner tables of the Sages' families. In early rabbinic tradition, in other words, the rituals of the meal penetrated the otherwise firm barrier between the world of ordinary experience and the world of Heaven. Eating a meal was a religious activity.

This was especially so at holy occasions. The Torah of Moses, for example, enjoins Jews to "sanctify" the Sabbath. It offers, however, few explicit instructions on how such sanctification is to be achieved. The Mishnah, for its part, assumes this is done by taking a meal. It records a series of disputes—

transmitted by the followers of two early-first-century Pharisees named Hillel and Shammai—regarding precisely how to sanctify the Sabbath at the Friday evening meal, which inaugurates the holy day. It is done by uttering a blessing called the *kiddush* (sanctification).

The followers of Shammai and Hillel, as the Mishnah represents them, agree upon many things concerning the kiddush. For one, the wine must be produced in purity and properly tithed before it is suitable for the meal. This common agreement sets the stage for their disagreements. They dispute, for example, whether the person making the blessing must cleanse the hands before or after mixing the wine in the cup. At issue is whether unwashed hands might convey uncleanness to the cup, thus invalidating the wine. Another dispute concerns whether a benediction is recited first in honor of the Sabbath day and then over the cup of wine drunk at the dinner—or vice versa.[13]

The disputes of the Shammaites and Hillelites regarding mealtime rituals provided generations of rabbinic disciples with food for thought. For our purposes, the interesting thing is not the theory behind each opinion, but the remarkable assumption shared by both parties. Each assumes that the Sabbath must be sanctified with blessings at a Friday night meal that includes wine. You will look in vain throughout the Torah of Moses for any such requirement. But it is assumed as a firm and uncontroversial fulfillment of a divine commandment to sanctify the Sabbath. The conflict concerns only the details of the procedure.

This dispute about the conduct of the Sabbath meal, and many similar disputes on related matters, may serve as a link between pharisaic notions of tradition and what later rabbinic Sages understood as Torah. To complete our speculative experiment, we offer the following proposal. Pharisaic tradition and rabbinic Torah share, at the very least, an interest in ritual actions. Some of these rituals, like the specific procedures for inaugurating the Sabbath, probably entered rabbinic Torah via the route of earlier pharisaic tradition. Others represent rabbinic developments of Judaic practices beyond explicitly pharisaic origins.

It is highly unlikely that all aspects of rabbinic ritual life originate in pharisaic traditions. In most cases, at any rate, the lines of connection are too blurred to trace. Common to both Pharisaism and rabbinic Judaism, however, is an attitude toward the nature of these ritual actions. Even though they may not be explicitly stated in the Torah of Moses, they are conceived as the fulfillment of the divine will. The Gospels, clearly enough, regard this as an absurdity and mock it as a sign of pharisaic hypocrisy. But it is certainly central to the rabbinic movement after the destruction of the Temple.

During the same post-70 decades in which the Gospel traditions were forming the image of the early-first-century Pharisees, the founders of the rabbinic movement were attempting to redefine the ritual life of Judaism. Rabban Yohanan ben Zakkai, a witness to the destruction of the Temple, is singled out in rabbinic writings as the originator of a number of ritual innovations. These made it possible to perform in the home or in public prayer services ritual acts once central to the services of the Temple. It was also in the post-Temple period that rabbinic traditions recorded a burgeoning interest in structuring prayer services that could serve as a replacement for the suspended Temple sacrifices.

Neither of these matters—performance of Temple rites in homes or the recitation of prayers instead of sacrifices—has any clear foundation in the Torah of Moses. For the Torah, the service of God was what Aaron and his priestly descendants did at the altar (e.g., Ex. 29:1–46) or what ordinary Israelites did by preserving the memories of God's redemptive acts (e.g., Deut. 6:1–25). But in rabbinic communities, a host of ritual practices was developed and accepted as received tradition, part of what it meant to live in continual conversation with the covenantal obligations imposed by the Torah.

If God required absolute obedience, and if the destruction of the Temple made many of his commandments impossible to fulfill, then it was only through traditions preserved outside the textual confines of scripture that Jews could begin to reconstruct their covenantal relationship with the God of Abraham, Isaac, and Jacob. It is in this sense that "ancestral tradition" and Torah become inseparably bound with each other.

The Rabbinic Written and Oral Torah

The question, of course, is *whose* tradition? We have learned, and ancient rabbinic Sages surely knew, that various traditions of interpretation and practice had for centuries shaped Jews' understanding of the Torah of Moses. Rabbinic Sages would have had no perception of the book of Jubilees as tradition, despite its antiquity, for they rejected its schedule of holidays.

An important rabbinic attempt to define a legitimate family tree of tradition is recorded in a third-century CE rabbinic work, the title of which is probably best translated as "The Founders" (*Avot*). It begins with the following assertion:

> Moses received Torah on Sinai, and passed it on to Joshua, Joshua to elders, and elders to prophets. And prophets handed it on to the men of the great assembly. They said three things: (1) Be prudent in judgment. (2) Raise up many disciples. (3) Make a fence around the Torah.

The passage continues with a lengthy list of later Sages, living well after the return from Babylonian exile, each of whom receives Torah from his predecessor and passes it on to disciples. This list of teachers, which includes pharisaic figures as well as rabbinic Sages known to have lived as late as the early third century CE, makes two intertwined claims. First, the tradition passed on as Torah by the rabbis begins with Moses and remains intact for well over a thousand years. Second, tradition is Torah *only* if it is transmitted by a rabbinic Sage. So much for Jubilees—and a host of other texts deemed by Sages to fall beyond the framework of Torah.

This list makes an extraordinary claim for the continuity of Mosaic teaching through the Sages. But even more interesting is the way in which Torah, received by Moses and passed on to his disciples, is distinguished from "*the* Torah of Moses," the actual document recording the Mosaic legislation. One builds "a fence" around the *textual* Torah of Moses with the *interpretive tradition* of Torah preserved by the rabbis. Indeed, in rabbinic perspective, it is precisely tradition that constitutes the "fence" around "the Torah" (Avot 3:13).

As Avot views things, *traditional* Torah passed on in rabbinic teaching constitutes a systematic safeguard against the violation of the *scriptural* Torah of Moses. Rabbinic Torah, as ancient tradition, enables Jews to properly embody laws, values, and norms of the scriptural Torah in their own pattern of life, even where these have no apparent warrant in Moses' book. That tradition, transmitted in rabbinic teaching and practice, is nothing less than Torah itself. It embodies in public and private life what God wanted for Israel when he revealed its basic outline, *the* Torah of Moses, to the entire community on Sinai. Thus, according to rabbinic Judaism, *rabbinic tradition and scripture together constitute Torah*; indeed, each requires and presupposes the existence of the other.

This perception of the inseparability of rabbinic tradition and the Mosaic scripture is expressed in rabbinic writings of the fourth and fifth centuries in a remarkably apt image. These writings, which we shall shortly discuss more extensively, speak from time to time of *two* Torahs having been revealed on Sinai. One of these, called the Written Torah, is the actual scroll of Mosaic teachings preserved as scripture and read in the synagogues. The written Torah includes, as its written extension and amplification, the entire canon of the Hebrew Bible as the rabbis defined it. The second Torah, called the Oral Torah, is claimed to have been transmitted to Moses by word of mouth alone and memorized. This orally preserved Torah has accompanied the Written Torah since the beginning and, indeed, constitutes the authentic interpretation of the Written Torah's many commandments. Most important of all, the only way this Oral Torah can be learned is by long and diligent discipleship to a rabbinic Sage who has committed the entire Torah, Written and Oral, to memory.

It is small exaggeration to say that the crucial human relationship of early rabbinic Judaism was between the Sage and his disciple. The disciple, a kind of apprentice rabbi, served his master as a butler and companion, much as his non-Jewish contemporary in the Hellenistic world might serve a philosophical teacher. In return, the disciple had the opportunity to study the Sage's every word and gesture as an exemplification of what it means to fully embody Torah. The essence of the Sage's teaching were his words of Torah and the way his behavior embodied Torah.

Mishnah Avot's Chain of Transmission Linking Mishnaic-Rabbinic Tradition to Sinai

The Prophetic Chain of Transmission

Moses
Joshua
the Elders
the Prophets

This chain carries the tradition of Torah through the period from Moses to the destruction of the First Temple (587 BCE).

Transmitters of the Early Second Temple Period

Men of the Great Assembly
Shimon the Righteous
Antigonus of Sokho

This chain carries the tradition of Torah from roughly the time of Ezra (450–400 BCE) to the early second century BCE. The Men of the Great Assembly and Antigonus of Sokho are known only from rabbinic texts.

The Age of The Pairs (Late Second Temple Period)

Yose b. Yoezer and Yose b. Yohanan of Jerusalem
Joshua b. Perakhyah and Nittai the Arbelite
Judah b. Tabbai and Shimon b. Shetakh
Shemaiah and Avtalion
Hillel and Shammai

Rabbinic tradition views the "The Pairs" as holding the offices of Patriarch and Supreme Court Justice respectively throughout the Hasmonean and early Roman Period in the Land of Israel (150–10). They are known primarily from rabbinic texts.

The Age of the Mishnaic Sages (Late Second Temple–Post Temple)

Rabban Gamaliel I
Rabban Yohanan b. Zakkai
Rabban Shimon b. Gamaliel I

Rabban Gamaliel II
Rabban Shimon b. Gamaliel II
Rabbi Judah b. Shimon b. Gamaliel

The title Rabban (Our Master) is a form of Rabbi (My Master) and appears first with these figures. All but Rabban Yohanan b. Zakkai are recalled in rabbinic tradition as having served as Patriarch. Rabban Yohanan is recalled as reconstituting the study of Torah in a seaport called Yavneh after the Destruction of the Temple in 70 CE.

Rabbinic tradition, then, worked in two ways. As a pattern of behavior learned by imitation, it was tradition transmitted simply by example. As an intellectual tradition, it was learned by studying and mastering the rabbi's oral teachings. To the degree that many Sages argued that their patterns of behavior were themselves based upon interpretation of the Torah of Moses, these two types of tradition were often fused into one and seen as continuous with the Mosaic revelation. It is for this reason that the actual literature of rabbinic Judaism, when it came to be composed into written texts, consisted almost entirely of words of Torah ascribed to specific rabbis and to depictions of how these words were exemplified by their deeds.[14]

The Literature of the Oral Torah

Sages routinely referred to the content of their traditional learning by the words *mishnah* (Hebrew) or *matnyta* (Aramaic). The best rendering of either term is "Repeated Tradition." By the early third century, there seems to have circulated a rather large Hebrew compilation of such repeated tradition. It was associated with the editorial work of the Patriarch Rabbi Judah.

Scholars still debate the degree to which this "Mishnah of Rabbi" existed in a written form. There is no doubt, however, that it was commonly memorized by rabbinic disciples and that much of their training was bound up in oral discourse about the interpretation of this text. This is what was "oral" about Oral Torah—it was *performed* in the course of its interpretation. Something very much like this early Mishnah is, at any rate, preserved in the copies of the Mishnah found in rabbinic manuscripts from the Middle Ages and onward into the printed books of the modern world.[15]

The work called Avot, from which we quoted earlier, is included in the Mishnah, along with more than sixty other treatises on various aspects of Jewish law. Each treatise, in whole or in part, is devoted to a specific legal topic and presents diverse rabbinic discussions about how to best implement the divine commandments contained in the Torah of Moses regarding that topic. The basic assumptions governing the compilation of the Mishnah are clear: God spoke once in the Torah of Moses and revealed his commandments; he continues to speak through the traditional Torah of the rabbis, which explains how to perform his commandments. These rabbinic explanations are called *halakhah* or "procedure"—that is, procedure for implementing the commandments. To follow the rabbis' halakhic procedures is to do God's will, as transmitted to Moses on Sinai.

The interpretive tradition of Oral Torah did not stop with the Mishnah but continued to grow in subsequent centuries as the Mishnah spawned later schools of technical interpretation. One important method of halakhic research was to identify and explicate those passages of the Written Torah that served as the basis for the specific procedures of Oral Torah. But the interests of rabbinic students of the Written and Oral Torah ranged far beyond strictly halakhic matters and included extended reflection upon other concerns central to the interpretation of the Bible—ethical issues, historical recollections, and theological speculation. These fell under the category of *aggadah*, "teachings" designed to foster a desire to serve God in obedience to the rules of halakhah.

Eventually, these two types of interpretive tradition were gathered together into immense, encyclopedic compilations of rabbinic teaching, *talmud* (Aramaic: "learning"). The most famous and important of these compilations are called the Talmud of the Land of Israel (edited ca. 425) and the Talmud of Babylonia (ca. 525). Both Talmuds are designed as Mishnah commentaries, offering line-by-line explorations of the Mishnah's halakhic applications and implications. Routinely, however, the Talmud's discussions include as well vast amounts of aggadic commentary on the Hebrew Bible. The Babylonian Talmud remains today the most revered classic of rabbinic teaching among observant Jews.

Other rabbinic teachings, on biblical interpretation in particular, were gathered together from the third to the seventh centuries in yet other large collections of lore called *midrash*, "interpretation" or "commentary." Unlike the Talmud, which is organized as a Mishnah commentary, works of midrash are normally organized around books of the Hebrew Bible or on scriptural readings assigned in the synagogue for specific holidays. Substantial collections of midrash focus upon the halakhic connections between the Written and the Oral Torah. Most of the surviving midrashic compilations, however, are dominated by aggadic discourses in which verses of the Written Torah are amplified by the traditions of the Sages' Oral Torah.

In all, half a millennium of rabbinic literary scholarship radically transformed the inheritance of the first 500 years of Judaic literary creativity. Midway in the first Judaic millennium, the collection of the Judaic scriptures received its final canonical stamp, and the task of fixing the texts of its vari-

Terminology and Chronology of Rabbinic Literature

In rabbinic literature it is convenient to distinguish between *types* of tradition in which knowledge was transmitted, *forms* of their transmission prior to their editing into finished compilations, and, finally, the *works* into which these traditions are compiled.

Types of Tradition

1. *Halakhah*—tradition about legal or ritual practice
2. *Aggadah*—tradition about history or theology

Forms of Transmission

1. *Midrash*—halakhic or aggadic tradition transmitted as an explanation of a biblical verse
2. *Mishnah*—halakhic or aggadic tradition transmitted without reference to a biblical verse
3. *Talmud*—analysis of a halakhic tradition

Major Compilations of Rabbinic Tradition

1. *Mishnah*—The halakhic collection supervised by Rabbi Judah the Patriarch in the Galilean city Tiberias, ca. 200.
2. *Tosefta*—A halakhic collection similar to, but larger than, the Mishnah, edited anonymously by 300 CE in Palestine. Tosefta means "supplement," that is, to the Mishnah.
3. *Mekhilta of Rabbi Ishmael*—A third- to fourth-century Palestinian midrashic compilation in which the legal portions of the Book of Exodus are provided with both halakhic and aggadic comment. All rabbinic authorities mentioned in this compilation are from the first to early third centuries.
4. *Sifra*—An almost exclusively halakhic midrash on Leviticus. It is probably from third- to fourth-century Palestine. All rabbinic authorities mentioned are from the first to early third centuries.
5. *Sifre*—A pair of midrashic works on Numbers and Deuteronomy, mixing both halakhic and aggadic types of tradition. Most authorities are identical to those of Sifra and Mekhilta.
6. *Bereshit Rabba*—An enormous compilation of aggadic traditions that comment on every verse of Genesis. It is rich in traditions in the names of third- and fourth-century Sages, and was probably edited in Palestine by the fifth century.

7. *Vayiqra Rabba*—This aggadic midrash focuses on Leviticus, using the first verses of the scriptural chapters as occasions for long homiletic discourses. Like Bereshit Rabba, it is probably from fifth-century Palestine.

8. *Talmud Yerushalmi*—The "Palestinian Talmud," a mostly halakhic commentary on the Mishnah (Palestine, ca. 425).

9. *Talmud Bavli*—The "Babylonian Talmud," compiling halakhic and aggadic materials into an encyclopedic commentary on the Mishnah (Mesopotamia, ca. 525).

ous books began in earnest. As a consequence, any literary works of Hellenistic Palestine and the Diaspora that might have competed for canonical inclusion were suppressed. This was the fate of Jubilees. Others, such as the Wisdom of Joshua ben Sira, enjoyed a quasi-scriptural status. This text is routinely cited in rabbinic literature but is officially excluded from the scriptural canon. Yet others, particularly if they were composed in Greek, were officially ignored. As we shall see in another context, however, theological and interpretive traditions found in them seem to have survived in rabbinic oral tradition as teachings of Sages.

Halakhic inquiry, for its part, had constructed a system of religious discipline that served as a whole to replace the ancient Temple's sacrificial media of atonement. Applying the textual tradition of the Written Torah to their lives through the ritual traditions of the Oral, rabbis and the Jews they influenced experienced an intimate sense of continuity between past and present, a trust that their pattern of life now conformed self-evidently to the original pattern handed by God to Moses. Supressing or transforming other worlds of Judaism, rabbinic Judaism created a religious world that, for many centuries, would appear to be the obvious embodiment of the world of the Mosaic Torah. By the early Middle Ages, any nonrabbinic Judaic world would have to define itself in categories provided by rabbinic Judaism itself.

Conclusions

We have argued three basic points in this chapter. The first is that the main scriptural texts of Judaism—the Torah of Moses and the epic that it introduces—emerged in the Persian period as part of a larger attempt to organize the Jews of Yehud around a program of religious-political regeneration. During the centuries after the return to Yehud, all of the inherited lore and law of ancient Israel was rethought and reinterpreted to produce a national history.

This history was not motivated by neutral curiosity about the past. Rather, the image of the past was shaped to interpret the present. In light of the past, the current historical moment appeared as the God-sent opportunity to once and for all correct the course of Israel's history.

The development of the scriptural canon unfolded through the successive attempts of Jews to interpret that covenantal history and apply it to their own situations. This constitutes our second main point. Judaic scripture did not happen all at once. The final canon resulted from centuries of reflective activity within various Jewish communities and did not achieve final resolution until roughly 500 years or so after the Torah of Moses began to dominate Jewish life in Persian Yehud.

Finally, we have stressed that the scriptures of Judaism were never rigidly distinct from the processes of tradition that gave them life in the various worlds of Judaism. All scripture started out as tradition; some literary traditions then became scripture, while others lived on as "commentary" or died away. The rabbinic tradition of Written and Oral Torah serves as a prime example.

It was rabbinic tradition that *created* the categories of Written and Oral Torah to distinguish scripture from tradition. Yet the rabbinic marriage of Written and Oral Torah enabled the Sages to portray the entire complex of rabbinic culture as stemming from the originating moment of Sinai. The rabbinic project, in hindsight, is not unlike that of Jubilees—to restate the Torah of Moses so that a body of interpretive tradition could determine its application. The rabbis, however, were in a position to make their revision part of the public policy of powerful empires.

Notes

1. The consequences of realizing that "scripture" has both a written and an oral dimension have only recently been considered by students of religion. An excellent place to begin is with William A. Graham, *Beyond the Written Word: Oral Aspects of Scripture in the History of Religion* (Cambridge: Cambridge University Press, 1987), pp. 9–48.

2. The best overall introduction to scripture in the comparative study of religion is found in Frederick M. Denny and Rodney L. Taylor, eds., *The Holy Book in Comparative Perspective* (Columbia: University of South Carolina Press, 1993).

3. Most commonly, this debate is played out in reference to the composition of the Torah of Moses itself. The discussion is bound up with the "Documentary Hypothesis," an attempt to isolate distinct ancient literary works used in the composition of the present Torah of Moses. Richard Elliott Friedman, *Who Wrote the Bible?* (New York: Harper & Row, 1987), pp. 15–32, offers a fine account of the history and significance of this hypothesis.

    All attempts to date those source documents (as well as their very existence) are, however, conjectural. Examples of the range of opinions held by most contemporary scholars may be found in James A. Sanders, *Torah and Canon* (Philadelphia: Fortress Press, 1972), and in Thomas L. Thompson, *The Historic-*

ity of the Patriarchal Narratives (Berlin: Mouton de Gruyter, 1974). Both authors regard the destruction of Yehudah as a crucial event in the process that led postexilic Jews to edit earlier Israelite historical and legal texts into the present Torah of Moses. R.N. Whybray, *The Making of the Pentateuch: A Methodological Study* (Sheffield: JSOT Supplement, 1987), has recently offered a powerful argument against the idea that the Torah of Moses contains earlier written documents.

4. You can find more ample treatment of the argument advanced earlier in Friedman, *Who Wrote the Bible?*, pp. 217–233. He, however, is more confident than I that the Torah of Moses is the handiwork of Ezra. A more technical work, which links the Torah of Moses to an anonymous postexilic composer of oral tradition, is Whybray, *The Making of the Pentateuch*, pp. 221–242. The opinion that the Torah of Moses reached its present form in the last century prior to the destruction of Yehudah is presented in Yehezkel Kaufman, *The Religion of Israel: From Its Beginnings to the Babylonian Exile*, tr., M. Greenberg (New York: Schocken Books, 1972), pp. 153–211.

5. An excellent brief introductory treatment of the history of the canon of the Hebrew Bible is the essay by Roger T. Beckwith, "Formation of the Hebrew Bible," in Martin Jan Mulder, ed., *Mikra: Text, Translation, Reading and Interpretation of the Hebrew Bible in Ancient Judaism and Early Christianity* (Assen/Maastricht and Philadelphia: Van Gorcum and Fortress Press, 1988), pp. 39–86. This should be supplemented with James A. Sanders, "Canon," in David Noel Freedman, ed., *The Anchor Bible Dictionary, Vol. I* (New York: Doubleday, 1992), pp. 837–852.

6. Everything you will probably ever want to know about the Septuagint can be conveniently found in Emanuel Tov, "The Septuagint," in Mulder, *Mikra*, pp. 161–188.

7. Sample translations of this literature with helpful introductions and explanations can be found in M. De Jonge, ed., *Outside the Old Testament* (Cambridge: Cambridge University Press, 1985); Michael A. Knibb, *The Qumran Community* (Cambridge: Cambridge University Press, 1987); and George W.E. Nickelsburg and Michael E. Stone, eds., *Faith and Piety in Early Judaism: Texts and Documents* (Philadelphia: Fortress Press, 1983).

8. An accessible discussion of the rabbinic role in defining the canonical boundaries is that of Sid Z. Leiman, "Inspiration and Canonicity: Reflections on the Formation of the Biblical Canon," in E.P. Sanders, ed., *Jewish and Christian Self-Definition. Volume Two: Aspects of Judaism in the Greco-Roman Period* (Philadelphia: Fortress Press, 1981), pp. 56–63. Those with some biblical Hebrew can consult his masterpiece on the subject, *The Canonization of Hebrew Scripture: The Talmudic and Midrashic Evidence*, 2nd ed. (New Haven: The Connecticut Academy of Arts and Sciences, 1991).

9. For other examples of conversations between writings within the scriptural canon, see Michael Fishbane, *The Garments of Torah: Essays in Biblical Hermeneutics* (Bloomington: Indiana University Press, 1989), pp. 3–18. Fishbane's enormous book on this phenomenon, *Biblical Interpretation in Ancient Israel* (Oxford: The Clarendon Press, 1985), is technical. But no one who works through it will ever again think that biblical writings came to be "just so."

10. A good edition of this text for students is in the translation of O.S. Wintermute, "Jubilees," in James H. Charlesworth, ed., *The Old Testament Pseudepigrapha. Vol. II* (Garden City, NY: Doubleday & Company, 1985), pp. 52–142. Wintermute's introduction to the translation is on pages 35–51. I have adapted Wintermute's translation in the quotations that follow.

11. There isn't space enough in this chapter to do justice to the history of Jewish scriptural interpretation in this early period. I recommend the texts mentioned in note 7 and the fine overview in James L. Kugel and Rowan A. Greer, *Early Biblical Interpretation* (Philadelphia: The Westminster Press, 1986), pp. 13–106.

12. Because of the connection of rabbinic Judaism with earlier pharisaic traditions, discussions of rabbinic origins are often veiled ways of arguing for the truth of Christianity over Judaism or vice versa. An important attempt to see the question of the Pharisees and the rabbis with clarity was begun a generation ago by Jacob Neusner. It is summarized conveniently in Jacob Neusner, *From Politics to Piety: The Emergence of Pharisaic Judaism*, 2nd ed. (New York: KTAV, 1979). For a good summary of the current thinking on pharisaic issues, see Anthony J. Saldarini, "Pharisees," *Anchor Bible Dictionary, Vol. V*, pp. 289–303. The rabbinic inheritance from the Pharisees is summarized by Jacob Neusner, *From Testament to Torah: An Introduction to Judaism in Its Formative Age* (Englewood Cliffs, NJ: Prentice Hall, 1988), pp. 15–65.

13. The discussion comprises the eighth chapter of the mishnaic tractate Berakhot ("Blessings"). You can follow it, and its later career in talmudic tradition, in Jacob Neusner, *Invitation to the Talmud: A Teaching Book*, Rev. ed. (San Francisco: Harper & Row, 1984).

14. The most useful undergraduate introduction to the development of the idea of Oral Torah and the nature of its texts is Jacob Neusner, *The Oral Torah: The Sacred Books of Judaism. An Introduction* (San Francisco: Harper & Row, 1986). For a rather different perspective on the same questions, compare Hyam Maccoby, *Early Rabbinic Writings* (Cambridge: Cambridge University Press, 1988).

15. The exact nature of rabbinic oral literature is still debated by scholars. One view, which holds that texts of Oral Torah were transmitted for centuries without writing, is represented by the influential study of Birger Gerhardsson, *Memory and Manuscript: Oral Transmission and Written Tradition in Rabbinic Judaism and Early Christianity*, tr., Eric J. Sharpe (Lund, Sweden: Gleerup; Cophenhagen, Denmark: Munksgaard, 1961).

For a discussion that concludes that many texts were known in written form at an early date, you can consult Hermann L. Strack and Guenter Stemberger, *Introduction to the Talmud and Midrash*, tr., Marcus Bockmuehl (Edinburgh: T & T Clark, 1991), pp. 35–49. This is the best reference work for scholarly opinion about the history and literary characteristics of all genres of rabbinic literature.

Three

Symbolic Vocabularies and Cosmic Structures

Introduction

Religious worlds, we hold, "posit various orders of reality and help individuals and groups to negotiate their relations with those orders." This is true for the worlds of early Judaism as well. All of them were grounded in more or less explicit conceptions of the cosmic order. They articulated these conceptions in terms of a clear vocabulary of core symbolic ideas. We discuss what we mean by "symbolic vocabularies" momentarily. For now, we point out that even though Judaic conceptions of the world's order were hardly uniform throughout our period, the symbolic vocabulary used to articulate these conceptions migrated with remarkable regularity throughout the entire millennium at hand.

This chapter traces that migration. It explores the ways in which a limited repertoire of symbols and ideas was incorporated into comprehensive Judaic conceptions of reality. First, we must isolate the surprisingly small cluster of such symbols or ideas. We can then better appreciate how Jews used them to think about and organize the various kinds of knowledge they had of the world. We notice that this knowledge was often congruent with what surrounding non-Jewish populations knew about reality. What made the Jews' worlds Judaic was the distinctive symbolic vocabulary through which their own knowledge was expressed.

The Judaic Symbolic Vocabulary

We begin with the common word "symbol." For the present purpose, a symbol is a word or an object around which multiple meanings seem to gather, like filings around a magnet. Just as magnetic fields are visible only in terms of the patterns made by the filings, the meanings of symbols are intelligible only in terms of the way humans actually use them. In general, religious symbols are words or objects that serve as highly compressed expressions of entire conceptions of reality.[1]

Think of the symbol of a cross (+). It has meanings that can be circumscribed. In a mathematical context, it indicates a certain way of combining numbers. To those who read the Latin alphabet, it represents the letter *t* and thus stands for a certain sound. But take the cross and enlarge it to a height of 6 feet or so; place the enlargement on the narrow wall of a rectangular building. It will be hard not to read the symbol as standing for the Savior revered by Christianity.

In its new context, the cross is the Cross; it addresses the most comprehensive conceptions of the world that Christians may entertain. Among different Christian worlds, moreover, there are real differences about what that shared symbol means. All these different meanings, though they may be in conflict, are the "real" meanings of the symbol. As historians of religion, our job is not to determine which Christians are using the symbol "correctly." This is for Christian theologians to determine. Rather, we try to understand the symbolic meanings in each Christian setting.

This begins our exercise in interpreting symbolic meanings. We explore the crucial symbols through which Judaic worlds have expressed their most comprehensive understandings of reality. We can focus upon five fundamental symbolic ideas. All of them, in varying degrees, figure prominently in early Judaic conceptions of the world. In their simplest forms, these ideas are the God of Israel, Torah, the People Israel, Exile, and Messiah.

Since more than one symbol seems always to figure in Judaic conceptions of reality, we can think of them together as constituting a kind of vocabulary. They are a small repertoire of symbolic terms through which Jews conventionally expressed their various conceptions of the world. This basic vocabulary of symbols made its first appearance clustered in the writings of Persian Yehud, playing an important role in the canonical narrative that structures the Hebrew Bible. It remained central as well throughout the ancient Jewish literature that competed with the scriptures for the attention of diaspora and Palestinian Jews.

God-Torah-Israel

The story at the heart of the Hebrew Bible concerns a single and sovereign God, the Creator of Heaven and Earth, who called into being a special people, Israel, to build for him a dwelling place in the world he created. The means of communication between God and Israel was, of course, Torah, the divine instruction. It was disclosed in stages: first to Abraham, then to Moses and Israel on Mt. Sinai. During the years of desert wandering, it was heard in the Tent of Meeting. Later, it sounded forth from the Temple in Jerusalem, God's dwelling place, to priests and prophets. Israel's compliance with the teachings of Torah sealed the covenantal relation of God and his people. In the name of that relationship, Israel called upon God for protection and sustenance as it tried to create, in the Land of Israel, the kind of social order desired by God.

The triad of God-Torah-Israel is a fundamental assumption of early Judaic world. In such worlds, God is rarely understood apart from his simultaneous relations with the world as its creator, with Torah as its revealer, and with Israel as its covenant partner or redeemer. Likewise, Torah rarely stands solely for a piece of wise or useful guidance. Rather, it is something that comes from God as a message for Israel. Israel, to complete the triad, is rarely simply the name of an ethnic group. In Judaic usage, it commonly denotes a people living in covenantal relation to God through the guidance of Torah.

Messiah and Exile

In light of this triad, we can appreciate the significance of the final key terms. Just as God-Torah-Israel represents an interrelated complex, so, too, do Messiah and Exile. The English word "Messiah" renders the Hebrew *mashiakh*. In its simplest meaning, it denotes "one who is anointed with oil." More expansively, it identifies a person consecrated to a divinely appointed task. In the Torah of Moses, particularly in the book of Leviticus, this term is used frequently to describe Aaron, the officiating priest charged with conducting the sacrificial service in the Tent of Meeting.

In the ceremony consecrating him to his task, specially prepared olive oil was poured on his head (Lev. 8:12) and other parts of his body. So, in the priestly sense, the Messiah is the priest whose sacrificial service in accordance with Torah sustains the covenantal relationship between God and Israel. This sense of the term was retained in a number of Jewish writings from Hellenistic Palestine in particular (pages 105–106). But more often it was overshadowed by a more prominent connotation.

This is the meaning of the term "Messiah" in the historical and visionary writings collected in Nevi'im as well as in some of the Psalms of Ketuvim. In these writings, the priestly usage of Leviticus is supplanted by a royal image. Messiah refers to one anointed to serve as king over the Israelite people in its Land. The original anointee was Saul, the first man appointed as king over Israel (I Sam. 8–10). The most famous Messiah was David, remembered in the historical writings of Nevi'im and Ketuvim as the standard against which all future kings would be evaluated (e.g., I Ki. 11:5–13, II Chron. 29:1–3).

By extension, the term also refers to all descendants of David's line who sat on his throne. All were Anointed Ones, sanctified by the oil poured upon them to the sacred task of governing Israel on its land in loyalty to God's Torah. All enjoyed and benefited from the vow that God is said to have made to David, a covenant no less binding than the general covenant with Israel: "Your line on the throne of Israel shall never end, if only your descendants will look to their way and walk before me as you have walked before me" (I Ki. 8:25).

Now, as the historical books of Kings and Chronicles tell the story of Israel's kings, it becomes clear that most of them did not "look to their way and walk before" God as David is said to have done. All but a few are depicted as morally unworthy of the covenant promise in their trust. One after the other, these books recall, Israel's kings sinned against God, introduced idolatrous worship into his Temple, polluted the land with wickedness, and caused (or permitted) Israel to go astray. Indeed, as the writings in Nevi'im tell the story, Israel became so estranged from God under such Anointed Ones that he raised up the Babylonian Empire to destroy the kingdom begun by David.

Israel, to use a colorful image from Leviticus 18:28, was "vomited out of the land," shipped in captivity to Babylonia. The failure of Messiahs to fulfill their covenant tasks explains the powerful role of our final symbolic term, Exile, in the Judaic symbolic vocabulary. Messianic corruption resulted in Exile; the reversal of Exile, in turn, was associated with the restoration of a proper royal Messiah who would once and for all fulfill the Davidic role.

Some prophetic visionaries, such as the exiled priest Ezekiel, held out hope for a future day when an anointed Davidic heir would once again sit on the throne of a just Israelite Kingdom. Speaking on behalf of God, Ezekiel promised that then "my servant David shall be king over them; there shall be one shepherd for all of them. They shall follow my rules and faithfully obey my laws. . . . I will be their God and they shall be my people. And when my sanctuary abides among them forever, the nations shall know that I the LORD do sanctify Israel" (Ezek. 37:24–28).

Neither the scriptural canon nor other early streams of tradition offer a consistent image of how the Messiah will draw Exile to a close or even of who that Messiah might be. Not all scriptural or nonscriptural traditions even imagine that a Messiah of any kind will figure in the conclusion of Exile. We explore this diversity of conception in detail later in this chapter. For now, we observe that the basic symbolic vocabulary of Judaic worlds draws the imagination in two different directions.

God, Torah, and Israel constitute the *vertical or spatial axis* of Judaic

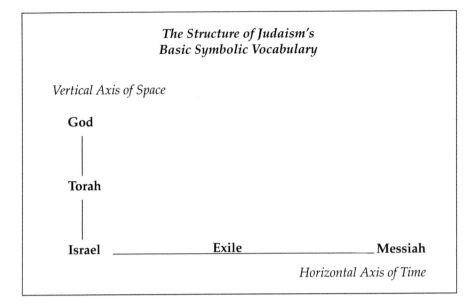

worlds. Exile and Messiah complement this with a *horizontal or historical axis*. Within these symbolic axes, early Judaism identified and defined the significance of everything else in the cosmos. Along one or another of these lines or another, all things of importance found their place and their meaning. Sometimes, Judaic worlds articulated rather harmonious syntheses of these two directions; at other times, the imagination of early Judaism focused upon one to the neglect of the other.

We consider now how specific worlds of early Judaism used the vocabulary we have described and how broadly they applied it. As the words of a dictionary of the English language can be used to make fresh statements, all of them different but all English, so, too, this particular vocabulary was used to describe many types of worlds, all different but all Judaic. Moreover, not all elements of the vocabulary issue into meaningful statements in every Judaic world, just as no English book uses every word in the dictionary. But normally, the presence of one symbolic element implies and evokes at least implicit judgment about the meaning of the others.

Worlds Constructed Along the Vertical Axis

Judging from the surviving literary sources, some groups within early Judaism showed a marked tendency to imagine the world almost exclusively in terms of the vertical axes of the Judaic symbolic vocabulary. In these worlds, the structure of the created order and the beings that populate it were of much greater interest than its temporal dimension. If time proved interesting at all, the past, rather than the future, dominated discussion.

The most interesting past was generally not the immediate past, counted in decades or even centuries. More commonly, it was the distant past described in ancient writings, canonical and otherwise, that were believed to have been recorded in times when God still spoke directly to human beings such as Moses and other prophets. The interesting past, in other words, was disconnected from historical time. Leading to no future, its relevance for the present was as a source of moral instruction. The past was a fable.[2]

In the worlds of early Judaism, two different but often complementary traditions of knowledge regarding the nature of the created order and the meaning of the past captured the attention of reflective Jews. We discuss each on its own and then trace the ways in which they mutually shaped each other in the construction of concrete Judaic images of the cosmos.

The Wisdom Traditions of the Middle East

One tradition, richly represented in Persian Yehud and later in Palestine, had deeply informed the priestly and scribal cultures of ancient Yehudah. Its historical roots extended back beyond Israelite culture to the great city-states and empires of Egyptian and Mesopotamian civilization—a tradition that celebrated wisdom (Hebrew: *hokhmah*) and revered the image of the Sage (*hakham*) or the Elder (*zaken*).[3]

This Middle Eastern tradition of wisdom treasured authoritative teachings from past Sages as reliable sources of knowledge and guidance. Much of this knowledge took the form that moderns might call a mixture of science and ethics. It was fascinated by the phenomena of the created order, cataloging their various relations, seeing in them intimations of the wisdom of the Creator of the World. It held out the promise, moreover, that understanding the design of the Creator could enable one to negotiate all of life's moral and intellectual challenges. Upon the basis of such authoritative traditions and penetrating observations, a wise and just society could be built under the guidance of Sages and righteous kings.

In ancient Israel, the main bearers of this tradition of wisdom were probably priests associated with religious shrines and the Temple, scholars associated with royal courts, and scribes. The results of their work were transmitted in a variety of literary genres. Chief among these were stories about the acts of ancient heroes, pithy observations on the human condition, catalogs of the various phenomena of the natural order, and, to an important degree, compendia of wise and just laws.

Parts of the Torah of Moses reflect this tradition. The stately description of the creation process in Genesis 1:1–2:3, for example, establishes the world as an ordered realm in which all things have their proper place and role.

God's comprehensive wisdom, furthermore, is contrasted with the imperfect, but perfectible, wisdom of humans. The human struggle toward wisdom is embodied in the story of Joseph, a gifted, but immature dream interpreter, who grows in self-knowledge and compassion on his way to becoming a principal deputy of the Egyptian Pharoah (Gen. 37–50). The book of Deuteronomy, proclaims that the laws of God constitute Israel's "wisdom before the nations" (Deut. 4:6)

The Middle Eastern scribal tradition of wisdom appears in other scriptural writings as well, most of which reached their canonical forms well before the first centuries CE. Many psalms, of which Psalm 119 is the most prominent example, celebrate God's commandments and teachings as an unfailing source of wisdom for those who obey: "How I love your Torah! It is my speech the entire day!" (Ps. 119:97). The first six chapters of the canonical book of Daniel focus in large part on the deeds of a hero noted for wisdom and piety. Similarly, the canonical collection of proverbial wisdom (Proverbs) and its sole example of abstract reflection upon life's meaning (Ecclesiastes) are both associated with Solomon, reputed by tradition to be the wisest of Israel's kings. Job, another ancient wise man, is the central figure in the canon's most sustained attempt to confront the problem of why righteous people suffer.

Beyond the scriptural canon, a number of Hebrew and Aramaic writings continued the tradition of compressing the practical wisdom of a lifetime into memorable epigrams. One of the best known is the Wisdom of ben Sira, attributed to an early-second-century BCE scribe named Joshua ben Sira. In Greek translation, it became part of the canon of the Septuagint. In it, sentiments such as the following are common: "To fear the LORD is the root of wisdom, and her branches are long life" (Sir. 1:20). The third-century CE rabbinic compilation of proverbs, Avot, is a rather late expression of the same tradition of proverbial wisdom: "Rabbi Hananiah ben Dosa says: He whose fear of sin dominates his wisdom will preserve his wisdom; he whose wisdom dominates his fear of sin will not preserve his wisdom" (Av. 3:9).

The Philosophical Traditions of Greece

But for all its influence, the tradition of Middle Eastern wisdom competed and combined with another. This second tradition linked the Judaic imagination to the Mediterranean world west of Egypt. It originated among the fifth-century BCE Ionian philosophers (*philosophos* means "wisdom lover") and extended to the various philosophical and rhetorical schools of the Hellenistic world, such as the Stoics, Cynics, and Epicureans.

Moral wisdom was for the Greek philosophers, as for their Middle Eastern counterparts, of primary importance. Where philosophy differed was in its emphasis. The Middle Eastern tradition saw the highest expression of wisdom in the capacity to master and act upon knowledge transmitted from the past. Greek philosophy, in contrast, celebrated the use of one's rational powers as a way of criticizing and perfecting received wisdom.

Philosophical teachers such as Socrates and his most famous disciple, Plato, developed ways of using logical argument as an antidote to the false beliefs transmitted as tradition. More than a purely psychological power, reason was viewed as a central element of all reality—an eternal and unchanging substance, the abiding foundation of all things that came into and passed out of being in the empirical world. Using reason to deduce the principles of reality, the philosopher united himself with the source of all things. He then knew how to act ethically in accord with cosmic norms. On the basis of such norms, moreover, just laws could be legislated by wise political leaders for the creation of an orderly society.

The literary expressions of Greek philosophical wisdom are diverse. In addition to fragmentary records of teachers who preceded Socrates, they include Plato's descriptions of Socrates' philosophical dialogues, as well as the systematic treatises of Plato's disciple Aristotle. A common literary pursuit among the Hellenistic heirs of Plato and Aristotle was to compose philosophical commentaries on ancient poetic works. A prime subject of such commentaries were the great epic works of Homer, the *Iliad* and the *Odyssey*. These epics were indeed the canonical texts of Hellenism, analogous in their own way to the Torah's place in the cultures of Judaism.

The goal of such commentaries was to demonstrate that the apparently irrational, naive myths and legends of the great Homer expressed profound truths about nature and morality. Allegory was the preferred method of interpretation. The allegorist would show how each troubling passage of a mythic episode could be connected to a suitable lesson taught by philosophical tradition. In this way, the allegorist saved the prestige of the Homeric epic by showing its integral connection to the best traditions of philosophical wisdom.

Greek philosophy, especially the allegorical method of interpreting ancient writings, played a profound role in the cultural lives of Greek-speaking Jews and was particularly influential in shaping the way they translated and interpreted their growing canon of scriptural texts. The Judaic form of philosophical tradition culminated in the first century CE in the writings of the first systematic philosopher in the history of Judaism, Philo of Alexandria. He was, as well, a master allegorist of the Torah. He applied the best of his skills to uncover the philosophical message behind the stories and laws written by Moses, whom he regarded as the first and greatest of the philosophers. We shall meet him again further on.[4]

Syntheses of Middle Eastern and Greek Traditions

Both these traditions of knowledge stemmed from independent cultural resources. Yet patterns of cross-fertilization within various Hellenistic Judaic settings are everywhere apparent.

Recall, for example, the Septuagint, the Greek translation of the Torah.

This translation consistently rethinks Hebrew conceptions within the philo-sophical terminology of Greece. A telling passage is the rendering of the di-vine name in Exodus 3:14. When Moses confronts the presence of God in a burning bush, he inquires after the name of the divinity who sends him to bring Israel out of Egypt. The Hebrew text records the divine answer as *ehyeh asher ehyeh*, an obscure reply that seems to mean, "I will become what I will become." The Septuagint, however, translates the Hebrew as *ho on*, "I am Be-ing." Hellenistic readers understood this term as a reference to the eternal Source of All Being, beyond the decaying matter of existence, discussed by the philosophers. Thus, the philosophical concept of divinity as a single source of all empirical reality, essentially uninvolved in the shifting events of human history, was joined to the Israelite conception of the God of Israel as the unique and only God who acts to redeem his one and only people. It was "Being" who redeemed Israel from Egyptian slavery.[5]

Just as Greek-speaking Jews adapted Greek terms to the expression of Hebrew ideas, so, too, did Aramaic and Hebrew speakers make their own the Greek intellectual heritage. The advice of the first-century BCE Sage Hillel: "what is hateful to you, do not do to your friend" (BT Shab. 31a), is a bit of practical wisdom that circulated throughout the Jewish Mediterranean. It ap-peared as early as the third or fourth century BCE in a Hellenistic Jewish novel entitled Tobit (4:15). The most famous version, of course, is preserved in Je-sus of Nazareth's name by Christian tradition, but it is also found in the writ-ings of the fifth-century BCE Greek historian Herodotus, as follows: "I will not myself do that which I account blameworthy in my neighbor." In this and other examples, wise sayings recorded in the names of Jewish teachers res-onate richly with the background, if not the exact words, of the Greek literary tradition.[6]

Thus, Greek culture was "nativized" by Jews and became a medium for expressing their own unique perspectives on reality. The combining of such traditions of wisdom in the worlds of Judaism was, for the most part, entirely unconscious. Few, apart from political ideologists, set out self-consciously to unify—or to separate—Judaism and Hellenism. Rather, Jews assumed that whatever is held to be true by reasonable people and is good for a person to know and to do was disclosed within the revered texts transmitted from the Jewish past.

Whether represented as Greek *sophia* or Hebrew *hokhmah*, wisdom in ancient Judaic worlds found its concrete expression in the symbolic figure of Torah. Torah, as these traditions imagined it, transcended the scriptural Torah of Moses, although Torah was certainly exemplified there. Torah, rather, was a principle of cosmic order. The canonical book of Proverbs (chap. 8–9) portrays wisdom as being God's companion from the beginning of time. The image was refracted throughout the worlds of ancient Judaism. It in-formed many of Philo's descriptions of Torah as a divine *logos* (word, princi-ple) or *nomos* (law, structure) through which Being conceived the world into existence. All that exists is as it should be because the world's structure is undergirded by divine thought, Torah.

For their part, nonphilosophical Hebrew writers such as Joshua ben Sira often equated hokhmah with a cosmic principle placed into the particular care of Israel: "Before time he created me, and I shall remain forever. In the sacred tent I ministered in his presence, and so I came to be established in Zion." (Sir. 24:9–10). The tradition moved directly into rabbinic thinking as well. In a famous comment on the first verses of Genesis, a rabbinic Sage described Torah as a blueprint of reality that even God must consult before creating the world. We discuss this text on page 115. In Mishnah Avot, one of the first pieces of wisdom the reader encounters is: "On three foundations does the world rest: on the Torah, on the Temple Service, and on acts of human generosity" (Av. 1:2).

The Space of the Cosmos and Its Inhabitants

Judaic forms of Greek and Middle Eastern wisdom traditions incorporated the symbols of God, Torah, and Israel into larger understandings of the cosmos as a unified whole. Let's begin to explore this.

Both wisdom traditions agreed in imagining the God of Israel as a divine King who reigned over an enormous cosmic realm. The same way human emperors had counselors and ministers who effected their will, so, too, God was served by a staff of heavenly ministers and messengers. Scripture, of course, mentions at times a "divine council" convened by the God of Israel (e.g., Ps. 89:6–8). It often describes as well divinely appointed messengers, such as the mysterious *malakh* ("messenger") who announced the good news of Samson's conception to his barren mother (Jud. 13:3). Here, and elsewhere, the Septuagint translated the Hebrew term malakh as *angelos*, the Greek word for "messenger." In the worlds of early Judaism, however, these divine counselors and angelic messengers were imagined against a cosmic canvas much broader than that articulated in most of scripture.

In the polytheistic pantheons of Hellenism, cosmic rulers routinely deployed a retinue of less powerful gods as their emissaries. Jews articulated this understanding of things within their own symbolic vocabulary, introducing the necessary modifications. The God of Israel, accordingly, filled the position occupied by Zeus or other cosmic rulers, such as the goddess Isis. Angels played a role very much like that of the minor gods in non-Jewish Hellenistic worlds.

The distinction between Greek gods and the angels of the God of Israel, however, was of crucial importance to many philosophically oriented Jews. They joined Stoics and others in denigrating the immoral behavior of the gods who populated the religious worlds of Hellenism. Few Jews, of course, would invest any effort in allegorical sanitizations of tales of divine lust and patricide, such as those common in Greek myth. Similarly, few would have been prepared to offer angels the sacrificial forms of worship that non-Jews offered to their gods. Nevertheless, Jewish monotheism, grounded in the structure of the Judaic symbolic lexicon, blended well with the philosophical monotheism of non-Jews, who regarded worship of the lesser gods as superstition, even if it served a patriotic purpose.

Unlike the gods of the Greek myths, the angels of the Judaic worlds were for the most part beyond moral reproach. Jews indeed knew of rebellious angels. Satan, or related figures such as Samael and Belial, loomed increasingly large in the Judaic worlds of antiquity. In some cases, a mere heavenly advocate, Satan or analogous figures, could also appear as a malevolent source of opposition to God's power. But for the most part, the angels populating Judaic worlds did only what their King commanded them to do and carefully avoided the embarrassing moral lapses of Hellenistic gods. Some angels might have once fornicated with human women (e.g., Gen. 6:1–4), but, unlike the randy drunkard Dionysius, they had since learned to restrain themselves.[7]

Despite this difference with regard to the gods, Jews agreed with their neighbors that all divine and angelic activity took place against the backdrop of vast cosmic spaces. God's dwelling was at the apex of a cosmic structure that began with the twelve astral constellations of the Zodiac. Beneath the stars was a series of seven heavenly spheres, each governed in its workings by the power of one of the seven fixed planets. Angelic messengers populated these spheres and moved up and down the cosmic ladder on their various tasks. Humans lived at the bottom, on earth.

Most humans stayed there until their bodies died, at which time their souls would confront one of two destinies. Souls devoted in life to wisdom and good works would float effortlessly up the cosmic ladder to return to the source of their being in the divine world. Others, coarsened by a life lived in the pursuit of folly or sin, would descend beneath the earth, cut off from the divine world until cleansed of the effects of earthiness.

This underworld, of course, had its own population of demonic figures, corresponding to the angels of the heavenly order. The philosophically minded may have discounted them, but archeological discoveries from Egypt to Mesopotamia attest to the attempts of Jews to use incantations and other ritual practices to prevent such demons from interfering in their fortunes—or to encourage them to interfere in the fortunes of enemies (see Chapter Five). Later rabbinic Sages, we shall learn, knew quite a lot about them.

Some few souls, and we return to them in Chapter Six, had mastered the mystery of liberating the soul from the body even in life. They could enjoy spectacular disembodied tours of the heavens. Philo, for example, describes one of his own such tours.[8] Others, divorced from philosophical circles but sharing some traditions with the rabbinic Sages, claimed to do so themselves by invoking the aid of an angelic teacher, the Prince of the Torah.

The Satan as a Source of Cosmic Evil

The biblical canon knows of a mysterious figure, the Satan, who seems to inhabit the heavenly regions as a kind of adviser or messenger of God (e.g., Job 1:6, Zach. 3:1–2). The name itself means "obstructor" or "adversary"; and in canonical settings, he seems to obstruct human designs. Throughout much of the history of early Judaism, however, the Satan's image grew to cosmic proportions, as he came to be perceived as a source of cosmic evil in opposition to God.

In the community that formed in the Dead Sea region of Qumran, it was clear that the Satan could have human allies on earth. The following text is from a document called "Curses of Satan and His Lot" (4Q286–7). It is probably part of a set of curses used by the Qumran community against its human adversaries. The translation is from G. Vermes, *The Dead Sea Scrolls in English* (Penguin: New York, 1990), p. 61.

Afterwards they shall damn Satan and all his guilty lot. They shall answer and say, Cursed be Satan in his hostile design, and damned in his guilty dominion. Cursed be all the spirits of his lot in their wicked design, and damned in their thoughts of unclean impurity. For they are the lot of darkness and their visitation is for eternal destruction. Amen,

---

What made this cosmic structure part of a distinctly Judaic world vision was, of course, the place of the God of Israel at the top and, obviously, the significance of the Jews at the bottom.

For most Hellenistic geographers and ethnographers, the Jews were an exotic curiosity, and their Land lay at the backwaters of civilization. Only Jews found a central role for Israel in the human order. But here we find an important point of geographical differentiation among the Jews. Most philosophically oriented Jewish works were written in the Greek-speaking Diaspora, whereas works more centrally in touch with Middle Eastern traditions were written in Hebrew or Aramaic by Palestinians. This perhaps explains why Palestinians tended to exceed diaspora writers in according the Land of Israel a distinctive role in the structure of the world's space.

Philo of Alexandria, for example, routinely portrayed the people Israel as the philosophical nation par excellence, commissioned by its lawgiver, Moses, to embody the highest truths of wisdom through its loyalty to the specific laws of the Torah of Moses. Thus, Israel as a national group is of central importance within the human order. It exemplies and transmits the wisdom that lies at the heart of all reality. But the Land of Israel for Philo tended

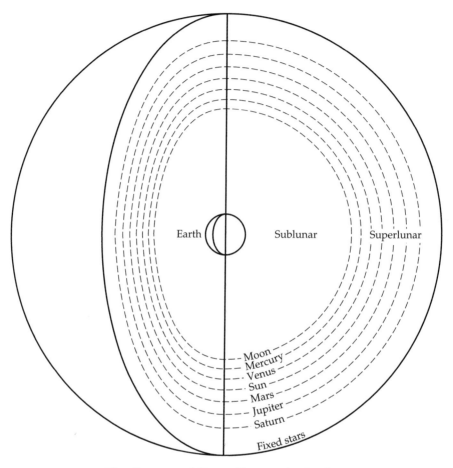

The Cosmos of Greco-Roman Antiquity

Jews, along with other members of Greco-Roman culture, conceived the Universe as a series of concentric spheres with the earth at the core and the ethereal sphere of the fixed stars at the periphery. Various categories of divine beings, conceived in early Judaism as angels, populated the realms between them. In the religious worlds of Hellenism, including Judaism, the spatial movement from the core to the periphery corresponds to a progressive refinement of being, from coarsest materiality to the most rarified spirituality.

Source: Luther H. Martin, *Hellenistic Religions: An Introduction.* Copyright © 1987 by Oxford University Press, Inc. Reproduced by permission.

to be shorn of concrete significance. To be sure, it served as a home for the Temple, in which priestly philosophers offered sacrifices that drew attention to important philosophical principles. The Land served as a vehicle for the expression of a variety of virtues, such as love for one's country. But the Land had no broader cosmic significance. The entire cosmos was the text within which the divine thought expressed itself, and the Torah given to Israel offered the code for deciphering that text. The Land of Israel, however, was neutral—equal to other lands, surely, but no higher.[9]

In Palestinian traditions of wisdom, to the contrary, the Land of Israel in general, and Jerusalem and its Temple in particular, figure prominently. A good example is the work of the Jerusalemite scribe Joshua ben Sira. Earlier we noted his concern to point out that the universal law of Torah makes its presence concretely known in Zion. Accordingly, the post-exilic history of the Land, which interested Philo hardly at all, was of great interest to ben Sira.

Ben Sira concluded his book by recounting all the heroes of Israel's past, beginning with Abraham and ending with the High Priest of his pre-Hasmonean day. In each, he found a model of wisdom and piety capable of being emulated in the present. The most loving attentions of the Cosmic King, who rules the whole universe, were elicited by the lavish grandeur of the sacrificial service offered in the Temple. That service culminated in a moment of union and communion between God and the Temple assembly as, under the raised hands of the priest, Simon, "they bow in worship to receive the blessing from the Most High" (Sir. 50:21). For all the cosmic importance of wisdom, the most intense experience of the God of the Universe remains available only in Jerusalem, the place of that God's choosing.

The worlds imagined within the wisdom traditions pay little explicit attention to the future-oriented historical concerns represented by ideas such as Exile or Messiah. They are absent almost entirely in Philo and reflect his larger disinterest in the Land of Israel as a geographical reality. But even Palestinian traditions of wisdom underplay orientations toward the future.

Joshua ben Sira's history of Israelite heroes, for example, shows little interest in the theme of Exile. His recollections of David, like those of Philo, offer no clue that in other Judaic worlds David could be imagined as a coming political leader who would preside over the end of Exile. Rather, ben Sira's King dwells safely in the past among vanished heroes. He is an ancient embodiment of wisdom and piety, not a hope for the future. The Messiah of interest to ben Sira, to the contrary, is the High Priest of Jerusalem. Here though, the messianic function is not political or historical, but liturgical. His sacrificial service and utterings of the priestly blessings, we have seen, establish and maintain the lines of communication that link Israel on earth to its God in Heaven.

It is always the world of vertical space that engages the imagination of ben Sira and other proponents of this stream of the wisdom tradition. Even centuries later, after the Jews of Palestine and the Diaspora had risen in messianic wars against Rome, tractate Avot and the rest of Rabbi's Mishnah remained almost entirely silent on the question of Exile and the role of the Messiah in bringing its end. For instruction on how the historical plane of experience could figure in the structure of Judaic worlds, therefore, we look elsewhere.

Worlds Constructed Along the Horizontal Axis

Greek-speaking Jews, as well as those at home in Aramaic or Hebrew, inherited more than wisdom traditions. They inherited as well the visionary tradition of Israelite literature—a tradition rich in concern for the moral fabric of Israelite society and its prospects for the future. The most influential works in this tradition had been gathered in the canon of Nevi'im. They were attributed to poets and preachers known collectively as prophets, spokespersons for God.

The largest canonical collections of visionary prophecies were gathered in the names of Isaiah, Jeremiah, and Ezekiel. But tradition transmitted as scripture twelve comparatively small works in the names of other prophets, equally charged with visionary promises. These writings often present dialogues between the prophets and the God of Israel, in which the prophet is commissioned to proclaim how divine interventions would shape Israel's and the world's future in response to Israel's loyalty or disloyalty to God. In most of these writings, Exile—as a threat or as an accomplished fact—is the fundamental issue; and the character of redemption from Exile, including the nature of the redeemer from Exile, is a prominent topic.[10]

The Redeemer in the Canon of Nevi'im

Works compiled and edited after the destruction of Yehudah in 587 BCE offer particularly rich explorations of the messianic theme. Here the redeemer of Israel is portrayed as a figure appointed by God. The diversity of these messianic conceptions is, in fact, extraordinary, especially in light of the exclusive focus of the later rabbinic and Christian traditions upon a Messiah of the House of David.[11]

One post-exilic visionary poet, whose songs now appear in chapters 40–55 of the book of Isaiah, employs a remarkable array of non-Davidic images through which to imagine the redemptive plan of God for Israel. In the following passage, for example, he extends the notion of a divinely anointed king entirely beyond the Israelite framework. For him, God's Messiah is none other than the Persian emperor Cyrus, who destroyed the Babylonian captors of Israel.

Note how the prophet interprets Cyrus' victories as the redemptive work of the God of Israel on behalf of his scattered people (Is. 45:1–6):

Thus says the LORD to his Messiah, to Cyrus, whose right hand I have grasped to subdue the nations before him and strip kings of their robes . . . I will give you the treasures of darkness and riches hidden in secret places, so that you may know that it is I, the LORD, the God of Israel, who call you by your name. For the sake of my servant Jacob, and Israel my chosen, I call you by your name, I surname you though you do not know me. I am the LORD, and there is no other; besides me there is no god. I arm you, though you do not know me, so that they may know, from the rising of the sun and from the west, that there is no one besides me; I am the LORD, and there is no other.

A Persian document from this period, the Cyrus Cylinder, suggests that the King credited his victories to the power of Marduk, the chief god of the Babylonian pantheon. In Cyrus' view, Marduk had invited Cyrus to punish Babylonian impiety. But the Hebrew prophet affirms that the new world order under Cyrus is nothing but the hand of Israel's God at work on behalf of a penitent community.

Cyrus is not the only figure upon whom Isaiah focuses the lens of messianic interpretation. In other passages, which became important for early preaching regarding Jesus' Messiahship, the prophet speaks of a servant of God who "was wounded for our transgressions, crushed for our iniquities; upon him was the punishment that made us whole, and by his bruises we are healed" (Is. 53:5).

Elsewhere in Isaiah's discussion of this servant, however, the redemptive sufferer seems to be Israel. Its suffering is borne in service of God's cosmic plan (Is. 49:1–7):

The Lord called me before I was born, while I was in my mother's womb he named me. . . . And he said to me, "You are my servant, Israel, in whom I will be glorified.". . . He says, "It is too light a thing that you should be my servant to raise up the tribes of Jacob and to restore the survivors of Israel; I will give you as light to the nations, that my salvation may reach to the end of the earth." Thus says the LORD, the Redeemer of Israel and his Holy One, to one deeply despised, abhorred by the nations, the slave of rulers, "Kings shall see and stand up, princes, and they shall prostrate themselves, because of the LORD, who is faithful, the Holy One of Israel, who has chosen you."

The identity of this divine servant is given as Israel, but the servant is also to "raise up the tribes of Jacob." Is Israel, then, its *own* redeemer? The prophet's text is never explicit.

In other post-exilic collections of visions, Israel's redeemer is never imagined as anyone but the God of Israel. An excellent example is the prophet whose visions are collected in chapters 9–14 of the book of

Zechariah, who lived in the Jerusalem community of Persian Yehud. For him, Exile was a fact of life even in the homeland. But he looked forward to an auspicious end to Exile at the conclusion of a cataclysmic world war in which the God of Israel would emerge as the visible ruler of the earth.

The following passages, probably from the late sixth century BCE, echo for centuries in later Jewish and Christian thinking about the end of history (Zech. 14:1 ff.):

> See, a day is coming for the LORD, when the plunder taken from you will be divided in your midst. For I will gather all the nations against Jerusalem to battle, and the city shall be taken and the houses looted and the women raped; half the city shall go into exile, but the rest of the people shall not be cut off from the city. Then the LORD will go forth and fight against those nations as when he fights on a day of battle. On that day his feet shall stand on the Mount of Olives, which lies before Jerusalem on the east; and the Mount of Olives shall be split in two from east to west by a very wide valley. . . . Then the LORD my God will come, and all the holy ones with him. On that day there shall not be neither cold or frost. And there shall be continuous day. . . . On that day living waters shall flow out from Jerusalem, half of them to the eastern sea and half of them to the western sea; it shall continue in summer as in winter. And the LORD will become king over all the earth; on that day the LORD will be one and his name one. . . . Then all who survive of the nations that have come against Jerusalem shall go up year after year to worship the King, the LORD of hosts, and to keep the festival of Sukkot. . . .

The end of Israel's Exile is, for this visionary, the end of all history as it has been known since the expulsion from the Garden. "Living waters" will spring up as in Eden, and Jerusalem's Temple will serve as the new Garden of humanity, where the God of Israel alone will be acknowledged by the entire world as its King.

A Diaspora Vision of Redemption

In addition to visions such as these, transmitted in the canonical works of prophecy, both Greek-speaking and Aramaic-speaking Jews were familiar with other works that described visions of the future communicated by God or angels to ancient seers. Greek culture, for example, had for some centuries preserved oracles concerning the future in the names of prophetesses known collectively as Sibyls. These oracles were communicated in Greek poetic forms and were represented as messages from various gods. Jews throughout the Greek-speaking world, and especially in Egypt, preserved their own collections of Sibylline Oracles, which used Greek poetic conventions to deliver messages of distinctly Judaic import.

Especially during the era of Roman domination in the first century CE, many such oracles expressed violent hatred of Roman rule and the conviction of imminent liberation at the hands of a divinely sent redeemer. The following example, from first-century CE Egypt, is framed in the past tense, by way of anticipating the coming redemption (Syb. Or. 5:414–430):[12]

> For a blessed man came from the expanses of heaven with a scepter in his hands which God gave him, and he gained sway over all things well, and gave back the wealth to all the good, which previous men had taken. He destroyed every city from its foundations with much fire and burned nations of mortals who were formerly evildoers. And the city which God desired, this he made more brilliant than stars and sun and moon, and he provided ornaments and made a holy Temple, exceedingly beautiful in its fair shrine, and he fashioned a great and immense tower over many stadia touching even the clouds and visible to all, so that all faithful and all righteous people could see the glory of eternal God, a form desired. For terrible things no longer happen to wretched mortals, no adulteries or illicit love of boys, no murder, or din of battle, but competition is fair among all. It is the last time of the holy people when God, who thunders on high, founder of the greatest Temple, accomplishes these things.

The "blessed man" of this passage has no messianic name, but he is clearly more than a human king, arriving as he does "from the expanses of heaven with a scepter in his hand." His victory is more than a political one, for it changes the nature of time, inaugurating an era in which "terrible things no longer happen to wretched mortals." He reigns over a transformed human community as God's deputy.

Redemption in the Palestinian Apocalypses

The Diaspora proved hospitable to the visions of Jewish Sybils, but the real home of speculation about the end of history in early Judaism was the Land of Israel. Many surviving Hebrew and Aramaic texts, written from the late-third-century BCE until the close of the first century CE, used the rhetoric of scriptural prophecy to articulate ever more concretely imagined scenarios about a coming resolution to the catastrophe of Exile. These texts were invariably presented as the record of revelations to ancient visionaries. Contemporary scholars often classify them collectively as "apocalyptic" literature, from the Greek word for "revelation."[13]

Such apocalypses were normally mediated by angelic interpreters (not unlike the book of Jubilees, see pages 74–78). Sometimes, as in chapters 7–12 of the scriptural book of Daniel (written at the outbreak of the Maccabean wars), the narrator describes a perplexing vision on his bed, which an angel comes to explain. At other times these visions take the form of heavenly journeys guided by the interpreting angels.

The content of many such visions is a dramatic, highly imagistic portrayal of the end of time. Events of this cataclysm include the redemption of Israel from Exile, the punishment of those Jews and non-Jews deemed to have impeded God's plans for redemption, and the restoration to God of sovereignty over the world. In more than a few such writings, God's coming kingdom is presided over by a superhuman Messiah, often of Davidic origins. In others, the Messiah is just as likely to stem from a non-Davidic Israelite hero, for example, a descendant of a royal figure such as Joseph or of the priestly clan Levi.

The heavenly journey of the visionary is so common in these writings that we should consider one example.[14] The following vision is preserved in a second-century BCE work called the Book of the Watchers, which is now the first part of a larger collection called I Enoch. The narrator, Enoch, is a figure from pre-Flood times who appears briefly in Genesis 5:25 as one who "walked with God."

Now we learn where he went. Dreaming on his bed one night, Enoch sees the heavens open up. Suddenly (I En. 14:8–25):[15]

> I saw the clouds: And they were calling me in a vision; and the fogs were calling me; and the course of the stars and the lightnings were rushing me and causing me to desire; and in the vision, the winds were causing me to fly and rushing me high up into heaven. And I kept coming into heaven until I approached a wall which was built of white marble and surrounded by tongues of fire; and it began to frighten me. And I came into the tongues of fire and drew near to a great house which was built of white marble, and the inner walls were like mosaics of white marble, the floor of crystal, the ceiling like the path of the stars and lightnings between which stood fiery cherubim and their heaven of water, and flaming fire surrounded the walls, and its gates were burning with fire. And I entered into the house, which was hot like fire and cold like ice, and there was nothing inside it; so fear covered me and trembling seized me. And as I shook and trembled, I fell upon my face and saw a vision. . . . And I observed and saw inside a lofty throne—its appearance was like crystal and its wheels like the shining sun; and I heard the voice of cherubim; and from beneath the throne were issuing streams of fire. . . . And the Great Glory was sitting upon it—as for his gown, which was shining more brightly than the sun, it was whiter than snow. None of the angels was able to come in and see the face of the Excellent and the Glorious One; and no one of the flesh can see him—the flaming fire was round about him, and a great fire stood before him. No one could come near unto him from among those that surrounded the tens of millions that stood before him. . . . Until then I was

prostrate with my face covered and trembling. And the LORD called me with his own mouth and said to me, "Come near to me, Enoch, and to my holy Word." . . .

At the top of the cosmos, in the highest level of the universe, is the Palace of God, surrounded by angels and bathed in a brilliant light emanating from the Throne Room. Upon the Throne sits God himself, too brilliant to gaze upon, but speaking, nonetheless, in human language to his loyal subject Enoch. What he explains, in the discourse that follows this vision, is the origin of human sin that befouls the earth and causes the sufferings of history. It all began when the angelic Giants of Genesis 6 descended to frolic with the daughters of men.

The Connection of Past, Present, and Future

We have seen enough of early Judaism's conceptions of the historical process to ask an obvious question: what distinguished visions such as Enoch's from the larger conceptions of reality of Hebrew and Greek wisdom tradition? It was, in part, an insistence upon the relation of past and future. The past was no longer a static picture of various patterns of human virtue or vice. Rather, figures such as Adam and Eve, or the Giants, did things in the past that still shaped the present. For this reason, figures from the past could be represented as sources of urgent messages about the present and the immediate future.

Past and present, that is, were bound together in a unified movement toward a future that was about to culminate in the cataclysmic end of time itself. Ancient heroes were held to be important transmitters of these visions because they lived when God still spoke directly to his prophets rather than through the written records transcribed in books. In the near future, however, it was often hoped that God would once again speak directly to his community still living in the End of Days. For the time being, the study of the heroes' preserved words was important because they contained the information needed to know the timing of the cataclysm and how to prepare for it.

Timetables became important. On pages 74–78, we discussed how the book of Jubilees developed a complex scheme of ancient chronology. Now the future as well was placed on schedule. When, in particular, would redemption come? Often the compilers of visionary writings described signs—wars, the reversal of natural processes, starvation, and the like—that would portend the coming time.

Many of these, revealed in response to the direct questions of Ezra the scribe, are listed in a first-century CE work called IV Ezra: "Infants a year old shall speak with their voices, and women with child shall give birth to premature children at three or four months, and these shall live and dance. Sown places shall suddenly appear unsown, and full storehouses shall suddenly be found to be empty; and the trumpet shall sound aloud, and when all hear it, they shall suddenly be terrified. At that time friends shall make war on friends like enemies, and the earth and those who inhabit it shall be terrified . . ." (IV Ezra 6:21–24).[16]

But more important than the timing itself was knowledge about the details of the redemptive events. God's detailed response to Ezra's questions on this matter bears repeating (IV Ezra 7:26 ff.)

> For behold, the time will come, when the signs which I have foretold to you will come to pass; the city which now is not seen shall appear, and the land which now is hidden shall be disclosed. And everyone who has been delivered from the evils that I have foretold shall see my wonders. For my son the Messiah shall be revealed with those who are with him, and those who remain shall rejoice four hundred years. And after these years my son the Messiah shall die, and all who draw human breath. And the world shall be turned back to primeval silence for seven days, as it was at the first beginnings; so that no one shall be left. And after seven days, the world, which is not yet awake, shall be roused, and that which is corruptible shall perish. And the earth shall give up those who are asleep in it; and the chambers shall give up the souls which have been committed to them. And the Most High shall be revealed upon the seat of judgment, and compassion shall pass away, and patience shall be withdrawn; but judgment alone shall remain, truth shall stand, and faithfulness shall grow strong. . . . Then the pit of torment shall appear, and opposite it shall be the place of rest; and the furnace of Gehenna shall be disclosed, and opposite it the Paradise of delight. Then the Most High will say to the nations that have been raised from the dead, "Look now, and understand whom you have denied, whom you have not served, whose commandments you have despised!" . . . thus he will speak to them on the day of judgment—a day that has no sun or moon or stars, or cloud or thunder or lightning or wind or water or air, or darkness or evening or morning, or summer or spring or heat or winter or frost or cold or hail or rain or dew, or noon or night, or dawn or shining or brightness or light, but only the splendor of the glory of the Most High, by which all shall see what has been determined for them. For it will last for about a week of years. This is my judgment and its prescribed order; and to you alone have I shown these things.

Note that in Ezra's conception, the Messiah is a curiously amorphous figure. On the one hand, as God's "son," he is a kind of angel. But, unlike an angel, he is to die; like Moses, he is not to preside over the final redemption. His kingdom of four hundred years is the first stage of a final dissolution of all reality, a return to the state of pre-creation. The important moments follow only thereafter: the resurrection and the judgment of the dead, and the inauguration of a new world order under the direct rule of God, the Most High. Only then is the world at rest, a rest reproducing the peace of the Garden, prior to the hopeless rebellion that inaugurated human history.

The Vertical and Horizontal Axes in Tension

You have seen enough of the visionary literature of our period to grasp its essential thrust. The space of the cosmos was vast and imposing. But everything in it found its place between the Heaven of God and the earth upon which Israel served God. Even what was beneath the earth had its meaning in terms of what God and Israel did above. Thus far, the vertical emphases of the wisdom traditions and the horizontal emphases of the visionary traditions share much. At issue was the conception of time in these worlds.

When the spatial axis represented in the symbols of God-Torah-Israel dominated, Judaic imagination focused upon the place of the soul in the cosmic order and the means by which knowledge of Torah ensured restoration to God's domain at life's end. The past showed Israel how to live for immortality; its future was confined to the future of the soul after the body's death.

When, by contrast, Exile and Messiah governed the symbolic imagination of Jews, all time was colored by the fundamental fact of human alienation from God represented by the rebellious assertion of human self-determination. The destiny of the individual soul was bound with the collective destiny of Israel in history. Humanity was in Exile from God, a fact that resulted in the story of suffering and death that is human history. Israel was likewise in Exile.

All of time gained meaning, therefore, both in terms of its origins and in terms of where it was headed. Originating in creation and the Garden, it was headed toward a final goal that would reproduce its origins in a new form. Torah, in this vision of reality, was a source of guidance from the past that helped individuals and the entire community to prepare itself for the coming future reconstruction of the world.

For many, time was moving toward the moment when Israel and humanity would be reconciled to each other and God in an all-embracing kingdom. In other scenarios, only righteous Israelites alone would survive to enjoy the new Eden. But in either case, history, the great disrupter of stability and atemporal order, would be overcome in a new and final reorientation of all reality. In some views, that new reorientation would restore to the world direct rule by God. In others, his Messiah, Davidic or otherwise, served as the regent of God's dominion. But on any terms, it was a world that could not come without a radical transformation of space as well. A fundamentally new heaven and earth would witness the perfection of time.

Messianic Movements in Early Judaism

The vivid messianic longings expressed in apocalyptic writings seem to have been paralleled in a number of anti-Roman social movements in Palestine during the first and second centuries CE. These messianic movements, which attracted primarily a peasant following, all centered on a leader claiming the right to rule Israel as King. Accordingly, the movements were actively suppressed by Roman authorities. The Messiahs either died fighting or were executed as political criminals.

Judas b. Ezekias, 6 CE

Simon, 6

Athronges, 6

Jesus of Nazareth, 30–32

Menachem b. Judas, 66

Simon b. Giora, ca. 68–70

Shimon b. Kosiba, 132–135

With the exception of the movements surrounding Jesus of Nazareth and Shimon bar Kosiba, we know about most of them only from sketchy portraits in the writings of the first-century Jewish historian Josephus, who found them distinctly distasteful. Among the Messiahs, only Jesus seems to have attracted the claim to descend from the House of David. His is, as well, the only movement to have survived and thrived after the Messiah's death.

Source: Richard A. Horsely with John S. Hanson, *Bandits, Prophets, and Messiahs: Popular Movements at the Time of Jesus* (San Francisco: Harper & Row, 1985), pp. 88–134.

Horizontal and Vertical in the Rabbinic World

Predictions of the world's imminent transformation, of course, proved to be premature. In the history of early Judaic worlds, even the devastating historical wars of 66–73, 115–117, and 132–135 proved more a disruption than an absolute end. Surely, the Judaic world that emerged after the second century was increasingly modeled by rabbinic architects and builders. But they salvaged bricks liberally from the structures of imagination that preceded them and built their world on the old symbolic foundation: the spatial order of reality imagined through the symbolic axis of God-Torah-Israel and the future-oriented world of history captured in the axis of Exile-Messiah. By 650 CE, they had built a world that, with various expansions, renovations, and rewirings, would serve as home for a millennium.

The Cosmic Torah of the Master of the Universe

That world, especially in its rich reflection upon the vertical axes of God-Torah-Israel, preserved much of the scribal and philosophical temperament of earlier Judaic worlds. Among the Sages, as among earlier Jewish scribes and philosophers, Torah and wisdom were equivalent terms, transcendant cosmic realities that linked God to Israel in timeless relationship. This perception is fundamental to the earliest homiletic collections of rabbinic literature, such as tractate Avot, and receives elaboration in the midrashic and talmudic compilations of the fourth to sixth centuries.[17]

In the first century CE, Philo had compared God's creation of the world to the work of an architect (On Creation: 4). Now we find a similar image with a striking change: Torah is portrayed as the blueprint for reality. The idea appears in Genesis Rabbah, a fourth- to fifth-century Palestinian aggadic midrash on the book of Genesis. The rabbinic comment is inspired by Proverbs 8:30–31, which portrays wisdom as a child frolicking before God prior to creation (Gen. Rab. 1:1):

> The word "child" (*amon*) sounds like the word for "craftsman" (*oman*). The Torah says: "I was the Blessed Holy One's crafting tool." In everyday experience, when a human king builds a palace he doesn't build it out of his own imagination. Rather, he hires a craftsman. And the craftsman doesn't build it out of his own imagination either. Rather, he has designs and diagrams to help him plan the rooms and doorways. So, too, the Blessed Holy One looked into the Torah and created the world.

Indeed, the passage goes on to recommend a remarkable interpretation of the first sentence of the Torah of Moses. The plain meaning is: "In the beginning God created the heavens and earth" (Gen. 1:1). Underlying this rendering, however, midrash finds a deeper significance: "Through the Torah, God created the heavens and earth."

If anything, the rabbinic conception of Torah as a cosmic principle was perhaps more comprehensive than earlier conceptions, for it colored the concrete meaning of all terms with which it was connected. As we saw in the last chapter (see pages 82–85, Sages viewed Torah as, first of all, a written text. This Written Torah provided authoritative instruction in the history of Israel and in God's will for Israel. But Torah was also, as it proceeded from the mouth of the Sage into the ears of the disciple, a medium by which God spoke through a specific human relationship. The knowledge the Sage transmitted through his behavior and teaching was Oral Torah, a model of a life perfected in communication with God. Thus, in intellectual and moral training, Torah served as both a world-structuring principle and as a means of perfecting human being.

The disciple's task in this life, accordingly, was to labor in the study of Torah at the feet of rabbinic Sages, to perform deeds of Torah. Mishnah Avot 2:8 transmits the following advice in the name of Rabban Yohanan ben Za-kkai: "If you have learned much Torah, don't think so highly of yourself— what were you created for?" To study Torah, then, was to fulfill the purpose of one's creation.

In this sense, the reward of a life lived in Torah was, to a degree, a worldly one. It drew one close to the Sage and, through him, to the God of Israel on a daily basis. But, apprenticeship to a Sage in earthly life was merely preparation for eternal discipleship as a student of Torah before God. This is part of what Sages termed the life of the World to Come, an inheritance of the soul beyond death where it returns to Heaven with the souls of the righteous. Included, of course, are those of departed Sages. Thus, in aggadic homilies of the later midrashic and talmudic compilations, the soul can be imagined as studying Torah in Heaven with God and Moses.

As in pre-rabbinic traditions of Judaic wisdom, God remained for sages a cosmic King. He is routinely referred to in rabbinic writings as *ribbono shel ha'olam* (Master of the Universe). Rabbinic parables are particularly rich in imagining him in his royal role. The divine King who looks into the blueprint of the Torah is just one of numerous examples.[18]

But earlier wisdom traditions produced no image of God as heavenly Scribe or Philosopher. Their reticence stands in sharp contrast with the rabbinic willingness to portray God—for the purposes of aggadic rhetoric, at least—as an assiduous Master of Torah, as a dutiful copier of the Torah's text, or as the headmaster of the Heavenly Torah Academy (*yeshivah shel ma'alah*) who intervenes in the halakhic debates of earthly Sages (and can be over-ruled by them if he holds a minority opinion!). Rabbinic descriptions of the meaning of Torah and the cosmic lordship of God, then, draw freely from earlier Judaic wisdom traditions. But everything borrowed is transmuted in terms of the Sages' particular concerns and perceptions.

The People and the Land of Israel in the Cosmic Order

This pattern of borrowing and transmutation continues as other details of earlier Judaic worlds are also incorporated into the rabbinic cosmology. The rabbinic cosmos is the same seven-tiered structure known to earlier Judaic worlds, replete with its entire complement of angels and demons. What makes this a rabbinic cosmos is the way the symbol of Torah organizes the relations of the vast cosmic spaces. Rabbinic Sages and their special disciples used what they called "the secrets of Torah" to facilitate the heavenly journeys that earlier Jews might have attempted through philosophical contemplation or prophetic vision (see Chapter Six). As Masters of Torah, moreover, Sages knew how to use its secrets to avert the harmful effects of demonic activities.[19]

The Babylonian Talmud is particularly rich in depicting the demonic surroundings of everyday life. Demons (*shedim*) congregated in isolated places, ruins and outhouses. They inhabited the moon shadows of stone walls and the stumps of palm trees. They might even surround one's bed at night. But Sages could offer diagnoses of and protection from demonic activites, as the following suggests (BT Ber. 6a):

> Said Rava: ". . . One who wishes to know where demons are takes ashes and sprinkles them around the bed. In the morning he will see something like a rooster's footprints. One who wishes to see them must take the afterbirth of a black cat, and its offspring—the firstborn of the firstborn. Roast it in fire and grind it to powder. When he puts the ashes in his eye, he'll see them. . . ." Rav Bibi bar Abbaye did this and saw them. But he was stricken. Rabbis prayed for mercy for him and he was healed.

The Sages' prayers, a function of their Torah mastery, enabled them to avert the consequences when a colleague had mismanaged his powers. All the more so did their Torah empower them to manage other relations at all levels of the cosmos—the human, the angelic, and the divine.

Like all worlds built upon the symbolic triad of God-Torah-Israel, that of the Sages accorded special cosmic significance to the People Israel as well. Among this people, after all, the eternal Torah had come to rest in the world of time. Israel embodied within the world God's original plan for the entire human order—to incorporate all of life under the canopy of the divine will as expressed in Torah. Where the Israel of the Sages differed most from that of earlier wisdom traditions, however, is in the second aspect of the term's meaning—the Land of Israel itself.

Philo's lack of interest in the geographical space of the Jewish homeland is entirely foreign to the Sages. Rather, much more in the manner of Palestinian wisdom traditions, the Land of Israel is for Sages a special preoccupation. But its symbolic importance exceeds anything we know from the wisdom traditions of Palestine. For Joshua ben Sira, we have seen, the Land was important because of the Temple that stood upon it. Rabbinic Sages, however, lived in a world without a Temple. Nevertheless, in their view, the Land retained a holiness in its soil, which distinguished it from any other spot on earth.

The Mishnah expresses this viewpoint in a complex body of rules governing the tithing of food. As we saw in Chapter Two (pages 80–81), these attracted the attention of the Gospels' authors. Farmers were to offer tithes to priests, Levites, and the poor. From the Mishnah's perspective, however, these rules had more than a charitable function. They offered a procedure for respecting the holiness present in the land of Israel by treating its produce as a sanctified object. For this reason, priestly and levitical tithes needed to be separated even though, with the Temple gone, priests and Levites could no longer eat the offerings.

Sages expressed their views about the uniqueness of the Land of Israel in other ways as well. They regarded all foreign lands—the lands of "the Worshippers of Stars and Constellations"—as intrinsically "unclean," polluting the bodies of those Jews who lived in them. In contrast, the Land of Israel needed to be preserved from uncleanness so as to respect its intrinsic holiness.

A large part of the Mishnah's earliest ritual and legal traditions, therefore, is concerned to maintain the ritual purity of the Jewish body and the Jewish household in the Land of Israel. Scriptural sources, naturally, are combed for guidance in maintaining such purity. Sages ignored, however, the fact that the Torah of Moses imposes the need for purification only upon one entering the Sanctuary. For Sages, at least in legal theory, such purity was incumbent upon all Jews in the Land of Israel who wished to eat a simple meal at the level of holiness appropriate to a disciple of the Sages.[20]

It is as if, with the destruction of the physical Temple, the Land and the People of Israel had themselves absorbed the invisible essence that constituted its holiness. Laws that once protected the holiness and purity of the Temple and its personnel were now applied to the territory and the people that the Temple had sanctified. So, in this aspect of the vertical triad as well—the role of the Land and the People of Israel in the spatial structure of reality, the rabbinic world must be distinguished from the scribal and philosophical traditions upon which it drew. Constructed well after the Temple had passed into the images of legend, the rabbinic world embodied the Temple's sanctity in the surviving realities of the Land and the People of Israel.

Torah and Messiah in the Redemption of Israel

The rabbinic world embodied in the Mishnah was the first Judaic world of antiquity for which the Temple was never a physical presence or even a recent memory. It was the one Judaic world, therefore, in which the implications of Exile, in both geographic and cosmological dimensions, were most fully explored. And, as we have seen, once the symbol of Exile began to resonate, the early Judaic imagination was almost reflexively drawn to construct scenarios for its end.

Thus, as rabbinic teaching reached increasing definition from the third through the seventh centuries, Sages' understanding of the spatial order of reality—structured by the symbols of God-Torah-Israel—became ever more hospitable to a future-oriented perspective. Sages living in Palestine and Babylonia were equally displaced in space. The corrective had to be found in time, in a future in which Israel would be restored to the entirety of its Land, the Temple to its ancient mountain, and the world to its proper course. The question of Messiah had to be squarely addressed.

In their conceptions of Israel's ultimate redemption from Exile, Sages drew upon images and ideas from the entire scriptural and apocalyptic traditions at their disposal.[21] But they filtered these images and ideas through their own overriding commitment to the central, and richly complex, symbol of Torah.

A sample from a Babylonian collection of traditions about Messianic times gives some idea of the range of speculation on this matter and evokes our earlier discussions of the books of Zechariah, Jubilees, IV Ezra, and I Enoch in particular (BT San. 97a-b):

> Said Rav Katina: The world will exist for 6000 years and be destroyed for 1000, as it is said in Scripture: "And the LORD alone shall be raised up on that day" (Is. 2:11). Abbaye said: It will be desolate for two thousand years, as it is said: "After two days he will restore us, on the third day he will raise us and we shall live before him" (Hos. 6:2).
>
> Traditional teaching supports the view of Rav Katina as follows: Just as the law of the Sabbatical Year requires that fields lie fallow one of every seven years, so too the world will lie fallow for 1000 years of 7000, as it is said: "And the LORD alone shall be raised up on that day" . . . and it says: "A thousand years in your eyes are like a day that has passed" (Ps. 90:4).
>
> A tradition reciter from the school of Elijah reports: The world will last for 6000 years. Chaos will reign for 2000. Torah will reign for 2000. The Days of Messiah will last for 2000. But because of our numerous sins, those years have been taken away.
>
> Said Elijah the Prophet to Rav Judah, the brother of Rav Sala the Pious: The world will last at least eighty five Jubilees. And in the last Jubilee the Son of David will come. Rav Judah replied: In the first part or the latter part? Elijah said: I don't know. Rav Judah asked: Will the entire time pass before he comes or not? Elijah replied: I don't know. Rav Ashi commented: This is what he meant—until then, don't expect him; from then on, expect him.

These are familiar themes from earlier apocalyptic tradition. But the passage also illustrates why the rabbinic world must be distinguished from the apocalyptic world.

Principally, the compilers of the apocalypses had imagined the timing of the End as a hidden divine mystery, already foreordained. The secret could be disclosed only to ancient visionaries in highly coded riddles. Rabbinic Sages differ from this view. First, we note their scepticism regarding attempts to discover a foreordained moment of Messianic deliverance. Elijah the Prophet is uncertain, and some rabbinic authorities are even more emphatic: "Said Rabbi Jonathan: Let their bones explode, those calculators of the End! For people might say: 'Since he has not come, perhaps he isn't coming?' " (BT San. 97b).

But more important, Sages incorporated Torah into the Messianic design. Between the return to chaos and the ultimate reign of Messiah, the world is prepared by a reign of pure Torah, as we saw earlier. Moreover, their conception of Torah made it possible for Sages to argue that Messiah could come at any moment. As they imagined it, the conditions for his coming were intimately tied to Israel's own behavior. The same section from Sanhedrin contains the following story in which Elijah is again the hero:

> Rabbi Joshua ben Levi found Elijah standing at the entrance of the tomb of Rabbi Shimon ben Yohai. . . . He said to him: When is Messiah coming? Elijah replied: Go ask him yourself! He asked: Where does he live? Elijah replied: At the gate of the city. He asked: What are his distinguishing features? Elijah replied: He is sitting among the diseased poor. All of them untie and tie their bandages together, but he unties them one by one, thinking—"Should I be summoned, I don't want to delay."
>
> Rabbi Joshua ben Levi went to Messiah and said: Peace to you, my Master and Teacher! Messiah replied: Peace to you, ben Levi! . . . He asked: When is Master coming? Messiah replied: Today! Rabbi Joshua ben Levi returned to Elijah, who said: What did he say to you? Rabbi Joshua ben Levi replied: . . . He lied to me, for he said: "I am coming today"—but he did not come! Elijah replied: He was refering to this verse—"Today, if you will obey his voice" (Ps. 95:7).

This story assumes an intimate connection between the coming of Messiah and the condition of Torah among Israel. True, Torah was a cosmic principle with its mysteries. But it was expressed in a form that humans could comprehend without prophetic powers—the Written and Oral of the Sages. Messiah would come when Israel perfected its knowlege of and loyalty to Torah. Not prophets, but Israel led by Sages could bring Messiah.

And who would Messiah be? The Talmud uses the title "Son of David," which expresses the dominant rabbinic view that Messiah would be a descendant of the ancient royal house of Israel. But Sages were reticent to focus upon any living figure as Messiah. Early Jewish followers of Jesus of Nazareth, of course, had seen in him the fulfillment of messianic promises. But he had died a criminal's death and left the world in Exile entirely as it had been, tales of his resurrection notwithstanding.

The second-century hero of Israel's war against Rome, Shimon bar Kosiba, seems to have won the approval of some Sages as Messiah. Yet his failure made him, and those who supported his messianic candidacy, the butt of rabbinic jokes: "When Rabbi Akiva saw Bar Kosiba he said: This is King Messiah! Rabbi Yohanan ben Torta said to him: Akiva, grass will grow through your cheekbones and the Son of David will still not have come!" (PT Taan. 68d).

In rabbinic opinion, Messiah would surely be a warrior, defeating oppressive nations in battle, as many apocalyptic visions had imagined. And, of course, he would also be a King, ruling over the Kingdom established by God, as God himself had promised to prophets like Ezekiel. But of crucial importance was that he be a Sage, a Master and Teacher of Torah. These assumptions, perhaps, explain the rabbinic tendency to focus messianic attention upon the figure of David. Of all the figures known to scriptural tradition, or who enjoyed messianic status in the apocalyptic traditions, David most plausibly combined in a single figure all the criteria of Messiahship. As warrior, he had created the largest Israelite empire in history. And everyone knew he had been God's most beloved and loyal King. But most crucially, the reputed author of the book of Psalms could be imagined as both prophet and Sage, a Master of Torah. A story about David's miraculous alarm clock makes the point: "Rav Shimon the Pious said: David had a harp hanging over his bed. When midnight came, the north wind would blow on the strings, and the harp would play by itself. David would immediately arise and engage in Torah study till dawn" (BT Ber. 3b).

So the Son of David, descendant of a king who had studied Torah from midnight to daybreak, would come to redeem Israel from Exile. He would rebuild the "Fallen Tabernacle of David" (Am. 9:11), just as the last survivors of the Babylonian Exile had done. And it was he who would preside over the events promised by generations of apocalyptic visionaries—the resurrection of the dead to judgment and God's transformation of the universe back to its original harmony. But the day of his arrival depended entirely upon Israel. As we have seen, he could come even today—but only if Israel listened to God's voice as heard in the Torah of the Sage.

In this sense, the rabbinic world achieved a balance between its vertical and horizontal axes that seems to have been rare in other worlds of early Judaism. Within it, reflection upon the vertical axis of cosmic space drew one's attention inevitably to the horizontal axis of unredeemed time. Meticulous absorption in charting and embodying the fullness of Torah served to heighten anticipation of that time when, under the shadow of the restored Temple, all the world would stream to Rebuilt Jerusalem to bask in the fullness of the Divine Presence. Messiah would redeem the Exiles and hasten the day when God, Torah, and Israel would be One.

Conclusions

This chapter has brought you through a complex body of ideas and images. But the point has been a simple one. We have tried to show how Judaic worlds of antiquity imagined the structure of reality, how people came to arrange their knowledge of the world. We have seen that such knowledge was structured by five fundamental symbols arranged along vertical and horizontal axes. Along the vertical axis the symbolic triad of God-Torah-

Israel served as the structuring elements by which Jews arranged whatever they held to be true about the created order and the ancient past. Along the horizontal axis of Exile-Messiah, they plotted the meaning of the past, the possibilities of the present, and the promise of the future.

In order to illustrate this, we focused upon three model worlds. The first, represented by the wisdom traditions of ancient Judaism, portrayed a world deeply committed to the symbols of the vertical axis, one that ignored or at least underplayed the symbolic meaning of Exile and Messiah. The second, represented by various prophetic and visionary writings within and beyond the scriptural canon, stressed the horizontal axis. It retained the cosmological structure known to wisdom traditions. But it used that structure as a backdrop to its own distinctive drama—the coming transformation of the world under messianic circumstances. Finally, we reviewed the rabbinic world structure, which for centuries embodied a rather precarious, but normally successful attempt to balance and integrate both symbolic axes. It inherited much from preceding Judaic worlds but altered everthing in light of its own distinctive emphasis upon the crucial symbol of Torah.

Notes

1. The concepts of "symbol" and "symbolic vocabulary" used in this chapter are close to the more detailed discussion of Robert S. Ellwood, *Introducing Religion: From Inside and Outside*, 3rd ed. (Englewood Cliffs, NJ: Prentice Hall, 1993), pp. 65–89.

2. James Kugel and Rowan A. Greer, *Early Biblical Interpretation* (Philadelphia: The Westminster Press), pp. 40–51, have a thoughtful discussion of how Jews apprehended their past during the Persian and Hellenistic periods. See also John J. Collins, *Between Athens and Jerusalem* (New York: Crossroad, 1983), pp. 25–59. During the centuries in which Jews were learning to see the past as a source of fables and lessons, the Greeks were doing so as well. See the marvelous work of Paul Veyne, *Did the Greeks Believe in Their Myths?*, tr., Paula Wissing (Chicago: The University of Chicago Press, 1988).

3. For an orientation to the Israelite tradition of wisdom, you may consult James L. Crenshaw, *Old Testament Wisdom: An Introduction* (Atlanta: John Knox Press, 1981). There is also a technical, but fascinating collection of essays by John G. Gammie and Leo G. Purdue, eds., *The Sage in Israel and the Ancient Near East* (Winona Lake, WI: Eisenbrauns, 1990). If you read through the latter volume's various essays on Israelite wisdom from pre-exilic through Hellenistic times, you will see how much my own discussion oversimplifies the actual complexity of the wisdom tradition.

4. See Collins, *Between Athens and Jerusalem*, pp. 137–194, for a fine overview of the Judaic forms of the Hellenistic philosophical tradition. A good introduction to Philo of Alexandria as a Judaic thinker in particular is that of Samuel Sandmel, *Philo of Alexandria: An Introduction* (New York and Oxford: Oxford University Press, 1979).

5. Elias J. Bickerman, one of the great modern students of Greek-speaking Judaism, offers a useful chapter on the translation techniques of the Septuagint in his *The Jews in the Greek Age* (Cambridge, MA, and London: Harvard University Press, 1988), pp. 101–116.

6. For the migrations of "do unto others" in particular, see Raymond F. Collins, "The Golden Rule," *The Anchor Bible Dictionary, Vol. II* (New York: Doubleday, 1992), pp. 1070–1071.

7. As you might imagine, discussion of ancient Judaic angelology is a rather esoteric academic discipline. A good place to go for an introduction is the multi-authored article "Angels and Angelology" in *The Encyclopaedia Judaica* (1972), 2, pp. 956–978.

8. See the Special Laws III:1 in F.H. Colson, tr., *Philo VII* (Cambridge, MA, and London: Harvard University Press and Heinemann, 1937), pp. 475–477, and On the Creation, 23, in F.H. Colson and G.H. Whitaker, tr., *Philo I* (Cambridge, MA, and London: Harvard University Press and Heinemann, 1929), pp. 55–57. Consult as well the excellent article by Peder Borgen, "Heavenly Ascent in Philo: An Examination of Selected Passages," in James H. Charlesworth and Craig A. Evans, eds., *The Pseudepigrapah and Early Biblical Interpretation* (Sheffield, England: Sheffield Academic Press, 1993), pp. 246–268.

9. Philo's disinterest in the Jewish political past in the land of Israel or its messianic future is discussed in Sandmel, *Philo,* pp. 102–110. For further discussion of Philo's views of the Temple and its priestly officiants, you may consult Jean Laporte, "The High Priest in Philo of Alexandria," in David T. Runia, David M. Hay, and David Winston, eds., *Studia Philonica Annual, 3: Heirs of the Septuagint: Philo, Hellenistic Judaism and Early Christianity. Festschrift for Earle Hilgert* (Atlanta: Scholars Press, 1991), pp. 71–82.

10. A good introduction to the setting of prophecy in Israelite society is by Robert R. Wilson, *Prophecy and Society in Ancient Israel* (Philadelphia: Fortress Press, 1980).

11. A common expectation among Jews of a messianic redeemer of Davidic descent did not emerge until the first century BCE. Excellent recent studies of the question are those of Kenneth E. Pomykala, *The Davidic Dynasty Tradition in Early Judaism: Its History and Significance for Messianism* (Atlanta: Scholars Press, 1995) and John J. Collins, *The Scepter and the Star: The Messiahs of the Dead Sea Scrolls and Other Ancient Literatures* (New York: Doubleday, 1995)..

12. I quote from the translation of John J. Collins, "The Sybilline Oracles," in James H. Charlesworth, *The Old Testament Pseudepigrapha, Vol. 1* (Garden City, NY: Doubleday & Company, 1983). See his introduction at that volume, pp. 317–324.

13. John J. Collin's introduction to this literature is the place to begin: *The Apocalyptic Imagination in Ancient Judaism* (New York: Crossroad, 1984).

14. An excellent profile of such journeys is that of Martha Himmelfarb, *Ascent to Heaven in Jewish & Christian Apocalypses* (New York and Oxford: Oxford University Press, 1993).

15. I quote the translation of Ephraim Isaac, in Charlesworth, *The Old Testament Pseudepigrapha* I, pp. 20–21.

16. This quote, and the one to follow, are from the translation of Bruce M. Metzger, in Charlesworth, *The Old Testament Pseudepigrapha I,* pp. 535, 537–538.

17. The most comprehensive survey of rabbinic ideas of Torah, which tracks as well the development of these ideas in different rabbinic texts, is that of Jacob Neusner, *Torah: From Scroll to Symbol in Formative Judaism* (Philadelphia: Fortress Press, 1985).

18. A fine study of rabbinic parables is that of David Stern, *Parables in Midrash: Narrative and Exegesis in Rabbinic Literature* (Cambridge, MA, and London: Harvard University Press, 1991).

19. Steven D. Fraade offers a helpful portrait of the early rabbinic sages until the third century in "The Early Rabbinic Sage," in Gammie and Perdue, *The Sage in Israel,* pp. 417–436. The most vivid portrait of the later Babylonian masters is that of Jacob Neusner, *There We Sat Down: Talmudic Judaism in the Making* (New York: KTAV, 1978), pp. 44–128.

20. The laws of tithing and uncleanness are highly complex. A good introduction to the tithing system is Alan J. Avery-Peck, *Mishnah's Division of Agriculture: A History and Theology of Seder Zeraim* (Chico, CA: Scholars Press, 1985), pp. 13–32. For the system of uncleanness, see Jacob Neusner, "History and Structure: The Case of the Mishnah's System of Purities," in Jacob Neusner, *Method and Meaning in Ancient Judaism* (Missoula, MT: Scholars Press, 1979), pp. 101–132.

21. A fine collection of essays on the various messianic traditions of ancient Judaism and their bearing upon rabbinic messianic ideas is found in Jacob Neusner, William S. Green, and Ernest Frerichs, eds., *Judaisms and Their Messiahs at the Turn of the Christian Era* (Cambridge: Cambridge University Press, 1987). For the development of rabbinic ideas between the second and the sixth centuries, see Jacob Neusner, *Messiah in Context: Israel's History and Destiny in Formative Judaism* (Philadelphia: Fortress Press, 1984).

Four

Social Foundations of Early Judaic Worlds

Introduction

Most Jews of the first Judaic millennium regarded themselves as part of an international people with whom they shared common historical and geographical origins. Although they hadn't shared a common language or territory since the destruction of Yehudah in 587 BCE, Jews recognized enough common traits to regard themselves as a distinct people within the larger, multi-ethnic environment of the Greco-Roman and Sasanian empires. Their self-perception coincided with the way their neighbors perceived them.[1]

A key element in this common perception was the understanding that Jews lived in accord with customs that distinguished them rather markedly from most other nations. It was, after all, the common customs of the descendants of Judean exiles that earned them the Greek name *ioudaioi* and their way of life the title *ioudaismos*, "Judaism." What, then, was this ioudaismos that caught the notice of Hellenistic observers from the fish markets of Alexandria to the hill country of Jerusalem and on to the rich farmlands of Mesopotamia?[2]

As we see in this chapter, it was not one, but many things. We begin our survey by sketching the broadest outlines of agreement among ancient Jews about what constituted the distinctive traits of the Jewish nation. That prepares us to identify and explore the areas and consequences of disagreement. We describe various kinds of communities created by Jews who desired to distinguish their way of Judaic life from those pursued by other Jews. Each community nurtured its own versions of the common Judaic symbolic vocabulary. Each cultivated distinctive types of religious leadership, enforced unique patterns of communal discipline, and defined varying kinds of social possibilities for men and women. Each was, at one and the same time, an example of Judaism and a unique social creation.

One consequence of the diversity of early Judaism is that the boundaries of different kinds of communities were not equally crossable. Some communities could be relatively closed to outsiders, others more open. An underlying theme of this chapter, accordingly, is precisely how diverse Judaic communities viewed Jewish and non-Jewish outsiders. We see that some of these outsiders became insiders, converts, either to Judaism as such or to a form of Judaism other than the one they were born into. Such converts routinely expressed their new self-understanding by taking up a new kind of Judaic life among other like-minded people. To convert was to enter a new social group with its own intensely experienced world.

Judaism as National Custom

Many striking impressions about early Judaism are preserved in the Greek and Latin writings of non-Jewish historians, ethnographers, philosophers, poets, and geographers of the Hellenistic world. Some of these authors observed Jews at first hand in their own cities or during travels to Judea, Syria, or points east. Other impressions were passed on as common knowledge—what "everyone" knew about the Jews. As with most amateur anthropology, much of this literature tells us more about the interests of the observers than about the lives of the observed. Some comments are flattering, presenting Jews as a barbarian ("stuttering," i.e., non-Greek-speaking) people whom even Greeks might do well to emulate; some are mean-spirited. Some observers regard the Jews as a race of philosophers; others, noting their tendency toward communal self-segregation, regard them as unsociable misanthropes, "haters of humanity." In any case, what drew the attention of most writers were exotic oddities.

Some Jewish Curiosities

The Roman historian Dio Cassius (160–230 CE) expressed himself in a way typical of many others, adopting a tone of detached, slightly amused condescension. In the course of describing the events leading to Rome's occupation of Jerusalem in 63 BCE, Dio offered his Greek readers the following observations of the Judean natives (Roman History, 37:16–17)[3]:

The country has been named Judea, and the people themselves Jews. I do not know how this title came to be given them, but it applies also to all the rest of mankind, although of alien race, who affect their customs. This class exists even among the Romans. . . . They are distinguished from the rest of mankind in practically every detail of life, and especially by the fact that they do not honour any of the usual gods, but show extreme reverence for one particular divinity. They never had any statue of him even in Jerusalem itself, but believing him to be unnameable and invisible, they worship him in the most extravagant fashion on earth. . . . They dedicate to him the day called the day of Saturn, on which, among many other most peculiar observances, they undertake no serious occupation.

Dio begins by pointing out that there are many, "of alien race," even Romans, who follow Jewish customs and are called Jews. We'll return to this point on pages 131–132. For now, we focus on what interests him: the Jews' exclusive worship of an invisible god and their odd reverence for Saturday, a day on which they do none of the normal work of the world.

The Jews were widely known as monotheists who, contrary to normal practice, tolerated no images of their divinity. Although many Hellenistic writers praised Judaic monotheism as a philosophically sound idea, the Jews' failure to respect the One God with a properly impressive figurative statue perplexed many. Had these anthropologists read the Septuagint's many injunctions against depicting the God of Israel in an image (e.g., Ex. 20), they might have remained perplexed; but they would at least have understood the source of the Jews' stubbornness on the matter.

Dio is correct as well in his notion that Jews refrained from working on the Sabbath (Hebrew: *shabbat*) as a way of dedicating themselves to the God of Israel (see Ex. 20:8–11). His reference to the "peculiar observances" associated with the Sabbath is vague. Pehaps it points toward patterns of communal worship or Torah study mentioned by first-century CE Jewish writers such as Philo and the Jewish historian Flavius Josephus.

Many Greek and Latin writers noticed an oddity in Jewish dietary habits. Plutarch (ca. 40–120 CE) composed an entertaining depiction of cultivated men engaging, in good Roman style, in thoughtful reflection at a meal. As the wine flows, conversation wanders to the arcane. Quite naturally, the topic of the Jews arises. Perhaps because of the culinary setting, attention turns to their well-known aversion to the meat of pigs and other delicacies treasured by civilized peoples.

It is asked: do they, perhaps, hate the pig or, to the contrary, hold the pig in some sort of reverence? (Dinner Conversations, 5:2–3)[4]:

"My impression," said Callistratus, "is that the beast enjoys a certain respect among that folk; . . . according to the story, it was the first to cut the soil with its projecting snout, thus producing a furrow and teaching man the function of a ploughshare. . . . So I think the Jews would kill pigs if they hated them, as the Magi (i.e., Persians) kill water mice; but in fact it is as unlawful for Jews to destroy pigs as to eat them. Perhaps it is consistent that they should revere the pig who taught them sowing and plowing, inasmuch as they honour the ass who first led them to a spring of water. Otherwise, so help me, someone will say that the Jews abstain from the hare because they can't stomach anything so filthy and unclean."

"No indeed," countered Lamprias, "they abstain from the hare because of its very close resemblance to the ass which they prize so highly. . . . The Jews apparently abominate pork because barbarians especially abhor skin diseases like lepra and white scale, and believe that human beings are ravaged by such maladies through contagion. . . ."

From here, the conversation passes on to other oddities about the Jews, including the possibility that their famous invisible deity is really Bacchus or Dionysis.

Plutarch's explanations of the Jews' dietary aversions are no more convincing than were many posed before and since. But he clearly knew something: pigs, hares, and asses are among the many animals of field, water, and air that are regarded in Lev. 11:1–46 and Dt. 14:3–21 as "unclean" and forbidden to Jews as food.

Jews as They Explained Themselves

Jews, of course, could always point to scripture (usually in Greek) to explain the origins of some of their most striking customs. But they were often unclear about how to defend those customs in terms that cultivated Hellenists might grasp. From the second century BCE until the first century CE, Jews writing in Greek expended much energy explaining the beneficial effects of such rules on Jewish moral and physical well-being.

A pioneer in this vein was the anonymous Egyptian Jewish writer of the Letter of Aristeas to Philocrates (ca. 150 BCE). The letter describes the circumstances that led to the translation of the Torah into Greek. But in the course of things, the author demonstrates the rational grounds of some Jewish customs that drew ridicule from Greek observers (Aristeas, 142–155)[5]:

To prevent our being perverted by contact with others or by mixing with bad influences, Moses hedged us in on all sides with strict observances connected with meat and drink and touch and hearing and sight, after the manner of the Law (*nomos*: Torah). . . . Do not take the contemptible view that Moses enacted this legislation because of an excessive preoccupation with mice and weasels or suchlike creatures. . . .

Everything pertaining to conduct permitted us toward these creatures and toward beasts has been set out symbolically. Thus the cloven hoof (e.g., Lev. 11:3), that is, the separation of the claws of the hoof, is a sign of setting apart each of our actions for good, because the strength of the whole body with its action rests upon the shoulders and the legs. The symbolism conveyed by these things compels us to make a distinction in the performance of our acts, with righteousness as our aim. . . .

The man with whom the aforesaid manner of disposition is concerned is the man on whom the legislator has also stamped that of memory. For example, all cloven-footed creatures and ruminants quite clearly express, to those who perceive it, the phenomenon of memory. Rumination is nothing but the recalling of the creature's life and constitution, life being usually constituted by nourishment. So we are exhorted through scripture also by the one who says thus: "Thou shalt remember the Lord, who did great and wonderful deeds in thee."

The point, one supposes, is that you are what you eat. Consumption of hoof-parting cud chewers encourages the ability to distinguish between right and wrong, just as it will enhance memory, the central faculty in the mastery of wisdom. Had Plutarch's diners only read Aristeas, they could have spared themselves a good deal of idle speculation about the motives of at least some Jews who refrained from pork!

The Jews, among a host of other barbarian types from urban society, were a favorite target for the Roman satirists. The first-century CE Persius, lampooning the sights and smells of the Sabbath in Rome's Jewish neighborhood, adds one other commonly noticed detail (Satires 5:180–184)[6]:

But when the day of Herod comes round, when the lamps wreathed with violets and ranged round the greasy window-sills have spat forth their thick clouds of smoke, when the floppy tuna's tails are curled round the dishes of red ware, and the white jars are swollen out with wine, you silently twitch your lips, turning pale at the Sabbath of the circumcized.

Persius is the first to observe a common Sabbath custom among Jews: eating fish and drinking wine. But he interests us in the present context because of his reference to circumcision, the surgical removal of the foreskin.

Many peoples (then and now) practiced circumcision as part of a boy's passage into manhood. But the Jews of antiquity (and now) were commonly thought to be unique in imposing circumcision on infants. Greeks and Romans saw it as a sign of extreme crudity, marring the beauty of the human form. Jewish men, for their part, believed it to be the mark of their descent from Abraham, who at God's command had circumcised himself at the age of ninety-nine as well as all the males of his household (Gen. 17:9–27).

One of the ablest interpreters of circumcision in early Judaism was

Philo of Alexandria. His massive explanation of the laws of the Torah, entitled The Special Laws, begins auspiciously with a vigorous defense of circumcision on a variety of grounds (Special Laws I, I)[7]:

> I will begin with that which is an object of ridicule among many people, . . . namely the circumcision of the genital organs. It is very zealously observed by many other nations, particularly by the Egyptians, a race regarded as pre-eminent for its populousness, its antiquity and its attachment to philosophy. And therefore it would be well for the detractors to desist from childish mockery and to inquire in a wiser and more serious spirit into the causes of which the persistence of this custom is due . . . .

Philo's first line of defense is to point out that the Egyptians, universally held to be a wise nation, are fond of circumcision. The Jews, by implication, are not fools.

He then proceeds to list four arguments for circumcision. These are grounded in hygienic explanations "handed down to us from the old-time studies of divinely gifted men who made deep research into the writings of Moses" (Special Laws I: II). But appeals to tradition are rarely enough for Philo. His final defense of circumcision, as we should expect, is philosophical:

> I consider circumcision to be a symbol of two things most necessary to our well-being. One is the excision of pleasures which bewitch the mind. For since among the love-lures of pleasure the palm is held by the mating of man and woman, the legislators thought good to dock the organ which ministers to such intercourse, thus making circumcision the figure of the excision of excessive and superfluous pleasures signified by one, the most imperious.
>
> The other reason is that a man should know himself and banish from the soul the grievous malady of conceit. For there are some who have prided themselves on their power of fashioning as with a sculptor's cunning the fairest of creatures, man, and in their braggart pride assumed godship, closing their eyes to the Cause of all that come into being. . . . The evil belief, therefore, needs to be excised from the mind with any others that are not loyal to God.

Circumcision, for Philo, is an outward sign that continually reminds its bearer of an inner truth: that pleasure is fleeting and that God alone is truly the creator of life. We cannot, of course, know who might have been convinced by Philo's argument. But that he felt obliged to make it indicates the centrality that he and other Jews ascribed to it in the domain of Jewish custom.

Together, then, with religious loyalty to an invisible god, the preservation of Saturn's day as a day of rest, and the avoidance of perfectly good foods, circumcision was one of the distinguishing traits of the Jews. The earliest writings that describe Jews as willing to fight and die in defense of their national customs are all associated with these same traits. Compelling descriptions are preserved in a Jewish work, written in Hebrew late in the second century BCE, entitled II Maccabees. It is preserved in Greek translation in many Old Testament canons.

Most of the book describes the rise of the Hasmonean kingdom, beginning in the revolt of the Maccabees against attempts to suppress distinctive Jewish customs. This suppression is vividly portrayed (II Maccabees 5:8–20):[8]

> At the suggestion of the people of Ptolemais a decree was issued to the neighboring Greek cities that they should . . . make the Jews partake of the sacrifices (to Zeus, the High God), and should kill those who did not choose to change over to Greek customs. One could see, therefore, the misery that had come upon them. For example, two women were brought in for having circumcised their children. They publicly paraded them around the city, with their babies hanging at their breasts, and then hurled them down headlong from the wall. Others, who had assembled in the caves nearby, in order to observe the seventh day [i.e., the Sabbath] secretly, were betrayed . . . and were all burned together, because their piety kept them from defending themselves, in view of their regard for that most holy day. . . . Eleazar, one of the scribes in high position, a man now advanced in age, was being forced to open his mouth to eat swine's flesh. But he, welcoming death with honor rather than life with pollution, went up to the rack of his own accord, spitting out the flesh, as all ought to go who have the courage to refuse things that it is not right to taste, even for the natural love of life.

Described here are more than "customs." Refusal to violate the Sabbath, eat pork, worship foreign gods, or spare their sons circumcision were principles of behavior for which some Jews would rather die than betray.

It is quite possible, of course, that Jewish writers focused upon aspects of Jewish custom that were the most visible to foreigners. In light of silence about less controversial customs, these may appear to stand out as particularly central. Nevertheless, the broad agreement across centuries and languages suggests that the traits we have isolated were indeed crucial markers of membership in the Jewish nation.

Conversion to Judaism

It is surprising that these customs seem to have proved most attractive to many non-Jews as well. Dio Cassius is only one of a number of writers who from the first century CE and onward pointed out that Jewish communities included people of non-Jewish birth. You'll recall that Dio knew of Romans who were called Jews after accepting Jewish customs.[9]

Perhaps the most famous of such converts was one Queen Helene of Adiabene, who—according to Flavius Josephus[10]—brought her entire country with her into the fold. Other writers speak of God Fearers (*theosebeis*)—non-Jewish women and uncircumcised men—who congregated at Jewish prayer gatherings, celebrated the Sabbath, and otherwise participated in Jewish national customs. Archeological inscriptions, moreover, reveal that at least some non-Jews, men and women of means, might contribute to the construction or repair of Jewish communal buildings as gifts to the Jewish community in whose life they shared.[11]

Since no writing from a self-professed God Fearer or convert has survived, it is difficult to know what motivated such men and women to attach themselves to the nation of Israel or what their experience in it was like. It is also difficult to know how the Jews they joined interpreted the converts' motives.[12] Greek and Latin writers who comment on the phenomenon of non-Jewish participation in Judaism seem to regard it as bizarre in the way that contemporary journalists cluck at the "cult phenomenon." And, to a degree, this may be part of the truth.

The Roman Empire knew a rich array of religious communities that served needs unmet by the ceremonial, essentially patriotic worship of the Roman Emperor. In addition to ancestral or national religions, there were many private religious associations that were multiethnic in character. Mithraism, for example, was composed primarily of soldiers in the Roman army, without regard for national origins. And, of course, Christianity grew increasingly popular after the first century as a multi-ethnic religious community. Members of such associations shared initiatory rituals, worshipful allegiance to a protective god or goddess, and celebration of communal meals. All this bound people of diverse backgrounds into a single fellowship offering loving companionship in this life and the next.

God Fearers probably regarded the Judaism they encountered as just such a private religious association. Its ancient origins in redemptive acts of God were well known. Members, moreover, enjoyed a richly evocative release from worldly concerns on the Sabbath. They observed subtle mysteries symbolized by prohibited and permitted foods and held an international membership, promising a meal and shelter wherever they traveled. And for men, circumcision into the covenant of Abraham offered an appropriately heroic initiation procedure.

The Basic Markers of Judaic Social Identity

Let us summarize the basic markers or outward signs of Jewish social identity in the middle centuries of our millennium. Ioudaismos included those born into the nation—a vast majority—and those who circulated within it as what might be called "associates." It was open in principle to those from outside, on condition of accepting the nation's collective discipline. Presupposed was exclusive loyalty to a single god, the God of Israel, as the sole ob-ject of religious veneration (precisely how, we discuss in Chapter Five).

Bound with exclusive loyalty to the God of Israel were a number of as-sociated observances that together and individually combined to create im-portant barriers between the free mixing of Jews and non-Jews. One was the day of rest, the Sabbath. Although no universal norms seem to have gov-erned its celebration, it was clearly honored as a day free of labor, an oppor-tunity to gather together to affirm loyalty to the God of Israel and membership in the community of Israel. While the world went on its course, the Jews separated from it to be among one another.

The dietary restrictions also served as an important marker of Jewish social separation. At the least, those who followed dietary rules could not share entirely in the meals of their non-Jewish neighbors. In light of the at-tention this attracted among non-Jews, it seems certain that Jews were often not subtle about this but used the custom as a way of limiting even permissi-ble socializing with non-Jews over food.

Circumcision, too, conveyed an important social meaning, for physical nakedness was important in the public expression of Hellenistic civic iden-tity. In the education of young men, as well as in city-wide cycles of public celebrations, athletic training and competition played a key role. Such com-petition was conducted by unclothed contestants. Their nakedness placed on display the perfection of the human form at the height of its skills. Partici-pants in such sport, like athletic heroes of our own day, were perceived to embody and celebrate the Hellenistic cultural heritage.

On such occasions, the "mutilated" Jewish male would clearly consti-tute a reminder of the ethnic boundaries that separated him (and his barbaric nation) from the rest of the world. Such separation only began with the body. Symbolically, however, it extended all along the spacial, vertical axis of real-ity. From the body, it reached upward into the highest summits of the cos-mos, pointing toward a God different from all others; from the body its implications spread outward throughout the human community, marking off "a people dwelling alone, and not counting itself among the nations." (Num. 23:9).

Natural and Intentional Judaic Communities

The customs that distinguished Jews from the non-Jewish world also served to distinguish Jews from one another. As we have seen, early Judaism had no central institution empowered to define a single pattern of living for all Jews. Rather, on the basis of certain core customs and relatively shared symbolic vocabulary, Jews everywhere formed a variety of communities. Each com-munity preserved its own traditions of Judaic expression. Out of these grew several quite discrete Judaic worlds.[13]

The term "sect," commonly used by historians of early Judaism to describe such communities, is not entirely appropriate here. Sects, as sociologists usually define the term, exist only in opposition to a central institution (sociologist use the term "Church") capable of prescribing standards of practice or belief. Usually, sects separate from a Church, claiming to be the sole legitimate community, which the Church has failed to represent. Correspondingly, the Church tries to repress the sect as a heretical departure from the true community. This model doesn't work for early Judaism, because, as we have seen, there was no central Judaic "Church" in antiquity from which Judaic sects could separate.

There is, however, a good deal of merit in trying to make some sense of the fragmented nature of Judaic religious society in our period. In our attempt to do so, we experiment with the term "intentional" Judaic communities. Many such communities were societies of like-minded people who made a self-conscious decision to join a group that they believed offered a form of Judaic life superior to others. Such intentional communities can be contrasted with "natural" Judaic communities. The latter, surely incorporating the vast majority of Jews, perceived Jewish ethnic bonds as the primary basis of communal boundaries.

These ethnic bonds were cemented through the national customs we discussed earlier in this chapter. Jews in natural communities shared certain common customs and recognized certain basic symbols as their own. But they were rather tolerant of wide ranges of behavior within the broad limits of Jewish social custom and recognized few official interpretations of the common symbolic vocabulary as binding upon individual belief. They seem to have been rather tolerant as well of God Fearers and other well-meaning non-Jews participating in communal life.

Members of intentional communities, by contrast, tended to have more careful rules for observing common Judaic customs, especially regarding the Sabbath or the dietary rules. Similarly, insiders tended to have a clearly defined understanding of "right" and "wrong" interpretations of Judaic scriptures and symbolic vocabulary. Often, acceptance of such rules and interpretations was taken as a sign of special loyalty to God. Members of the community were thus entitled to an enhanced status as the "remnant" or "elect" of Israel. Sometimes such communities could be very strict in requiring new Jewish members to abandon old ways of living. Presumably, it would be difficult for non-Jewish God Fearers to feel welcome in such settings.

But these are only generalizations. We begin our survey of specific communities with the Samaritans, who survive even today as a separate national group in the State of Israel. Their example will help us clarify how it is that a religious world can be Judaic, yet, at the same time, be regarded by itself and others as outside the community of Judaism. From the Samaritans, we turn to vigorous intentional communities. All of them made clear demands that initiates undertake radically new ways of living in conjunction with deeply changed self-understandings. These are the members of the Dead Sea community at Qumran, the Therapeutae of Egypt, and the early Jewish communities committed to the Messiahship of Jesus of Nazareth. We conclude, finally, with the emerging communities of rabbinic disciples.

The Samaritans: Israel but Not Jews

Those raised in cultures shaped by Christian traditions are used to thinking of the word "Samaritan" as a synonym for one who performs an unusual act of humanitarianism. The image, of course, comes from the famous parable of the Good Samaritan in the Gospel of Luke 10:29–37. A look at this parable will prove useful. To Jesus' reminder to "love your neighbor as yourself" (quoted from Lev. 19:18), an obtuse lawyer responds, "Who is my neighbor?" Jesus replies:

> A man was going down from Jerusalem to Jericho and fell into the hands of robbers, who stripped him, beat him, and went away, leaving him half dead. Now by chance a priest was going down that road; and when he saw him, he passed by on the other side. So likewise a Levite, when he came to the place and saw him, passed by on the other side. But a Samaritan while traveling came near him; and when he saw him, he was moved to pity. He went to him and bandaged his wounds, having poured oil and wine on them. Then he put him on his own animal, brought him to an inn, and took care of him. The next day he took out two denarii [coins], gave them to the innkeeper, and said, "Take care of him; and when I come back, I will repay you whatever more you spend." Which of these three, do you think, was a neighbor of the man who fell into the hands of the robbers?" He [the lawyer] said, "The one who showed him mercy." Jesus said to him, "Go and do likewise."

To understand the power of the parable, you have to know that Samaritans were regarded with great contempt by many Jews of that time. The "good Samaritan" of this parable is a figure chosen to shame people with pretensions to being righteous before God. The parable is intended to surprise its audience: *even* a Samaritan, a member of a despised minority, could fulfill a simple commandment of the Torah in a way that the powerful and privileged might well emulate.

Who were these Samaritans, and why did the Gospel writer take for granted that Jews had contempt for them?[14] To describe the "who" will help to answer the "why." The term "Samaritan," like the term "Jew," links a distinct people to a particular place, the district of Roman Palestine called Samaria (Hebrew: *shomron*), bordered by Judea to the south and the Galilee to the north. Samaritans claimed to be descendants of the ancient northern Kingdom of Yisrael. Its first king, Jeroboam, had broken away from Solomon's Yehudah-based Empire in 960 BCE. Under numerous subsequent

Samaria: Between Judea and the Galilee

Source: Based on Nicholas De Lange, *Atlas of the Jewish World* (Oxford: Equinox, 1984), p. 24.

dynasties, Yisrael pursued its own cultural and political life until it was destroyed by Assyria in 722 BCE. *Shomron*, the capital, lent its name to the remnant that still populated the area.

The Samaritans' claim to be the only authentic survivors of the exiled

Israelite nation, rather than their location, attracted unpleasant attention to them. From their homeland, which divided Roman Palestine between Judea and the Galilee, they denied the historical authenticity of the political and religious institutions of Jerusalem. This conflict between the Samaritans and the Judeans had persisted throughout the Hellenistic period. Its focus was the Temple.

Contrary to the long-standing tradition of most diaspora and Palestinian Jews, the Samaritans insisted that Mt. Gerizim in Samaria was the place that God had long ago chosen as the sole place from which to offer sacrifice. They built a Temple there and refused to acknowledge the legitimacy of the Temple in Jerusalem. The final break between the Samaritan and the Judean communities probably came during the Hasmonean period. The Hasmonean King, John Hyrcanus, for motives that might have been both practical and theological, destroyed the Mt. Gerizim Temple in 128 BCE. It was never rebuilt.

No doubt many who had worshipped there later blended into the larger Jewish population of Palestine and turned their loyalties to Jerusalem. But others continued to refuse submission to the centrality of Jerusalem, its Temple, its priesthood, and its royal dynasty. They were the creators of a distinctive Samaritan identity over against that of other Jewish Palestinians. They continued to offer sacrifices on Mt. Gerizim—a rite conducted by Samaritan priests up till the present—and developed their own complex social and religious traditions.

The crucial literary expression of this Samaritan identity was produced within a century of the destruction of the sanctuary on Mt. Gerizim. It was a distinctively Samaritan scripture, a version of the Torah of Moses. This Torah differed from the Torah preserved in rabbinic tradition in many minor ways, a trait it shares with other ancient versions of the Torah of Moses. But what distinguished it from all other Jewish or Christian versions was its preoccupation with Mt. Gerizim as a divinely appointed sacrificial site.

We can look at its rendition of the Ten Commandments in Exodus 20: 1–17. In the Samaritan version, the following comment is added to verse 17[15]:

> And it shall be, when the LORD your God brings you up to the Land of the Canaanites that you are about to inherit, you shall set up for yourselves great stones. Coat them with lime and write upon them all the words of this Torah. And when you cross the Jordan, set up these stones, concerning which I command you this day, on Mt. Gerizim. And build there an altar to the LORD your God, an altar of stones, . . . and offer up upon it burnt offerings to the LORD your God, and sacrifice peace offerings. And you shall eat and rejoice there before the LORD your God on that mountain, across the Jordan, toward the setting sun, in the Land of the Canaanite, who dwells in the Arevah, opposite Gilgal, near Elon Moreh, opposite Shechem.

These lines are composed of verses found elsewhere in the Torah (e.g., Deut. 11:29, 27:2–7, 11:30), but you won't find them after Exodus 20:17 in any Jewish or Christian Bible, ancient or modern.

Like all the versions of the Mosaic Torah we discussed in Chapter Two, the Samaritan Torah constitutes a community's judgment regarding the *true* revelation of God to Moses. In this case, that judgment was capable of surviving even after the rabbinic version of the Torah suppressed all its earlier competitors. Indeed, the Samaritan Torah is the basis of a rich body of Samaritan interpretive tradition that began in antiquity and reached great heights during the Middle Ages.

The Samaritan case offers one example of how far we can stretch the concept of a Judaic world. In many respects, the Samaritans were much like Jews. Like Jews, Samaritans were monotheists who revered the God of Israel. They honored the Sabbath as well, sharing many Sabbath customs with other Palestinian Jews. They circumcised their male children and avoided forbidden foods, as did the Jews. But, at the same time, they distinguished themselves from Jews. Their social relations with Jews were kept to a minimum. Moreover, they worshipped at their own sites and celebrated holidays on separate days in accord with their own calendrical system. Most important of all, while Jews and Samaritans would identify themselves as ethnic Israelites, the Samaritans would deny they were also Jews. Samaritans regarded Jews as a foreign people, as the Jews regarded them. Samaritan customs and the Samaritan conception of Israel's past served to define a Judaic religious world over against that of the dominant religious worlds of the Jews. Both communities shared key symbolic elements such as the vertical triad of God-Torah-Israel. And at least one Samaritan group, the first-century CE Dositheans, developed as well a powerful messianic movement based upon a redeemer of Mosaic rather than Davidic ancestry.[16]

These parallels and contrasts lead to an unavoidable conclusion; *the Samaritans' religious world is an example of a Judaic world that, in its own view as well as in the eyes of Jews, is not part of Judaism.* Neither the Samaritans nor the Jews regarded the religious world of the Samaritans as continuous with Judaism, yet the historian of religion must surely include the Samaritan world in any discussion of the worlds of early Judaism.

The Yakhad: The Converts of Israel in Damascus

As natural as Jewish identity in antiquity might have seemed to the Jews and those who wrote about them, there were many Jews who perceived their precise way of expressing Jewish customs as a self-conscious decision. What distinguished different Judaic communities was, among other things, the degree to which the decision to live in a certain kind of communal discipline was valued as a turning point in a person's devotion to the God of Israel.

One intentional Jewish community that stressed the need for an active choice of a new Judaic way of life seems, appropriately, to have called itself the *yakhad* (Community). Because it flourished in the Judean Desert south of Jerusalem, in a barren region called Wadi Qumran, contemporary scholars often refer to it as the "Qumran community." Founded early in the Hasmonean dynasty, it persisted for about two centuries, prior to its destruction during the revolt of 66–73 against Rome.

Some of the Yakhad's writings seem to have been preserved in a large library of many other ancient Jewish texts, now widely known as the Dead Sea Scrolls. In scrolls such as the Damascus Rule, the Community Rule, and others, we find numerous references to the Yakhad's leadership, initiation procedures, and other illuminating information. What emerges is a vivid picture of a community clearly committed to an ideal of total life reorientation—conversion—as the only way to be truly part of Israel's covenant relationship with the God of Israel.[17]

The circumstances of the group's origins are debated among historians. Some historians suspect that the Yakhad originated in a group of Jerusalem priestly families claiming descent from Zadok. Reputed to be a descendant of Aaron, Zadok had been appointed High Priest by King Solomon (I Ki. 2:35). His descendants dominated the Jerusalem Temple throughout much of the history of ancient Yehudah and, it appears, were installed in the High Priesthood during the Persian and Hellenistic periods as well. This changed in the wake of the Maccabean wars. By 152 BCE, the High Priesthood was filled by members of the non-Zadokite Hasmonean family (see Chapter One, pages 37–41). The founders of the Yakhad, it is argued, may have been demoted or deprived of their due by the new order. We'll return to the Yakhad's recollections of its origins momentarily.

Since the discovery of the community's writings and communal buildings, many historians have tried to link the Yakhad to one of the Jewish groups mentioned in the writings of Flavius Josephus, Philo, and other ancient writers. Most contemporary historians believe that the Yakhad was part of a community known in ancient Greek-language sources as the Essenes, a monastic group reported to have lived in the Dead Sea area. This is likely, but the Qumran texts do not yield any obvious Hebrew equivalents of the name "Essene." Moreover, there are many ways in which ancient descriptions of the Essenes do not match the profile of the literature at Qumran.

A more recent proposal links the Yakhad to another group that figured prominently in the Temple bureaucracy of the Hasmonean and Herodian administrations. This group is known in Greek writings as the Sadducees and in rabbinic texts as the Zadokites (Hebrew: *tzadukim*). They appear to have been in routine conflict with the early Pharisees about numerous legal and theological points. Until recently, these disputes were reported only secondhand in Josephus' writings and those of the rabbis. The publication of a fragmentary text called the Halakhic Letter (Hebrew: *miktzat ma'aseh torah*) from among the Qumran scrolls, however, reveals that the writer of this letter held

The Dead Sea Wilderness Region

Source: Based on H. Shanks et al., *The Dead Sea Scrolls After Forty Years* (Washington, D.C.: Biblical Archeology Society, 1991, 1992), p. x.

some legal views ascribed in the Mishnah to the Sadducees. Because the Yakhad seems also to have been hostile to the Pharisees, it is indeed possible that the Yakhad and the Sadducees had some traditions in common.

There is one major difficulty in linking the Yakhad's Zadokites too

Archeological Remains of the Yakhad

The ruins on the far left seem to have housed a communal dining room. The function of many of the rooms remains unclear. The ruins sit on a prominent bluff (center) overlooking a *wadi*, or dried riverbed (on the right).

Source: Sonia Halliday Photographs

firmly to the Sadducees. The latter are universally portrayed as wielding great power in the Jerusalem Temple in the Hasmonean and Herodian times—precisely when the founders of the Yakhad seem to have been deprived of their Zadokite prerogatives. Perhaps before us is the record of two priestly groups *each* claiming authentic Zadokite lineage. One dominated; the other went into exile in the Judean wilderness. In any event, closer identification of the Yakhad with the Sadducees, Essenes, or any other group must await further historical research.[18]

It is obvious, however, that the nature of the Yakhad as a religious community was bound up with its principled opposition to the official Jewish administration controlling the Temple. Its calendrical system, for example, was a solar calendar similar to that of the book of Jubilees and thus contradicted the calendar by which the timing of Jerusalem's Festivals was calculated. The Yakhad's opposition began shortly after the Hasmonean victory over the Seleucids. Some of their writings recall the rise to power of a Wicked Priest who, after a brief period of favorable rule, "forsook God and betrayed the precepts for the sake of riches."[19] In response, the founders of the Yakhad and other sympathizers seem to have left (or were forced to leave) Jerusalem. They created their own priestly community centered in the caves of Qumran. Satellite communities existed throughout southern Judea.

Claiming priestly descent through Zadok, the Yakhad's founders interpreted their separation from Jerusalem as a self-exile of the pure and holy genuine priests from the impure political appointees who had gained control of the Temple. Unlike most worlds associated with priestly groups, however, theirs was deeply marked by the horizontal or historical axes of Judaic symbols. They awaited a time in the near future when God would restore the true descendants of Zadok to the Temple service in a cosmic battle. This war, between the Children of Light (the Yakhad) and the Children of Darkness (other Jews and their imperial supporters), would usher in the end of time and the direct rule of God.[20]

The Yakhad's communal discipline must be interpreted against this background. Although its writings are not in total agreement about all aspects of the Yakhad's structure and government, there is enough agreement to permit some useful generalizations. It is clear, to begin with, that the Yakhad's view of priesthood was complex. On the one hand, in accord with universally held assumptions, it was inherited through one's family. On the other, one could assume certain priestly prerogatives through a transformation of one's moral life. This is reflected in the social composition of the group. The leaders seem to have been priests by family lineage, but many members were clearly not of priestly families. Their priestly status, rather, was acquired by their commitment to living in accord with a rigorous communal discipline.

We quote from the Damascus Rule's interpretation of a verse from the canonical book of Ezekiel (Damascus, 3–4)[21]:

> "The Priests, the Levites, and the sons of Zadok who kept the charge of my sanctuary when the children of Israel strayed from me, they shall offer me fat and blood" (Ezek. 44:15). The "Priests" are the converts of Israel who departed from the land of Judah, and the "Levites" are those that joined them. The "sons of Zadok" are the elect of Israel, the men called by name who shall stand at the end of days.

This statement contains the Yakhad's self-understanding in a nutshell. Ezekiel's references to various orders of inherited priesthood are systematically expanded to include nonpriests who have taken up the community's life.

The Hebrew *shavei yisrael* literally means, the "returners of Israel," the elect who have separated themselves from the rest of Israel and, in preparation for the end of days, have returned to the true service of God. With the Jerusalem Temple polluted, the members of the Yakhad saw their own communal life as a pure sacrificial offering that alone brought atonement and purification from the increasingly heavy weight of Israel's sinfulness.

According to the Damascus Rule, returners were viewed as having entered a "New Covenant in the land of Damascus" (that is, Exile—Qumran).[22] The commitment to this New Covenant was total, involving one's entire personhood and possessions. Thus the Community Rule (Community, 1):[23]

> All those who freely devote themselves to [God's] truth shall bring all their knowledge, powers, and possessions into the Community of God, that they may purify their knowledge in the truth of God's precepts and order their powers according to His ways of perfection, and all their possessions according to His righteous counsel. . . .

In order to prepare for this total commitment, returners served a period of training at the fringes of the community and learned how to follow its specific interpretations of the rules of the Torah. Both the Damascus Rule and the Community Rule list scores of such rules that govern all areas of personal life, interpersonal relations, hierarchies of communal authority, and ritual matters.

According to the Community Rule, individuals had to demonstrate over a period of two years their suitability to join the community. During this testing period, prospective members were denied full participation in the community's ritual meals. Finally, after standing an examination before a council composed of communal leaders, "if it be his destiny . . . then he shall be inscribed among his brethren in the order of his rank for the Torah, and for justice, and for the pure meal; his property shall be merged and he shall offer his counsel and judgment to the community."[24]

The borders of the Yakhad, obviously, were not easy to cross. One was required to become cleansed physically and spiritually so as not to pollute the common life that constituted the Yakhad's sacrificial offering. Converts could move from outside the group to the inside only by becoming a disciple, learning in a period of initiation the distinctive lifestyle that distinguished the wise and pious from the ignorant and wicked. It is difficult to imagine that those born of non-Jewish parents (by any definition of Jewishness) could have been considered as initiates. This was a community of "Israel" open only to those born into the Jewish nation willing to commit to the true path of covenantal life.

What was communal life like? Despite rigid hierarchies based upon priestly birth and knowledge of scripture, it was characterized by an overall sense of powerful community. Thus, the Community Rule: "These are the

The Community Rule of the Yakhad

This photograph shows column 7 of the Community Rule, which spells out behavior expected of initiates into the Yakhad. The paragraph at the top of the column begins as follows:

> If any man has uttered the Venerable Name even though frivolously, or as a result of shock, or for any other reason whatever, while reading the Book or praying, he shall be dismissed and shall return to the Council of the Community no more. If he has spoken in anger against one of the Priests inscribed in the Book, he shall do penance for one year and shall be excluded for his soul's sake from the pure Meal of the Congregation. But if he has spoken unwittingly, he shall do penance for six months. Whoever has deliberately lied shall do penance for six months. Whoever has deliberately insulted his companion unjustly shall do penance for one year and shall be excluded. . . .

Source: Photograph by John C. Trever. Courtesy of the School of Theology at Claremont, Ancient Biblical Manuscript Center.

ways in which all of them shall walk, each man with his companion, wherever they dwell. The man of lesser rank shall obey the greater in matters of work and money. They shall eat in common and pray in common and deliberate in common."[25] A focus of communal life was a communal meal presided over by hereditary Priests. These meals seem also to have served as teaching occasions at which "there shall never lack a man among them who shall study the Torah continually, day and night, concerning the right conduct of man with his companion."[26]

Some writings of the Yakhad speak of a mysterious Teacher of Righteousness (*moreh tzedek*), an inspired leader raised by God, who disclosed to the original members of the Yakhad important mysteries contained in scripture. It is unclear how his authority was inherited or transmitted in later generations. What seems beyond doubt, however, is that scriptural study at Qumran, under a series of figures who held the title of Interpreter of the Torah (*doresh hatorah*), was regarded as a kind of revelatory experience.

Gathered around the Interpreter, members felt in the presence of prophecy, as the Torah's "hidden things" (Dt. 29:28) became manifest to all. This was especially so, perhaps, in the teaching of new initiates. "When they have been confirmed for two years in perfection . . . they shall be set apart as holy. . . . And the Interpreter shall not conceal from them, out of fear of the spirit of apostasy, any of those things hidden from Israel which have been discovered by him."[27]

Let us make a few observations at this point. Before us is a small, cohesive society viewing itself as the "true" Israel. Unlike the Samaritan example, however, this claim was not historical or ethnic in focus. Rather, it was entirely moral. "Israel," to be sure, is a historical people for the Yakhad. But the *true* Israel is the community of Jews who penitently returned to the service of the God of Israel. Whereas the Samaritan communities might have regarded themselves as the *original* Israelite people, the members of the Yakhad seem to have viewed themselves as the *last* Israelite people.

The members of the Yakhad, as an expression of their conversion to the New Covenant, had separated themselves from the rest of Israel. Their identity as Israel was grounded in this conversion, a moral transformation of each individual member. Those Jews who remained loyal to the corrupt regime of Jerusalem—and to their non-Jewish imperial allies—were doomed to destruction in the coming war in which the forces of Light would overwhelm those of Darkness. The morally transformed would prevail.

The Yakhad's communal style of life was entirely centered on the act of conversion that brought one into the community of Light. Elaborate initation disciplines filtered out those whose original conversion proved insincere. Once fully incorporated into the community, however, the initiate enjoyed an intense life structured around obedience to detailed rules for living and submission to the teachings of charismatic leaders gifted with prophetic powers.

What did the Yakhad share with other Judaic communities? Not much, if we use as our standard the relatively open-bordered "natural" Jewish communities described by Hellenistic writers. The Yakhad maintained a detailed body of rules that governed their observance of Jewish custom. This discipline served as a way to exclude other Jews who might have, for example, revered the Sabbath or avoided forbidden meats, but who observed such customs in accord with different rules. In addition to establishing a social distance from other Jews, the discipline surely served to limit interactions with non-Jews.

Most important, the Yakhad understood its way of life as a conscious rejection of a person's own past. Entering the community was the beginning of a new, redeemed life, a life free of earlier sins and untainted by others who continued to sin. In the new community, one found fellow travelers upon a road that would lead to the coming redemption. Redemption would confirm that the choice made in conversion was the only choice to be made.

The Therapeutae: An Israel for Women

The decision to leave one form of life and, through moral transformation, enter another more intensely lived community is a common pattern among Jewish groups in antiquity. Whether men and women made such decisions together as households or independently as individuals is hard to specify. Given the communitarian atmosphere of the Qumran Yakhad, for example, it is probable that a married man's entry into the community would automatically include his wife and children. But could a married woman, regarded as part of her husband's household, make a decision on behalf of her husband and children? We do not know. An unmarried woman would be unlikely to be able to take up life in the Yakhad or in one of its outlying communities independently of a male sponsor, such as a brother or a father.

In one community, however, it is certain that the project of personal transformation was begun only by people without families. This is a community of first-century CE Egyptian Jews, known in Greek as Therapeutae. The Greek name seems to mean "Healers" or, perhaps, "Worshippers." They practiced a life of prayer, ascetic discipline and study on the outskirts of Alexandria. Among them, men and women joined equally of their own free will and pursued a common discipline in sexually segregated societies.

All our information about the Therapeutae comes from Philo of Alexandria, who discusses them in detail in his book *On the Contemplative Life*.[28] They serve him as a model of what it means to live in pursuit of philosophical knowledge and the loving service of God. Since Philo is our only source of information—and so clearly uses the Therapeutae to model his own ideas of virtue and piety, it is hard to be sure that his picture is any more accurate than are those of Greek and Latin writers on the Jews. On the other hand, Philo had a generally dismal view of women, regarding them as lustful and unsuited to intellectual pursuits, making it hard to imagine him inventing a group of women philosophers. By reading his account carefully, we can draw some cautious conclusions.

In Philo's view, Therapeutic men and women (the latter are called by the feminine form, Therapeutrides) pursued an identical discipline in their separate communities. They passed their days living alone in simple huts, undisturbed by the needs of children or the tempests of sexual relationships. Let Philo describe their way of life in his own words (Life 25–28)[29]:

> In each house there is a consecrated room which is called a sanctuary or monastery, and closeted in this they are initiated into the mysteries of the sanctified life. They take nothing into it, either food or drink or any other of the things necessary for the needs of the body, but laws and oracles delivered through the mouth of prophets, and psalms and anything else which fosters and perfects knowledge and piety. They keep the memory of God alive and never forget it, so that even in their dreams the picture is nothing else but the loveliness of divine excellences and powers . . .
>
> Twice every day they pray, at dawn and at evening; at sunrise they pray for a fine bright day . . . in the true sense of the heavenly daylight which they pray may fill their minds. At sunset they ask that the soul may be wholly relieved from the press of the senses and the objects of sense and, sitting where she is consistory and council chamber, to herself pursue the quest of truth. The interval between early morning and evening is spent entirely in spiritual exercise. They read the holy scriptures and seek wisdom from their ancestral philosophy by taking scripture as an allegory, since they think that the words of the literal text are symbols of something whose hidden nature is revealed by studying the underlying meaning.

Philo here describes the ideal of philosophical existence in terms distinctive to Jews.

Although contemplation of God is the objective that these Jews share with Greco-Roman philosophers, the source of philosophical study is not Plato, Aristotle, or the writings of the Stoic teachers, but the Torah of Moses and the writings of the prophets, as filtered through the interpretive lens of philosophical allegory. Through it, these men and women are initiated into the ultimate mysteries of holy living. Philo, we sense, would feel very much at home among them.

Men and women mingled only in celebration of the Sabbath and the late spring festival of Shavuot. Philo depicts the Sabbath celebration as a philosophical discourse offered by a senior male member of the community in a house set aside for communal functions. Here men and women sat separately, divided by a partition that, according to Philo, served two purposes: "the modesty becoming to the female sex is preserved, while the women sit-

ting within earshot can easily follow what is said, since there is nothing to obstruct the voice of the speaker" (Life, 33).[30] After the discourse, members
shared a simple communal meal of bread and salt seasoned with herbs.

The Shavuot celebration seems also to have taken the form of a philosophical discourse and common meal, but with an added feature—communal song. Philo interprets these hymns as commemorative in nature,
re-enactments of the songs sung by Israelite men and women upon their redemptive passage through the waters of the Red Sea after the liberation from
Egypt (Ex. 15).

His admiration of the participants shines through his description of
their song (Life, 88–89):[31]

> It is on this model above all that the choir of the Therapeutae of either
> sex, note in response to note and voice to voice, the treble of the
> women blending with the bass of the men, create an harmonious con-
> cert, music in the truest sense. . . . Thus they continue till dawn, drunk
> with this drunkenness in which there is no shame, then not with heavy
> heads or drowsy eyes but more alert and wakeful than when they
> came to the banquet, they stand with their faces and whole body
> turned to the east and when they see the sun rising they stretch their
> hands up to heaven and pray for bright days and knowledge of the
> truth and the power of keen sighted thinking. And after the prayers
> they depart each to his private sanctuary once more to ply the trade
> and till the field of their philosophy.

In this song, the purest mingling of male and female takes place, the mingling of ethereal voices divorced from physical desire and passion. Male and
female transcend each other in that most Hellenistic of liberations, liberation
from the limitations of the corrupt, mortal body.

Philo's description of the women attending the Shavuot celebration offers insight into the women attracted to this sort of community and a clue
into what it offered them as women in particular. He (Life, 68) describes
them, on the whole as:[32]

> aged virgins, who have kept their chastity not under compulsion, like
> some of the Greek priestesses, but of their own free will in their ardent
> yearning for wisdom. Eager to have her [Wisdom] for their life mate
> they have spurned the pleasures of the body and desire no mortal off-
> spring but those immortal children which only the soul that is dear to
> God can bring to the birth unaided, because the Father has sown in her
> spiritual rays enabling her to behold the verities of wisdom.

Let us reflect on this in light of other things we have learned about the
Therapuetae.

In order to have engaged in the strenuous Therapeutic discipline of textual and philosophical study, women would have had to be highly educated. In Philo's Egypt, this would have been the privilege of very few men, not to mention women. This suggests, therefore, that the Therapeutics in general came from an exclusive sector of Egyptian Jewry. The Therapeutrides must have been well-born as well.

These women are described as older "virgins" (Greek: *parthenoi*). In the Greek of Philo's day, this term could refer either to a young woman without a legitimate sexual partner, a woman who had never had sexual relations, or one who had ceased to have them. This suggests that these women were either unmarried throughout their lives or, if married at one time, were now freed of that relationship by the death of their husbands or, perhaps, by divorce. What made it possible to become a Therapeutride, therefore, was a combination of social privilege and freedom from the responsibility of caring for a husband and family. The only children they cared for, as Philo puts it, were the immortal conceptions of the mind, impregnated there by the seeds of God's own Word.

The Therapeutrides, then, were a community of single women who separated from families and social obligations to pursue a life of disciplined study and reflection upon Wisdom (that is, Torah and philosophy). It would be exciting to find a text produced by a Therapeutride who reflected upon her experience in this women's Israel. Unfortunately, we can draw inferences only from Philo.

Women within this community enjoyed two kinds of freedom. On the one hand, they were inducted into the essential mysteries of God and constituted a spiritual elite within the larger community of Israel. The freedom from ignorance offered by knowledge of Torah was fully theirs in a way few Jews of that day, men or women, would ever enjoy. On the other hand, this initiation also freed them from their culturally defined roles as caregivers and as childbearers. Husbandless and childless, they became free to create themselves anew as souls who, responsible to no one but God, were no longer defined by common expectations of what women might do or be. This choice of community, of course, had broad implications. It was a choice not only against other styles of life available in the Egyptian Jewish community, but against the dominant Hellenistic conceptions of what a woman could hope for and become.

The Jesus Communities: An Israel for Jews and the Nations

Another communal setting that proved particularly attractive to a wide range of married women, as well as to an equally broad spectrum of men, were the numerous communities of born-Jews and non-Jews who gathered together for common meals and ritual celebrations in the name of the Messiah, Jesus of Nazareth.[33]

The designation of these groups as "Christian" was coined in Syria in the second century CE, a century after Jesus' death. But, like Judaism, a broad term like "Christianity" hardly does justice to the diversity of these communities, either in first-century CE Palestine or throughout the Mediterranean and Middle East for some centuries thereafter. Here we can only hint at the details of what, from the perspective of those beyond the Jewish nation, became the most important intentional community ever created within Judaism.[34]

Christian leaders of the second to fourth centuries commonly noted the survival of various sorts of Jewish Christians who constituted a curious or even threatening minority presence within the emerging universal Church. Some of these were understood to be communities of ethnic Jews who celebrated Jesus' Messiahship, while others seem to have been, at least in part, ethnically non-Jewish. What troubled Bishops about such groups was their tendency to observe some or all of the common Jewish national customs.

Circumcision and a persistence in celebrating Jewish Sabbaths and Festivals seem to have been fairly common. In some groups, women were said to use their menstrual periods, in accord with Mosaic law (Lev. 15:19 ff.), as an excuse to abstain from sexual relations with their husbands. Groups such as the Nazoreans and the Ebionites were believed even to preserve their own gospel traditions in Hebrew or Aramaic, in addition to (or instead of) the Greek Gospels used by most Christian communities.

We do not know which, if any, of these communities preserved any real continuity with Jesus' original disciples, the Jewish founders of what had become Christianity. For that matter, the lives and beliefs of the original disciples of Jesus are difficult to reconstruct from the Gospel traditions recorded near the end of the first century CE. Historians are usually cautious in claiming to know what Christianity was like before it began to claim an identity distinct from Judaism. Most Jewish devotees of Jesus in the mid-first century CE, however, would likely have been surprised to hear that their communities were anything but an expression of Judaism.

Rather, they had chosen to pursue a particularly intense form of Judaic communal life. This life, with its own discipline, brought them into routine relation with the God of Israel, through his chosen Messiah. Jesus, to be sure, had not conquered Rome in a victorious battle; rather, he had been executed for political crimes against the Roman state. But Jesus' disciples claimed that his death had been followed by a miraculous resurrection. This miracle threw a surprising light on all the messianic hopes of the Jewish people as preserved in the canonical scriptures.

The Messiah would indeed transform all the world and preside as Davidic heir over God's Kingdom. But his primary redemptive act was first experienced by individuals in their own lives. By conquering death on the Cross, Jesus was believed to have exercised a role previously reserved for God. He had conquered the power of death over those who accepted his self-sacrifice on their behalf. To place one's faith in Jesus' messianic self-sacrifice was to be reborn into a this-worldly immortality and placed in a new relationship to God. In hymns, prayers, and other forms of veneration, those redeemed from death by the Messiah commonly celebrated him as a heavenly being, hardly distinguishable from the God who had sent him.[35]

Like the Yakhad, the communities gathered in Jesus' name were grounded in personal conversions expressed by taking up a new way of life. Converts embarked upon the new life of immortality through a purifying baptism. They reconfirmed its power in a celebratory ritual meal (Greek: *eucharist*) in which members became part of the "Body of Christ" by symbolically consuming Jesus' body and blood in the form of bread and wine. They expressed it morally by living within the communities of those redeemed in Jesus.

Little in the communities we have described was not congruent with the symbolic vocabulary we have found in early Judaic worlds. Jews of the first century CE knew of heavenly beings who, like Jesus, were close to God and served as his agents. Some also preserved traditions that a messianic figure would die prior to the redemptive drama. True, the symbolic eating of the Messiah in the Eucharist would have struck many as extremely puzzling. But, for all that, Jewish communities founded in Jesus' name prior to 100 CE probably shared a good deal with most "natural" communities of Jews. Certainly they were no more idiosyncratic than, for example the Samaritans, the Yakhad, or the Therapeutae.

Indeed, the Jesus communities seem to have achieved a balance between "insiders" and "outsiders" rare within early Judaic communities. They represented an openness of boundaries similar to natural Jewish communities, even while cultivating an intense communal life characteristic of intentional communities. In terms of overall patterns of custom, for example, these communities would have appeared typically Jewish—preserving Sabbath rest, dietary restrictions, and circumcision. Like many natural Jewish communities (and unlike the Yakhad, for example), both Jews and non-Jewish God Fearers were welcome among them, even if they did not fully share the discipline of the group.

For initiates, rigid hierarchies based on social rank and wealth were relatively lax—more so, for example, than at Qumran. Women, too, seem to have enjoyed degrees of authority as prophets or teachers. It is difficult to find evidence of women in such positions in other Jewish communities of the period. Even the Therapeutrides, you'll recall, listened through a screen while men offered philosophical teaching. Women and men, finally, could become members on their own, without giving up families who remained outside the fold.[36]

These messianic communities seem, then, to have been well integrated into the spectrum of Judaic communities of the mid-first century CE. Yet, by the end of that century, it had become clear to many that the Jesus communities were not Judaism but something else. What had happened?

What happened, in essence, is that the message of Jesus' redemptive conquest of death had become more attractive beyond the communities of Judaism than within them. Increasing numbers of non-Jews had associated themselves with the Jesus communities. In some cases, non-Jewish members were required, as part of their conversion, to accept the patterns of circumcision, Sabbath observance, and dietary customs common to most natural Jewish communities. In others, however, the question was raised—did participation in the redemptive common life require a convert to accept Jewish social customs?

The most important responses to this question were offered by Paul of Tarsus (died ca. 62 CE), a brilliant interpreter of early traditions about Jesus. A Greek-speaking Jew from Asia Minor, Paul had not known Jesus personally. But shortly after learning of Jesus' career, he became convinced that Jesus' death and resurrection had a unique significance. Paul had accepted a fundamental tradition that Jesus had risen to heaven upon his resurrection and would soon return as God's messianic agent to preside over the resurrection of the dead, the judgment of humanity, and the perfection of human history. To this, Paul added his own distinctive insight: Jesus' resurrection as Messiah was the first act of a redemptive drama that would incorporate Israel and the non-Jewish nations into a single body of humanity redeemed from sin and death. Messiah had come to redeem not only Israel, but all humans who trusted in the power of his self-sacrifice.[37]

Paul, a man of intense energy, possessed remarkable rhetorical skills. He became one of the most successful of many messengers of the redemptive good news (*euangelion*, Gospel) then traversing the Roman Empire. The New Testament's book of Acts offers a description of his evangelizing practice as it was recalled by Christian tradition a generation after his death. Entering a city, Paul would set up teaching in a Jewish community in which God Fearers were numerous. There, he would try to prove that various verses from the canonical scriptures contained predictions of Jesus' redemptive death.

Sometimes, as in Lystra in southern Turkey, for example, he made himself a disruptive presence and was beaten and thrown out (Acts 14:19–20). Often enough, as Acts relates matters, both Jews and God Fearers would find his proofs and teaching convincing. Under his guidance, they would create a special community (*ekklesia*, church) in which to pursue a new form of life "in Christ." Initiation into such a life began with baptism, which purified the soul from sin and enabled its rebirth into new life, and continued in light of retellings of the stories of Jesus' miracles and teachings designed to evoke his presence. It often reached peaks of ecstatic experience, interpreted as prophetic inspiration.

All this involved, as you might guess, a radical reinterpretation of fundamental elements in the symbolic vocabulary of Judaism. One of Paul's principal messages was that in the community of those redeemed in Christ, ethnic distinctions between Jew and Greek were meaningless. Israel, that is,

Adoration of Jesus as Messiah and God as Ruler:
A Striking Liturgical Theme in Early Judaism

The prominent role of Jesus as an angelic or divine figure for early Christians should not obscure the deep roots of such devotion in the traditions of early Judaism. Below is a case in which a liturgical tradition of Christian prayer surfaces centuries later among non-Christian Jews.

This passage from an early Christian hymn is quoted by the apostle Paul in his letter to a community he founded at Philippi in Macedonia (Philippians 2:5–11). The letter was probably written around 60 CE and testifies to a very early form of worshipful adoration of Jesus as divinely appointed Messiah:

> Therefore God also highly exalted him and gave him the name that is above every name, so that at the name of Jesus every knee should bend, in heaven and on earth and under the earth, and every tongue should confess that Jesus Christ is Lord, to the glory of God the Father.

Compare the images of this passage with the one that follows. This hymn first appears in the literature of heavenly ascent that circulated at the fringes of rabbinic communities in the last centuries of our period. By the early Middle Ages, the hymn became part of the rabbinic New Year liturgy. In more recent centuries, it has come to be sung at the conclusion of every daily worship service.

> Therefore, we hope for you, our God, quickly to see the splendor of your power to banish idols from the earth and that the false gods be cut down; to perfect the world under the reign of the Almighty, and that all flesh and blood call upon your name that all the wicked of the earth turn to you. May all who dwell on Earth recognize and know that to you every knee must bend and every tongue must swear, and before you every living thing must kneel and prostrate; to the glory of your name they must give honor.

Most probably, the Pauline text reflects the way an earlier Jewish hymn to God was adapted to refer to Messiah Jesus. Were it not for this Pauline passage, our earliest reference to the hymn would come from the centuries-later version cited in the second passage.

Sources: Philippians quoted from *HarperCollins Study Bible* (New York: HarperCollins, 1993); Maaseh Merkavah revised from the translation of M. Swartz, *Mystical Prayer in Ancient Judaism* [Terbingen: Mohr (Paul Siebeek), 1992].

acquired a new meaning in Paul's symbolic vocabulary. It defined a fundamentally new human possibility, as explained in a letter to his community in Rome (Rom. 9:6–8):

> For not all Israelites truly belong to Israel, and not all of Abraham's descendants; but "It is through Isaac that descendants shall be named for you" (Gen. 21:12). This means that it is not the children of the flesh who are the children of God, but the children of the promise are counted as descendants.

As Paul's earliest interpreters phrased it, in distinction to Fleshly Israel (the Jews) stood Spiritual Israel (the Church). Members of the Yakhad, of course, had long ago made a similar distinction between true Israel, children of Light, and those who merely claimed the name Israel, Children of Darkness. But this Spiritual Israel, Children of the Promise, defined an unprecedented community of both Jews and gentiles. All nations were entitled to the redemption offered by Christ's conquest of death and sin.

Paul's reinterpretation of the meaning of Israel is, in fact, part of a much more fundamental restructuring of the received Judaic symbolic vocabulary. As a sign of the universality of the redeemed life, Paul cautioned non-Jewish members of the Church from adopting the customs that had distinguished Jews from non-Jews. Whereas Jews might commonly view circumcision or dietary laws as signs of Israel's special relation to God, Paul regarded them as signs of confusion about the truer meaning of redemption.

In other words, Paul subordinated the symbol of Torah, which represented the body of Jewish covenantal customs, to the symbol of Messiah. Messiah, not Torah, now constituted the link between God and the Spiritual Israel. Accordingly, works of the Law (*nomos* or Torah), such as circumcision, would never help non-Jews establish a proper relation with God. This was possible only through works of faith (*pistis*) in the redemption offered by Christ to Jew and Greek (Rom. 9:30–32):

> What then are we to say? Gentiles, who did not strive for righteousness, have attained it, that is, righteousness through faith; but Israel, who did strive for the righteousness that is based on the law, did not succeed in fulfilling that law. Why not? Because they did not strive for it on the basis of faith, but as if it were based on works. They have stumbled over the stumbling stone. . . .

It is, perhaps, Paul's subordination of Torah to Messiah, his collapsing of the vertical and horizontal axes of Jewish symbolic thought into one another, that most clearly distinguishes his religious world from other early Judaic worlds.

To be sure, Paul had vigorous opponents among other early Jewish apostles. Many saw little harm in the preservation of Jewish customs in the churches. But his general approach prevailed and ultimately entered the canonical tradition of what became Christianity. A result of his success was that churches became dominated by non-Jewish converts for whom Jewish customs would have no particular meaning. Jewish converts to the community of Christ, by contrast, may have been much more comfortable retaining their customs within exclusively Jewish churches, even if they acknowledged that this was not a norm for all members of the Body of Christ. Such churches became marginal, however, once the link of Christian identity to Jewish national custom had been severed in most communities by the devaluation of the place of Torah in the new life.

In the meantime, most Jews outside the Jesus communities refused Jewish fellowship to uncircumcised non-Jews who ate pork and violated the Sabbath, yet who insisted that the Messiah had made them the True Israel. Churches, therefore, grew increasingly estranged from even the most loosely defined Judaic communities. What had begun as yet another intentional Jewish community was becoming a new kind of world altogether, built on an entirely new pool of converts.

But the parting of these worlds would take some time to solidify. Centuries after most Christians had lost any sense of ethnic connection to Jews, the tirades of Christian bishops against "Judaizers" within the Universal Church were matched by the curses of rabbinic masters against Jewish "deviators" (Hebrew: *minim*) and "sinners" (*posh'ei yisrael*) who had been seduced into disobeying the Torah and defiling the sanctity of God's name.

The Rabbinic Communities: An Israel of Discipleship

The history of Christianity, we have seen, begins in one sort of Judaic intentional community. The character of Judaism, for the past fifteen hundred years, has been deeply stamped by another. We speak, of course, of that form of community in which the rabbinic Sage played the complex role of moral guide, legal authority, and model of human perfection.

We have already seen in Chapter Two that the Pharisees of the first century CE may have provided much of the inspiration for later rabbinic tradition. And certain aspects of the Yakhad's communal life—especially the cultivation of complex rules for expressing communal membership—also have their rabbinic parallels. But the rabbinic communities of the third to seventh centuries created their own unique style of life, their own patterns of community.[38] Unlike the Yakhad or the Therapeutae, rabbinic communities formed no exclusive wilderness enclaves. Rather, more like the messianic communities in Jesus' name, they lived as families in towns and villages, in the midst of other Jews and non-Jews. After the Bar Kosiba war, the center of such communities was in the northern Palestinian province of Galilee. From there, new communities spread to other Jewish areas of the Mediterranean and the Middle East on the heels of rabbinic refugees or patriarchal emissaries.

The distinctiveness of rabbinic communities lay in their complex body of rules for performing the customs common to all Jews of antiquity—as well as the customs distinctly their own. Like the Yakhad, however, members of rabbinic communities insisted that full access to the life of the community was open only to those who accepted compliance with these rules. Of particular importance, therefore, were rules that regulated social relations between insiders and outsiders. These were summarized in the Mishnah by 200 CE and became the subject of complex developments in subsequent centuries.

Rules for the preparation of food, for example, helped to limit the range of Jews with whom families might eat common meals. Nearly all Jews, as we have seen, refused to eat certain meats. But rabbinic communities would eat meat that had been slaughtered and examined only in accordance with complex rabbinic procedures. Moreover, they interpreted a scriptural prohibition against boiling a goat in its mother's milk (e.g., Ex. 23:19) as a prohibition against cooking meat and dairy foods together. Such fastidiousness, apparently unknown in other Jewish communities, prevented Jews observing these rules from eating in the homes of Jews who did not.[39]

Other important rules regulated the celebration of the Sabbath and the Festivals. These could have important social implications. Consider, for example, the rabbinic institution of a mixed domain (Hebrew: *eruv*) for the Sabbath. When a number of homes shared a common courtyard, rabbinic custom was to place a dish of food in the courtyard on Friday afternoon before the Sabbath fell. This food, placed in the name of all the residents, had the effect of turning the houses and the courtyard into a single "home." Legally defined as inhabitants of a single household, the several families were now free to share food and other household items with all their neighbors on the Sabbath. If, however, even one household refused to acknowledge the eruv, none of them could be joined together. Accordingly, outsiders to the rabbinic communities found themselves forced either to reject the eruv, and thus incur the displeasure of their neighbors, or to accept it and become, to a degree, participants in the Sabbath rhythms of the rabbinic community.[40]

Much rabbinic custom concerned marriage, that most important means of establishing social bonds. In the ancient world in general, marriage was not viewed primarily as a means of joining lovers together into a legitimate relationship. Rather, as much as anything else, it was a financial relationship between extended families. In a world of rigid social hierarchies, marriage enabled families to move up (or down!) the social ladder on the backs of their marriageable children.

To these concerns, which all Jewish families might have shared in contemplating a marital match, rabbinic families added others. They would marry off their sons and daughters only to families who accepted rabbinic rules for contracting and solemnifying marriages. Terms for dowries, maintenance, and settlements in the case of divorce would be set by rabbinic guidelines. Divorced men and women could remarry a member of a rabbinic community only if the divorce had been governed by rabbinic regulations. Such laws ensured that new families would be drawn into the rabbinic communities on terms that those communities had much power to define.[41]

All these rules, in addition to a host of others covering all aspects of life, were regarded in rabbinic communities as *halakhah*. You'll recall from Chapter Two that halakhah was understood as tradition that had been transmitted by an unbroken line of prophets and Sages from the most ancient of times and was providentially preserved only by the rabbis. By the third century and onward, halakhic norms were regarded as nothing less than part of revelation itself, the Oral Torah that God had transmitted to Moses on Sinai.

The Sages' possession of Oral Torah explains the character of the most important human relationship within rabbinic communities. This was the relationship between the Sage (*hakham*)—the Master of Torah—and his exclusively male disciples (*talmidei hakhamim*). The term "rabbi" originated as a form of address to any social superior. It means My Master. In rabbinic communities, however, it was a title conferred upon a disciple by a Sage. The title granted its holder the right to expound Torah in public settings, such as schools or other gatherings, to independently establish halakhic norms for other Jews, and to sit on rabbinic courts of law.

In addition to these teaching and legal privileges, however, the rabbinic Sage enjoyed another kind of authority. It was grounded in his complete mastery of scripture and his ability to recall, analyze, and apply to life traditions of rabbinic learning known as Mishnah, Repeated Tradition (see Chapter Two, pages 85–87). The Sage's power to shape the lives and consciences of his disciples lay in great measure in their perception of him. He represented a living embodiment of what Torah could mean in human life. The Written and Oral Torah were at his total command; they flowed from his mouth as life-giving waters do from a fountain.

While discoursing on Torah, he formed sentences and thoughts not in the Aramaic and Greek dialects of other Jews, but in the classic Hebrew phrases of the scriptures and the traditions of ancient Sages going back to Moses himself. His teaching, moreover, was not confined to his public discourses. Even his most common actions—the way he blessed his bread, uttered his prayers, purchased his vegetables, or cleaned himself in the latrine—could become sources of halakhah, disciplines by which disciples might pursue their own self-perfection. As an embodiment of Torah, he had as well penetrating insight into each disciple's character; his rebuke was devastating, while his advice and praise could set a disciple on his own path to perfecting the discipline of Torah.

Rabbinic communities probably began as collections of households in which the male heads were disciples of one or another Sage. Such households would have conducted their affairs in light of the Sage's teaching, as mediated through the householders, his disciples. Prior to the third century CE, it is possible that communities formed around the specific Sages might have had antagonistic relations with those formed around others. Reports about conflict between the first-century disciples of Shammai and Hillel may preserve memories of such social as well as legal conflict.

The Mishnah (Shab. 1:5; elaborated in PT Shab. 1:7, 3c), for example, recalls a day on which the disciples of Shammai "packed" a study session to ensure the suppression of the views of the disciples of Hillel. In another case, a Sage is told that he "deserved to forfeit his life" for following a prayer practice of the disciples of Shammai (Mishnah Ber. 1:3).[42] But from the time of Rabbi Judah the Patriarch's ascendancy in the late second century, the rabbinic communities seem to have displayed tolerance for the minority traditions among them.

In any event, minority viewpoints were carefully preserved, becoming part of the legal tradition awaiting the disciple's mastery. Rabbi's Mishnah is rich in reports of Sages' disputes regarding details of halakhic practice as well as in views regarded as superseded. Indeed, it is largely composed of such disagreements. The mishnaic tractate Eduyot 1:5 contains an important justification for preserving them:

> Now why do they record the opinion of an individual in addition to that of the majority, since the halakhah accords with the majority opinion? So that when a court prefers the minority opinion it may rely upon it.

In other words, minority positions were carefully preserved so that, through judicial creativity, they might one day re-enter tradition and have new life. The value of such views was stressed, a few centuries after the compilation of the Mishnah, in a famous passage of the Babylonian Talmud. In response to a dispute between the disciples of Hillel and Shammai, a Heavenly Voice is said to have rung out, declaring: "Both opinions express the views of the Living God—but the halakhah conforms to the view of the disciples of Hillel!" (BT Eruv. 13b).

From the third century and afterward, then, halakhic disputes appear to define legitimate ranges of difference within a community rather than the norms of mutually exclusive societies. The Babylonian Talmud portrays on nearly every page the diversity of rabbinic custom as practiced by different teachers until well into the sixth and seventh centuries. At any rate, the differences rabbinic groups preserved among themselves were insignificant in comparison to the differences between rabbinic communities on the whole and nonrabbinic Jewish communities. To enter a rabbinic community was to undergo a kind of conversion, not to Judaism, but to the Torah tradition embodied by a particular Sage. He and his disciples would become the guide of a new household into the orbit of halakhic discipline.

This rabbinic model of an intentional Judaic community was obviously distinct from the exclusivism cultivated at Qumran or the monasticism of the Therapeutae. In contrast, it sought to include the entire community of Israel. The rabbis, that is, were apostles of Torah in the same way that early Jewish followers of Jesus had been apostles of the Messiah. Historians still debate the degree of rabbinic enthusiasm for non-Jewish converts.[43] But there is no doubt that the Sages' primary interest was focused upon a fundamental social goal within ethnically Jewish communities. They wanted to govern Jewish society beyond the circle of immediate disciples, on the basis of rabbinic legal tradition as contained in the Oral Torah as a whole. Thus, as we saw in Chapter One, they sought and readily gained permission from Roman and Mesopotamian authorities to establish themselves as the justices of local Jewish courts and civic leaders of Jewish communities.

For the Sages, therefore, it was not enough to be a personal guide over a disciple's private quest. Seeking through moral suasion and personal example to convert Jewish individuals to the halakhic path, they also sought the political power to assert the authority of halakhic tradition as Jewish public law. As a religious style of life, halakhic tradition sought an inner transformation of natural Jews into a Holy People. As a social policy, however, halakhah sought to shape the public dimension of Jewish society according to rabbinic traditions, regardless of the inner feelings of the larger community.

If Jewish farmers in the Land of Israel could be made to sow and harvest their crops in accord with halakhic norms, if Jewish merchants in Tiberias or Antioch could be required to employ rabbinically regulated weights and measures, if Jewish litigants in Rome or Ktesiphon could be required to accept rabbinic mediation, then the transformation of the inner life of Israel would follow. All of Israel could become an intentional community of disciples inwardly as well as a natural community pursuing Jewish national customs in accord with rabbinic dictates.

Conclusions

This chapter has shown how a single religion can gain expression in a multiplicity of communal and social forms. If you want to imagine early Judaism as a single religious world, you need to account for the different sorts of communities Jews created within that world. Our study suggests that it is better to imagine the various intentional communities as discrete Judaic worlds, societies with clear views regarding who was inside, who was outside, and why the distinction was crucial.

As we have seen, all certainly acknowledged a body of national custom that defined natural or ethnic membership in the Jewish people. But even such obvious social facts could be controversial, as in the case of the Samaritans, Israelites who refused to be Jews, has shown. Often, national custom was the point of departure only for a more crucial journey: the attempt to embody the national tradition in a communal form demanding intense personal reorientation. The communities we have studied shared the view that Jewish life required a kind of conversion, a transformation of the person. That transformation was conceived as more than therapy for unhappy personalities. The healing was achieved by reorienting people to reality itself, a reality that included, as its principal foundation, the God of Israel. Life in these communities was conceived as continuous pursuit of such reorientation.

Notes

1. The question of how ancient Jews understood their relationship to Jewish and non-Jewish "others" or outsiders is an important one, for it helps us to see how they viewed themselves as well. A scholarly, but instructive, article on this topic is that of Y. Amir, "The Term *ioudaismos*: A Study in Jewish-Hellenistic Self-Identification," *Immanuel* 14 (1982), pp. 34–41. A useful collection of articles on the question has been edited by Jacob Neusner and Ernest S. Frerichs, *"To See Ourselves as Others See Us": Christians, Jews, "Others" in Late Antiquity* (Chico, CA: Scholars Press, 1985).

2. For the century immediately surrounding the emergence of Christianity, the most comprehensive source of information on the diversity of Judaism is E.P. Sanders, *Judaism: Practice & Belief, 63 BCE–66 CE* (London and Philadelphia: SCM Press and Trinity Press International, 1992).

   A manageable survey extending a few centuries forward, with an excellent bibliography, is that of Tessa Rajak, "The Jewish Community and Its Boundaries," in Judith Lieu, John North, and Tessa Rajak, eds., *The Jews Among Pagans and Christians in the Roman Empire* (London and New York: Routledge, 1992), pp. 9–28. More in-depth discussions of various diaspora Jewish communities can be found in the essays collected in Shaye J.D. Cohen and Ernest S. Frerichs, eds., *Diasporas in Antiquity* (Atlanta: Scholars Press, 1993).

3. The translation is adapted from Menahem Stern, ed. and tr., *Greek and Latin Authors on Jews and Judaism, II: From Tacitus to Simplicius* (Jerusalem: Israel Academy of Sciences and Humanities, 1980), p. 351.

4. The translation is adapted from Menahem Stern, ed. and tr., *Greek and Latin Authors on Jews and Judaism, I: From Herodotus to Plutarch* (Jerusalem: Israel Academy of Sciences and Humanities, 1976), p. 555.

5. The translation is adapted from R.J.H. Shutt, "Letter of Aristeas," in James H. Charlesworth, *The Old Testament Pseudepigrapha, Vol. 2* (Garden City, NY: Doubleday & Company), pp. 22–23.

6. The translation is from Stern, *Greek and Latin Authors, I*, p. 436.

7. The translation of this and the following passage is from F.H. Colson, tr., *Philo VII* (Cambridge, MA, and London: Harvard University Press and Heinemann, 1934), pp. 101–105.

8. The translation is from Wayne A. Meeks, ed., *The HarperCollins Study Bible: New Revised Standard Version with the Apocryphal/Deuterocanonical Books* (New York: HarperCollins, 1993), pp. 1703–1704.

9. A clear effort to identify the kinds of non-Jews who became attracted to Judaism is available in Martin Goodman, "Jewish Proselytizing in the First Century," in Lieu, North, and Rajak, *Jews Among Pagans and Christians*, pp. 53–78.

10. He discusses the events in his *Jewish Antiquities* 20.2.1–5, translated by Louis H. Feldman, *Josephus: Jewish Antiquities. Books 18–20. Vol. 9* (Cambridge, MA, and London: Harvard University Press and Heinemann, 1969), pp. 399–419.

11. Such contributors are discussed in Rajak, *Jews Among Pagans and Christians*, pp. 22–24, and in a technical but fascinating article by Ross S. Kraemer, "On the Meaning of the Term 'Jew' in Greco-Roman Inscriptions," in *Harvard Theological Review* 82 (1989), pp. 35–53.

12. The richest amount of information comes from rabbinic literature. The rabbis, however, were more interested in the legal status of the converts than in their psychological profiles. The best recent discussion of rabbinic attitudes toward the convert is that of Gary G. Porton, *The Stranger Within Your Gates: Converts and Conversion in Rabbinic Literature* (Chicago: The University of Chicago Press, 1994).

    A useful survey of Jewish attitudes toward converts prior to 70 CE is that of Scot McKnight, *A Light Among the Gentiles: Jewish Missionary Activity in the Second Temple Period* (Minneapolis: Augsburg/Fortress Press, 1990). For the later Roman Empire, you can consult Martin Goodman, *Mission and Conversion* (Oxford: Oxford University Press, 1994).

13. In addition to the articles under "Judaism," in David Noel Freedman, ed., *The Anchor Bible Dictionary, Vol. III* (New York: Doubleday, 1992), pp. 1037–1089, Alan F. Segal, *Rebecca's Children: Judaism and Christianity in the Roman World* (Cambridge, MA: Harvard University Press, 1986), pp. 39–67 offers a manageable discussion of the varieties of Judaic communities in Palestine and the Diaspora. An excellent discussion of Palestinian forms of Judaism in particular is that of James D.G. Dunn, "Judaism in the Land of Israel in the First Century," in Jacob Neusner, ed., *Judaism in Late Antiquity, Part 2: Historical Syntheses* (Leiden: E.J. Brill, 1995), pp. 229–261.

14. The most complete preliminary introduction to the history of the Samaritan community is the article by Robert T. Anderson, "Samaritans," in *Anchor Bible Dictionary, Vol. V,* pp. 940–947.

15. I translate the text of August Freiherr von Gall, ed., *Der Hebräische Pentateuch der Samaritäner* (Giessen, Germany: Topelmann, 1918), p. 158.

16. The ancient sources regarding the Dosithean movement are all analyzed in Stanley J. Isser, *The Dositheans: A Samaritan Sect in Late Antiquity* (Leiden, The Netherlands: E.J. Brill, 1976).

17. The Dead Sea Scrolls, first discovered in 1947, have often been sensationalized as containing "secrets" about Jesus, the origins of Christianity, or other aspects of ancient Judaism. Speculation was heightened by the excessive delays in publishing many of the manuscripts. Since the early 1990s, however, the entire collection has become available.

    These scrolls (mostly in partially decomposed fragments) contain, for the most part, copies of biblical books or works of biblical interpretation. Some texts, however, are theological or historical tracts possibly representing the ideas of the group's leaders. A useful overview of the religious world emerging from the Yakhad's writings can be found in Johann Maier, "The Judaic System of the Dead Sea Scrolls," in Jacob Neusner, ed., *Judaism in Late Antiquity, 2,* pp. 84–108.

18. To appreciate the full range of views on the origins and nature of the Yakhad, and especially the new perspectives raised by the "Halakhic Letter," it is best to compare the recent works of two excellent scholars, James C. VanderKam, *The Dead Sea Scrolls Today* (Grand Rapids: Eerdmans Publishing Co., 1994) and

Lawrence H. Schiffman, *Reclaiming the Dead Sea Scrolls* (Philadelphia: Jewish Publication Society, 1994).

19. I quote from the Commentary on Habakkuk, translated in G. Vermes, ed. and tr., *Dead Sea Scrolls in English*, 3rd ed. (London: Penguin Books, 1987), p. 287. The fourth edition of this valuable work reached me too late for use in the present volume. Another excellent and up-to-date translation is that of Florentino Garcia Martinez, *The Dead Sea Scrolls Translated: The Qumran Texts in English*. Tr., Wilfred G.E. Watson (Leiden, The Netherlands: E.J. Brill, 1994).

20. This battle is described in the War Rule. See Vermes, *Dead Sea Scrolls*, pp. 105–127.

21. Ibid., p. 85.

22. Ibid., p. 90.

23. Ibid., p. 62.

24. Ibid., p. 70.

25. Ibid., p, 69.

26. Ibid., p. 69.

27. Community Rule, 8. In ibid., p. 73.

28. My discussion of the Therapeutae is based upon the pioneering article of Ross S. Kraemer, "Monastic Jewish Women in Greco-Roman Egypt: Philo Judaeus on the Therapeutrides," Signs 14 (1989), pp. 342–370. This has been incorporated into a more general chapter on "Jewish Women's Religious Lives and Offices in the Greco-Roman Diaspora" in Ross Shepard Kraemer, *Her Share of the Blessings: Women's Religions Among Pagans, Jews, and Christians in the Greco-Roman World* (New York: Oxford University Press, 1992), pp. 106–127.

29. Translated by F.H. Colson, *Philo IX* (Cambridge, MA and London: Harvard University Press and Heinemann, 1917), pp. 127–128.

30. Ibid., p. 133.

31. Ibid., pp. 167–169

32. Ibid., p. 155.

33. "Christ" is not the family-name of Jesus, but a Greek word (*christos*) that means "anointed one," equivalent to the Hebrew *mashiakh* or Aramaic *meshikha* ("Messiah"). The name "Jesus" is an English form of the Greek *iesous*, which corresponds to the Hebrew *yeshua*, a common form of the name "Joshua." The native Aramaic of the earliest generation of Jesus' Jewish Palestinian followers was rapidly replaced by the Greek spoken by both Jews and non-Jews outside of Palestine and Syria.

34. The question of Christian origins has generated a massive body of scholarship on the nature of "Jewish Christianity." The best orientation is provided by the following two articles: Gottfried Schille, "Early Jewish Christianity," in *Anchor Bible Dictionary, Vol. I*, pp. 935–938, and Stephen G. Wilson, "Jewish-Christian Relations, 70–170 CE," *Anchor Bible Dictionary, Vol. III*, pp. 834–839.

    For greater depth, you may consult Paula Fredericksen, *From Jesus to Christ: The Origins of the New Testament Images of Jesus* (New Haven: Yale University Press, 1988), Larry W. Hurtado, *One God, One Lord: Early Christian Devotion and Ancient Jewish Monotheism* (Philadelphia: Fortress Press, 1988), or Jack T. Sanders, *Schismatics, Sectariaus, Dissidents, Deviants: The First One Hundred Years of Jewish-Christian Relations* (Valley Forge, PA; Trinity Press International 1993).

35. The best discussion of how early Christians applied to Jesus forms of veneration that other Jews reserved for angelic figures or God is found in Hurtado, *One God One Lord*, pp. 100–114.

36. Kraemer, *Her Share of the Blessings*, pp. 128–156, offers a lucid description of women in Christian communities of the first century after Jesus' death.

37. A good account of the psychology of Paul's conversion as reflected in his thought is offered by Alan Segal, *Paul the Convert* (New Haven: Yale University Press, 1990), pp. 96–116. Lloyd Gaston, *Paul and the Torah* (Vancouver: University of British Columbia Press, 1987) is a fine place to start a study of Paul's conceptions of Israel and Torah.

38. The closest thing to an introductory account of rabbinic communal life from its origins through the rise of Islam is that of Jacob Neusner, *From Testament to Torah: An Introduction to Judaism in Its Formative Age* (Englewood Cliffs, NJ: Prentice Hall, 1988). Neusner's book focuses more on the intellectual traditions of the Sages than on their communal forms. Yet, it is the best place from which to move on into more technical studies, of which I mention only one: Lee I. Levine, *The Rabbinic Class of Roman Palestine in Late Antiquity* (Jerusalem and New York: Yad Izhak ben Zvi and Jewish Theological Seminary, 1989).

39. For a taste of the rabbinic dietary rules you might consult the mishnaic tractate Hullin ("Common Food") in Jacob Neusner, ed. and tr., *The Mishnah: A New Translation* (New Haven: Yale University Press, 1988), pp. 765–786.

40. The rules for the courtyard *eruv* are in the mishnaic tractate Eruvin, chaps. 6–7, in ibid., pp. 218–223.

41. Rabbinic rules for these matters are gathered in the various tractates of the Mishnah's third Order, the Order of Women. They are all translated in ibid.

42. These and other traditions about these two famous bodies of disciples have been collected and studied from the perspective of legal history by Jacob Neusner, *The Rabbinic Traditions About the Pharisees Before 70, Part II: The Houses* (Leiden, The Netherlands: E.J. Brill, 1971).

43. The pros and cons are fully explored in Martin Goodman, *Mission and Conversion*, and Gary Porton, *The Stranger Within Your Gates*.

Five

Ritual Space
and Performance
in Early Judaism

Introduction

In an earlier discussion of the symbolic vocabulary of Judaic worlds (Chapter Three, pages 96–113), we explored how Jews imagined the structure of the cosmos and how they thought about their place in the past and the future. Judaic worlds, although differing on certain details, were routinely built upon shared images of the cosmos and the various orders of being from heaven to earth. You might have wondered how people came to such conceptions and why they were held with such conviction. Much more was involved than the fact that knowledge of the heavenly order was contained in venerable writings.

We see in this chapter that these conceptions were convincing because people could correlate them to their personal experience. For them, the highest reaches of the heavens were more than matters of speculation or belief, for aspects of the heavenly world could be made present in a concrete form in their own earthly communities. Similarly, the vanished time of the past and the "not yet" of the future could be made tangible, to some degree, in the here and now. This experiential component of Judaic conceptions of reality was made possible through ritual.

It is as difficult to define ritual as it is to define religion. For the purposes of our discussion, it will be helpful to interpret ritual as a certain kind of performance. From this perspective *rituals are stereotyped, frequently repeated combinations of action and speech that normally occur in a particular place set apart for the purpose of the performance.* The physical space surrounding the ritual actors becomes a kind of stage and the observers a kind of participating audience.

This use of a dramatic analogy points out that, like a play, ritual creates a setting that dislodges the sense of everyday reality. In its place, there emerges a representation of the way things, beyond superficial appearances, really are or might be. In the time occupied by the ritual, that is to say, the physical and social surroundings of the mundane world are penetrated by worlds beyond the everyday.

A clearing in a field surrounded by stones or a room decked out with sanctified objects becomes a place to experience some world or aspect of reality other than that known in normal space and time. People gathered within such spaces, accordingly, share to a greater or lesser degree in this reorganization of perception. They permit themselves to become part of the drama they witness; they find their place in the world evoked by the drama. Accordingly, their acceptance of that world's reality is grounded in the powerful testimony of personal experience.[1]

The Jerusalem Temple, at the center of the political and religious life of the Jews, provided the most widely recognized "official" ritual setting in ancient Judaism. We, therefore, describe the ritual space it created, some of the rituals performed there, and the elements of the heavenly world it represented to those who thronged to it. Both before and after the Temple's destruction, however, other kinds of less majestic ritual spaces served as settings for performance that brought the heavenly order or other times and places into experience. We examine two such spaces in particular, the synagogue and the home.

Each in distinctive ways provided a setting for re-creating or reinterpreting experiences originally reserved for Temple priests and the commoners who observed its spectacles. But just as important, each represented elements of Judaic worlds that were neglected by the particular sacrificial focus of the Temple. In examining the synagogue and the home as ritual settings, we devote most of our attention to the ritual performances of the rabbinic halakhic tradition. Of the Jewish literatures of antiquity, rabbinic writings offer the clearest examples of how ritual performance relates to the worlds of the performers.

The Jerusalem Temple as a Ritual Center

Most surviving information about the Second Temple concerns the massively renovated structure begun under Herod. The work started about 20

Herod's Temple Viewed from the Southwest

Source: Reproduced by permission of the artist, Leon Ritmeyer, and Hershel Shanks, Editor, Biblical Archaeology Society.

BCE and was completed less than a decade before the Temple's destruction in 70 CE. This was one of the largest Temple complexes of its time, encompassing more than 169,000 square yards. Like its Solomonic, Persian, and Hasmonean predecessors, Herod's was housed on a low hill adjoining the eastern wall of Jerusalem, facing the Mount of Olives. The Temple included a main Sanctuary, a courtyard for sacrificial rites, and adjoining courtyards for visitors and worshippers. It stood at the center of an enormous, roughly rectangular terrace running to the north and south of the city wall. If Jewish writers of the time, such as Josephus, are to be believed, it was one of the marvelous national Temples of the ancient world.[2]

The Ritual Setting

In addition to its physical magnificence, Herod's Temple inherited the aura of sanctity enjoyed by its predecessors in Israel's historical memory. The Temple of Solomon, which stood for some three-and-a-half centuries prior to 587 BCE, had preserved the holiness of the desert Tent of Meeting, the first shrine established by Moses as a dwelling place for the God of Israel. The Second Temple, rebuilt by 515 BCE, was seen as the smaller, but still holy, embodiment of God's promise to dwell among his people. Herod's Temple was a far grander structure than its Persian or Hasmonean predecessors. Its very grandeur added to the international prestige of the God and People whom it represented and the Land it protected.

The Temple linked Jews to the world of heaven as well as serving as a visible link to the Jewish national past. Many regarded the Temple as the earthly manifestation of an ethereal palace that existed in God's domain. Moses was said to have seen the model on Sinai (Ex. 25:9, 40), and Ezekiel had been given a tour (Ezek. 40–48) by an angel. Some apocalyptic visionaries, like those of the Enoch tradition (Chapter Three, pages 110–111), described journeys of other ancient prophets to the Throne of God in a heavenly Temple.

In addition to its capacity to evoke speculation about its heavenly counterpart, the Temple was also viewed as a visual representation of the cosmos itself. Josephus, historian and priest, offers an example of such conceptions. He wrote that certain furnishings of the Temple served as reminders of cosmic realities. The embroidered curtain that covered the entrance to the main Sanctuary represented to him the main elements of creation: earth, air, fire, and water. Similarly, some of its inner furnishings recalled the cosmic order of the Zodiac and the four corners of the sea and earth.[3]

For most, to see the Temple on earth was to come as close as they ever would to heaven. Precisely because it was perceived to be an earthly version of a heavenly prototype, the Temple was a powerful symbol of the unity of all elements of God's cosmic design. Within its boundaries, the heavenly, earthly, and social realms were all joined into a seamless whole. Israelite priestly tradition, we saw in Chapter Three, tended to imagine the earth's surface as divided between the clean land of Israel and the unclean lands of the nations, the holiness of the Land and the commonness of all other space. The ground plan of the Herodian Temple mirrored this conception of things.

The Gentile's Court. We begin with the Temple's outer reaches. The main entrance and exits to the compound were the two Huldah Gates on the southern perimeter. Visitors entering from this direction found themselves under beautifully columned porticoes that opened into an enormous plaza. Opposite stood the sanctuary—a massive stone structure covered in marble, polished granite, and gold—surrounded by its own wall, running east and west across the central plaza. This plaza could be populated by any visitor to the Temple. But it was set aside especially for non-Jews who, out of courtesy or a sense of admiration for the God of Israel, might wish to make a sacrificial gift at his shrine. They could purchase a small goat or lamb from a merchant in the porticoed area and have it conveyed to a priest to be offered in their name.

But they could not penetrate any farther than this outer plaza. As non-Jews, the more holy precincts of the Temple area were closed to them. Signs in Greek and Latin made the point clearly: "No foreigner is to enter within the forecourt and the balustrade around the sanctuary. Whoever is caught

---

The Heavenly Model of the Sanctuary:
Revelations to Moses and Ezekiel

The theme of the heavenly, eternal model of the physical Temple is richly represented in the literature of the Second Temple period. It echoes in the canonical Scriptures as well. The first selection is set in the context of the revelation at Sinai, where Moses receives specific instructions from God regarding the construction of the wilderness Tent of Meeting. The second is part of a detailed description of the tour of the exiled prophet, Ezekiel, through the heavenly Temple.

> The LORD spoke to Moses, saying: Tell the Israelite people to bring Me gifts; you shall accept gifts from Me from every person whose heart so moves him. . . . And let them make Me a sanctuary that I may dwell among them. Exactly as I show you—the pattern of the Tabernacle and the pattern of all its furnishings—so shall you make it. Exodus 25:1–9
>
> Now you, O mortal, describe the Temple to the House of Israel, and let them measure its design. But let them be ashamed of their iniquities: When they are ashamed of all they have done, make known to them the plan of the Temple, and its layout, its exists and entrances—its entire plan, and all the laws and instructions, pertaining to its entire plan. Write it down before their eyes, that they may faithfully follow its entire plan and all its laws. Ezekiel 43:10–11

(*Translation: Tanakh* [Jewish Publication Society, 1988].)

---

will have himself to blame for his subsequent death."[4] In view of the extreme concentration of holiness within the Temple itself, a non-Israelite presence would be a violation of its sanctity and a defilement of its purity.

Courts of Women and Israelites. Not even Jews could enter the Temple at will. Those who wished to present offerings or witness the sacrificial service would have purified themselves, prior to entry, of any contact with death, bodily discharges, or other substances deemed to convey pollution to humans.[5] Only those who had immersed in water and were prepared for the sacrificial conclusion of their purification procedure could enter the Temple area. They would enter through a separate eastern entrance.

On the inside, a series of inner courts, separated by ascending steps and gates, guided a successively more exclusive group of visitors westward and

Floor Plan of the Herodian Temple

Key: 9–10: Huldah Gates; 13: Gentile Court; 21: Women's Court; 24: Nikanor Gate; 25: Outer Altar; 26: Israelite Court; 28: Priest's Court; 30: First Chamber of Sanctuary; 31: Holy of Holies.

Source: Th. Busink, *Der Tempel von Jerusalem* (Leiden: E. J. Brill, 1970, 1980), p. 1179. Reproduced by permission.

---

upward, toward the Sanctuary itself. A square outer court at the eastern end of the Temple, roughly 245 feet on each side, was designated the Women's Court. Jews of both sexes might gather there, but women normally could get no closer to the sacrificial service than the Nikanor Gate. It was centrally placed in a wall that divided the Women's Court from a second, smaller space called the Israelite Court. Unless women had the obligation to be involved in a purification sacrifice, they had to view the sacrificial acts from a balcony in their court. Men, however, could ascend the fifteen semi-circular steps through the Nikanor Gate into the Israelite Court, a narrow rectangular area 245 feet long and 20 feet wide.

The Priests' Court. The Israelite Court was bounded by a stone wall about a yard high. Jewish men of nonlevitical, nonpriestly descent could pass no farther unless they were obliged to engage in a purification sacrifice or other rite. But they had a clear view of the priestly activity, for before them lay the Priests' Court. Here, in a large space 245 feet long and 340 feet wide, the actual sacrificial rituals were performed by the priests to the musical accompaniment of the Levite's songs, cymbals, flutes, horns, and stringed instruments.

This court was dominated by the implements of the sacrificial rituals. On the northern end, cattle were slaughtered and butchered by priestly workers. In the center, toward the south, stood the altar, a cube 58 feet long on each side and almost 30 feet high. Priests would ascend a ramp to place on its fires the carcasses of slaughtered animals and to smear its four corners with sacrificial blood. To the east of the altar stood a large basin that provided fresh water for priestly ablutions.

The Sanctuary. Dominating the Priests' Court, at its easternmost end, was the Sanctuary. Its facade of pure white marble and gold plating stood about 182 feet high and was equally broad. Whereas Levites served within the Priests' Court, only priests, the holiest of the Israelite tribes, could walk up the twelve steps that led through golden doors into the eastern part of the Sanctuary. They entered a long, rectangular room (about 73 X 36 feet) illuminated by a seven-branched, golden candelabrum (*menorah*). At the eastern end stood a golden altar for incense and a golden table that held twelve loaves of bread, in accordance with the requirements of Exodus 25:23–30. Priests would daily clean and kindle the menorah, offer incense, and, on Sabbath Eve, change the loaves. But even they could penetrate no farther than this antechamber.

The Holy of Holies. At the extreme western end of the Sanctuary, behind an embroidered curtain, was the holiest, purest spot on earth, the Holy of Holies. It was a perfectly square room, about 36 feet on each side and equally as high. No one but the High Priest could enter it; and even then, he could do so only on the Day of Absolution (*Yom haKippurim*). This was the holiest day of the year, for on it the people of Israel and the Land itself were purged of the year's accumulation of sin.

In the wilderness Tent of Meeting and, later, in Solomon's Temple, this space had been the resting place of a large chest, the Ark of the Covenant, reputed to contain the Mosaic tablets from Sinai. The Holy of Holies also had once contained a throne of gold-plated models of angelic beings, Cherubim, whose wings sheltered the Ark and provided a throne for the hovering Glory (Hebrew: *kavod*) of God. From above the Cherubim, the scripture reported, God's voice had rung out to command Moses, Aaron, and generations of High Priests after them.

But these holy objects had been lost in 587 BCE. What remained, according to later rabbinic tradition, was a flat stone called the Foundation Stone. Upon it, some rabbinic Sages insisted, the world had been created. Their insistence upon this point highlights the cosmic function of the Holy of Holies itself. This room served as the meeting of heaven and earth, where all the forces of creation were present in their most intense form. At the center of the Temple's rings of holiness, therefore, was nothing at all, an emptiness filled with the potential of infinite presence. God's Glory or Presence (Hebrew: *shekhinah*), that part of his being capable of worldly embodiment, could descend through it from the heavenly Throne at any instant.

A Model of the Cosmos. This sketch of the Temple complex suggests how it modeled the relations of all dimensions of the world—the cosmic, the geographical, and the social. The Holy of Holies assured access to the upper reaches of heaven, drawing from them a flow of holiness that descended in progressively broader waves toward the lower regions. Because of its holiness, the Holy of Holies required extreme protection from pollution. Accordingly, all the world's geographical and social space was mapped out in relation to the Holy of Holies in terms of various levels of purity.

The non-Jewish nations, represented in the farthest outer court, stood at the borders of the world; at the center, within the walls of the Temple, was the domain of Israel. Thus, holy and common lands were represented in the world of the Temple complex and separated from each other as well. Moreover, within the confines of purity there were also divisions and grades. Jews were divided into classes, each finding a place in the Temple world matching its potential for holiness. Within this anthropology of holiness, men approached the holiest space more closely than women, priests and Levites more closely than male commoners, priests more closely than Levites, and the High Priest more closely than other priests.

In the hierarchy of heaven and earth, then, the High Priest, costumed in special vestments symbolizing celestial mysteries, stood more closely than any human to the world of heaven. He and his priestly kinsmen served as the human community that established and maintained connection between the various orders of being. Their labor in the Temple preserved all other orders of being from collapse. Upon them, the people of Israel, the Land of Israel, and, ultimately, the entire cosmos and its population all depended.

Ritual Activities

The ritual activities taking place in the Temple had an impact far beyond the boundaries of the Temple complex and the experience of its priestly officiants. As a ritual representation of the cosmos, it helped to define for Jews the nature of all space surrounding it as well. If the Temple was the hub or center of the world, everything else could be viewed as finding a place on a

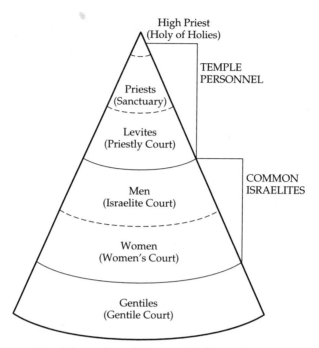

The Hierarchy of Human Holiness/Purity

The geographical space of the Temple buffers the Holy of Holies from penetration by sources of uncleanness. Holiness and cleanness are correlated values. This correlation can be represented graphically as a cone. At the base are those visitors to the Temple who are by nature beyond the continuum of holiness and cleanness. They are confined to the Court of the Gentiles. At the pinnacle is the High Priest of Israel, who enters the Holy of Holies itself in a state of absolute holiness and purity. Between are various gradations of Israelites, who can penetrate successively more exclusive Temple areas.

spoke emanating from that center toward the periphery of space. Thus, the outer reaches of the Jewish Diaspora could establish connections to the Temple despite huge distances. We can appreciate the Temple's capacity to transform the world around it by focusing on some typical activities.

THE TAMID OFFERING

The most frequently repeated sacrificial ritual was the twice-daily Perpetual Offering (Hebrew: *tamid*). At dawn and at dusk, a yearling lamb was slaughtered in the Priests' Court. To the accompaniment of fried wheat cakes and wine, its body was wholly burnt up on the altar's fires. These offerings were seen as the means to establish proper connection between the earth and the power that created and sustained it. Sacrifices returned a portion of the bounty of the Land of Israel—its meat, grain, wine, and oil—to its heavenly Lord. Satisfying the divine claim upon the Land of Israel, the priests cleared a path for divine blessing to pulse into the world through the altar. Such blessing protected the Land of Israel from blight and drought and enabled the world to remain firm on the foundations originally created by God.[6]

The ritual of sacrifice, upon which the life of the world depended, was itself dependent upon the taking of life. Called *avodah* in Hebrew, or "service," the sacrificial process was an arduous act of killing performed by a priest acting as a holy executioner. Struggling, bleating victims had to be bound, slaughtered, disemboweled, dismembered, and their parts disposed of in carefully prescribed ways. As sacrificial blood spurted from the throats of slaughtered lambs, priestly assistants collected it in bowls, stirring the hot blood to prevent coagulation until the officiating priest was free to sprinkle it on the horns of the altar, after which the carcass was placed upon the fire.

The culmination of the Tamid Offering was the pouring of wine upon the altar and the conferring of a priestly blessing upon the assembled community. A pre-Hasmonean writer, Joshua ben Sira, described it as follows around 180 BCE (Sirakh 50:16–21):

> Then the sons of Aaron shouted; they blew their trumpets of hammered metal; they sounded a mighty fanfare as a reminder before the Most High. Then all the people together quickly fell to the ground on their faces to worship their Lord, the Almighty, God Most High. Then the [Levite] singers praised him with their voices in sweet and full-toned melody. And the people of the LORD Most High offered their prayers before the Merciful One, until the order of worship of the LORD was ended, and they completed his ritual. Then Simon [the High Priest] came down and raised his hands over the whole congregation of Iraelites, to pronounce the blessing of the LORD with his lips, and to glory in his name; and they bowed down in worship a second time, to receive the blessing from the Most High.

When the spectacle of the victim's death and physical destruction was completed, the entire community in the Temple court acknowledged the priest's success in bringing the power of life anew into the world. The worshippers sent their own adorations of God skyward with the aromatic smoke of the sacrificial victims whose deaths they had witnessed.

Although the priests did the work, the participatory witness of a communal audience was a crucial part of the Temple's ritual life. The presence of witnesses, indeed, transformed the service from a private priestly rite into a public event that served as a tutorial in priestly conceptions of the world. These were made immediately tangible to the nonpriestly majority through the powerful media of massive architectural presence and ritual pageantry. Indeed, the experience of the Temple, rather than literary formulations of law and theology, were the primary means by which common Israelites would have identified with the biblical description of Israel as "a kingdom of priests and a holy nation." (Ex. 19:6)

PILGRIMAGE FESTIVALS AND THE SPACE OF THE DIASPORA

In addition to daily offerings and those of Sabbaths and New Moons, the Temple calendar provided for other grand public spectacles of sacrifice. These were the thrice-yearly mass pilgrimages associated with the spring harvest festival of Pesah (Passover), the early summer barley festival of Shavuot (Pentecost), and the autumnal New Year season that culminated in the festival of Sukkot (Booths). On these Pilgrimage Festivals, Jews from Palestine and many points in the Diaspora would stream toward Jerusalem.

There, males in particular were obliged to show themselves in the Temple with the Festival Presentation Offering required in the Torah of Moses (e.g., Ex. 23:14–18). Only part of this offering was burned; the rest served as the menu of a festive meal that men would share with their households. Few diaspora Jews could make frequent pilgrimages. It is likely, however, that most would return to their homes with vivid reports of the sights and sounds of the Temple, an encouragement to others to undertake a similar journey.

Thus, the calendar of Pilgrimage Festivals enabled the Temple to transform the entire Jewish Diaspora into a series of spokes emanating from the center of the Temple. Along these spokes, Jews could move back and forth between the center of the world and its circumference. The rhythms of the sacrificial seasons transformed the Temple into a kind of heart. Its beat circulated a stream of Jews throughout the body of Israel in a perpetual systolic-diastolic rhythm, geared to the cycles of the seasons.

THE TEMPLE RITUALS AND THE PALESTINIAN COUNTRYSIDE

For Jews who lived within the environs of Judea, the Temple's presence was a more regular, if slightly less spectacular, part of experience. Apart from the official Sabbath and Festival calendar, the random events of private life would also attract local Jews to the Temple. Men and women were obliged to celebrate their purification from moral or physical pollution by bringing an appropriate sacrificial animal to the Temple to be offered by priestly officiants. Communion offerings of cattle could be brought at various occasions as gestures of thanks for divine blessing. The poor participated for the relatively small price of a few pigeons or some grain meal.

The male Judean population was given an active role in the Temple's life-giving rituals apart from their personal sacrificial offerings. According to reports from many ancient sources, priestly and levitical families throughout the country were organized into twenty-four divisions (Hebrew: *mishmarot*), each of which provided a weekly rotation of sacrificial workers for the Temple. After a week of service, one division would be replaced by another throughout the year.[7]

Men of common origin were enlisted in these divisions as platoons of bystanders (Hebrew: *ma'amadot*). Some commoners would travel to Jerusalem with the priests and Levites of their towns, where they would officially witness the sacrifices as representatives of all Israel. Others would remain in their towns and villages. According to later rabbinic reports (Mishnah Taanit 4:2–3), they participated in the sacrifice by gathering at dawn and late afternoon, the times of the Tamid Offering, to read aloud from the first chapter of the book of Genesis.

At the moment the priests were sustaining creation through their sacrifices, villagers were intoning the story of the world's creation. In a real sense, then, through the bystanders, the ritual life of the priests extended beyond the Temple into the lives of the Judean population. Nonpriestly Jews could incorporate the Temple, as the center of the world, into their own experience around the Temple's actual borders.

Summary

For as long as the Temple stood, the social rhythms associated with its ritual schedule constituted the hub of reality for the Jewish communities of the homeland and the Diaspora alike. Few Jewish communities—the special case of the Samaritans comes to mind—entirely rejected the Temple's claim to be the unique meeting place of heaven and earth and the center of Jewish national unity in geographic dispersion. But that is not to say it enjoyed an absolute monopoly.

Far from it. Even those who revered the Temple and routinely shared in its celebrations participated frequently in other centers of ritual life. These, too, could evoke with power other dimensions of diverse Judaic worlds. When the Temple was destroyed, they began a steady rise to importance. Eventually, the Temple, as a heavenly reality without any physical expression in the material world, functioned as a metaphor for other spaces in which rather different rituals were enacted. One that became increasingly common from the first century CE and onward was the synagogue.

The Synagogue as a Ritual Center

The earliest mention of Jews gathering for religious celebrations outside the sacrificial setting of a Temple does not use the term "synagogue." Archeological remains from third-century BCE Egypt include Greek inscriptional references to an institution called the *proseuche* (prayer place) and suggestions that special buildings might have been set aside for this purpose. The Greek word *synagoge* appears later. It is as likely to refer to a community of people as permanent to the place in which they meet. Thus, the "synagogue of the Jews" often is a synonym for the Jewish community.

Additionally, Greek-speaking Jews used many other terms to describe the nature of their communal gatherings and the places in which they were held (e.g., *semneion* or "sanctuary"; *didaskaleion* or "place of instruction"; *sabbateion* or "Sabbath place"). In order to simplify our discussion, we shall use the term synagogue to designate all such public gatherings of Jews.[8]

It is from only the first century BCE and thereafter that archeologists find remains of buildings in the Diaspora and Palestine that seem to have served as permanent settings for the conduct of Jewish communal activities. Most of the earliest of these buildings are from lands to the west of Palestine, in Egypt and Greece (Delos, from the first century BCE). This has led many to suggest that the synagogue as both a social institution and a physical gathering place originated in the western end of the Jewish Diaspora. An expression of what we have called natural Jewish communities, the synagogue enabled them to celebrate a national identity and continue ancestral customs within the dominant non-Jewish environment.

In contrast to the diaspora situation, synagogues seem to have been less prominent in Palestinian Jewish society prior to the third century CE. One inscription from the late first century BCE, to be discussed later, mentions a synagogue in Jerusalem. But only three buildings likely to be synagogues have been found that existed prior to the late second century CE—those at Gamla, Masada, and Herodium. Jewish ethnic dominance within the Palestinian population, and the influential presence of the Jerusalem Temple, may have hindered an essentially diasporic institution from making much headway in the homeland until the Temple was destroyed. In any event, by the third century, the synagogue building was becoming as common in the areas of heavy Jewish settlement in northern Palestine, such as the Galilee and the Golan Heights, as it was in the Diaspora.

The Ritual Setting

Remains of synagogue buildings, most of which come from the second to sixth centuries, have been identified from Italy to Syria, with important examples in Asia Minor as well. Despite much stylistic diversity, many of these remains confirm reports from ancient writers that the synagogue was a multipurpose gathering place. In addition to teaching and prayer activities, they hosted a variety of other events, including legal proceedings, and might even have served to house travelers. This diversity of synagogue functions perhaps explains why neither the Greco-Roman Temple plans nor that of the Jerusalem Temple provided any architectural models for synagogue builders.

Architectural Conventions. Rather, their architectural inspiration was the repertoire of ground plans and facades commonly found on all manner of public buildings in the ancient world. Usually, there was an open central room with ample space for seating. Larger buildings had many adjoining rooms, presumably for a variety of functions. These aspects of its architectural design suggest that the synagogue was precisely what its Greek name implies: the hub of Jewish life in its town, a central gathering place of local Jews and others attracted to the community of Israel. Larger cities had more than one.

Despite its architectural inspiration, other aspects of the synagogue's design and decoration suggest that gatherings within it had more than a purely social meaning. In a variety of ways, the local scene of, for example, Sardis (Asia Minor) or Tiberias (Galilee) was routinely superimposed upon a more evocative one—that of Jerusalem. Consider the matter of spacial orientation. Although synagogues did not attempt to look like the Temple, in most of them from the third century and onward the seating faced toward the city in which the Temple had stood. Ruins from Italy, Greece, and Asia Minor direct the attention of audiences eastward toward Jerusalem, whereas those in Syria face west. In Galilee and the Golan Heights, to the north of Jerusalem, the synagogues commonly direct attention southward.

This spacial orientation discloses the synagogue's function beyond that of a simple meeting hall; quite literally, it was a place of reorientation. This particular hub of Jewish society was simultaneously a spoke in a much larger wheel, centered in Jerusalem. Jews gathered in one space but were immediately reminded of their relation to another. Synagogue artisans often enhanced this reorientation, self-consciously evoking at every opportunity the sacred space of the Temple.

Temple Symbolism. Most synagogues of this period had impressively carved doorways or other masonry that incorporated Temple ritual objects as symbols into the design. In addition to the *menorah* and *shofar*, symbols recognized as Jewish throughout the Greco-Roman world, artisans usually depicted the *lulav* (palm branch) and the *etrog* (citron), both of which played a prominent role in the Temple celebrations of the autumn festival of Sukkot. The intentions behind the selection of such objects are difficult to identify with certainty. Perhaps they mark off a particular building as belonging to the Jewish nation in Exile. But the persistant emphasis upon Temple objects

Synagogues of Palestine

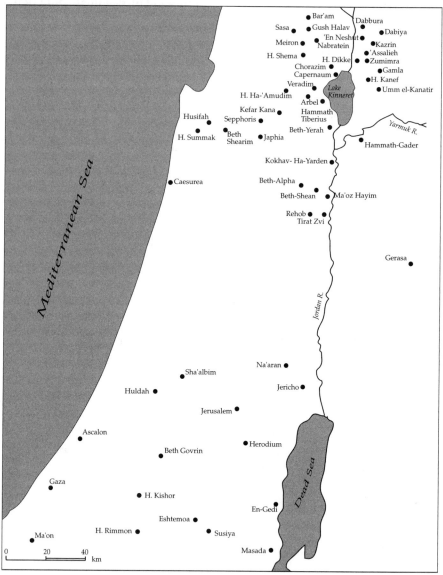

Range of Synagogue Remains, First to Sixth Centuries CE

As these maps demonstrate, there are dozens of archeological sites that have been identified, with various degrees of certainty, as the remains of synagogues.

Source: Maps on this and facing page based on Lee I. Levine, *Ancient Synagogues Revealed* (Detroit: Wayne State University Press, 1982), pages 2, 163.

Synagogues of the Diaspora

Typical Synagogue Floor Plans:
The Basilica

The earliest synagogue finds employ the "basilica" ground plan, as shown above. In this ground plan, the focus of worship is at the narrow end of a rectangular building. Often an indentation or "apse" was built into that wall, presumably for the purpose of reading the Torah or other ritual activity. The inner space is divided by rows of columns. This example is from a fifth- to seventh-century synagogue in Gaza.

Source: Israel Exploration Society, Jeruselum. Used with permission.

Typical Synagogue Floor Plans:
The Broadhouse

This drawing shows the ground plan of the synagogue of Dura Europos, destroyed by a Persian invasion in 256 CE. It employs the "broadhouse" model. In this structure, the focus of worship is on the long wall, rather than the short wall. In the present example, at the very top, a niche is carved into the wall for the Torah scrolls. The actual worship space is at the top of the ground plan. Beneath it is a courtyard for gathering. At the bottom are various rooms for diverse social functions.

Source: C. Kraeling, *The Excavations at Dura Europos*, Vol. VIII: *The Synagogue* (New Haven, Yale University Press, 1956).

Symbols from the Synagogue in Ostia, Italy

An important synagogue from the fourth century CE is found in Ostia, the port of Rome. The carvings shown here are entirely typical of symbols found throughout synagogues of the Diaspora and the Land of Israel. The seven-branched Menorah dominates the panel. From the left to right are other objects used in the liturgies of various Festivals—the lulav and etrog (Sukkot) and the shofar (Rosh Hashanah). The panel was placed in the niche used to store the Torah scroll.

Source: M. F. Squarciapino, *Archaeology* 16 (1963)

---

suggests that those who entered these synagogues wished to draw upon the Temple's cosmic symbolism to exalt their own more humble setting.

Synagogue Art at Bet Alpha. Indeed, the conception of the synagogue as a place for ritual, in addition to merely convivial or educational activity, is conveyed by other aspects of their interiors. Many synagogues were distinguished by artful mosaic tile floors. These can be particularly evocative of spaces and times far more enchanted than those of an urban street in the Byzantine Diaspora. The floor mosaic of the Galilean synagogue of Bet Alpha (ca. fifth century) is a superb and well-known example.

The mosaic, which occupies a rectangular space of about 17 × 32 feet in the main room of the building, is a composition of three separate panels, leading from the doorway and extending to the opposite wall facing Jerusalem. Upon entry, the eye first falls upon an illustration of Abraham's near sacrifice of Isaac (Gen. 22). For those who used this building, passage from the outer foyer through the doorway of the main room was a passage from everyday time and place into the time of the ancestors and prophets of the scriptural past. This room's space offered a visual evocation of the past, complementing the actual scriptural readings in which that past was presented in holy words.

The next panel, occupying the center of the room, can be interpreted in one of two ways, depending if one believes that the Torah's prohibition against creating carved images of God (Ex. 20:4–6) was routinely extended to mosaic art. Most interpreters assume that the central panel represents the sun as a chariot driver moving through the sky. It is possible, however, that the chariot driver is the God of Israel himself, guiding the sun chariot's team. In any event, the Sun Chariot and its horses are surrounded by zodiacal signs and symbols of the four seasons. Having reentered the Israelite past, the visitor was now asked to reflect upon the majestic cosmic setting presided over by the God of Israel. Thus, the synagogue evoked more than the biblical past, when God spoke face to face to Israel's ancestors. It urged its visitors to contemplate the expanded spaces of the cosmic order and to reflect upon the larger setting of their lives beyond the intimately known world of the human city.

The final panel fills the rest of the floor, directing attention to the Jerusalem wall's semi-circular enclosure (apse), which probably held the Torah scroll. This panel depicts a parted curtain behind which lies a series of images of the Temple's Holy of Holies, its menorahs, shofars, and other ritual objects. Lions, representing the Davidic dynasty, flank an image of the Ark of the Covenant. Having passed, at least in imagination, from the Israelite past through the vast spaces of the heavenly world, the visitor's attention arrives finally at the heavenly Temple—the eternal model of the building whose ruins alone were visible in Jerusalem.

What the High Priest had seen with his eyes of flesh once a year, the visitor to the synagogue could contemplate with the mind's eye at any time and anticipate as a reality in the messianic future. The Bet Alpha synagogue, in sum, evokes in its rather small space all that mattered in ancient Judaic worlds—the time of ancient Israel, the enormous spaces of God's universe, the timeless holy space of the Temple, and the future restoration of Israel. All are simultaneously present, presided over by the room's sole sacred object, the scroll of the Torah.[9]

Synagogue Art at Dura-Europos. In one remarkable case, the third-century synagogue unearthed in the Syrian town of Dura-Europos, illustrations were found not on the floors, but in a series of richly conceived wall paintings that surround an elaborate wall niche designed to hold the Torah scroll. Here, the biblical past and the eternal present represented by the Temple are prominent. These paintings seem to have been intended as a pictorial commentary on various biblical stories, a kind of visual "scripture" anticipating the famous stained glass art of Latin Christianity and the iconography of

The Bet Alpha Synagogue Mosaic

Source: Goodenough, E. R., *Jewish Symbols in the Greco-Roman Period*. Copyright ©1988 by Princeton University Press. Reprinted/reproduced by permission of Princeton University Press.

Byzantine churches. Jews who frequented this synagogue could read in its walls' images the entire history of God's saving activities on behalf of Israel even as the words describing these events were proclaimed from the Torah and prophetic writings. Facing Jerusalem, they could contemplate a vivid depiction of the Temple even as they sang Psalms that had once been performed there by levitical ancestors.[10]

The illustrations at Bet Alpha, Dura, and many other Byzantine synagogues are marvelous introductions to the imaginative life of the Jews who used them. They also raise important questions about the relationship of their communities to the rapidly growing rabbinic movement of the Roman and Byzantine period. Palestinian rabbinic literature of these centuries in particular generally disapproved of the representational images in synagogue decoration, such as Bet Alpha's Sun Chariot and astrological figures (cf. PT Avodah Zarah 4:1, 43d; 3:3, 42d).[11] Surely, Dura's representation (just to the right of the Torah niche) of Pharoah's daughter bathing unclothed in a river would have been regarded as immodest in rabbinic circles, despite the painter's intention to celebrate the providential sparing of Moses from the Nile.[12]

Synagogue Communities and the Sages. One likely interpretation of the gap between rabbinic sensibilities and the reality of the Byzantine synagogue is that synagogues were not the centers of rabbinic authority that they would become in late medieval and modern times. Indeed, as we shall see on page 192, the rabbinic Sage had no official role in the synagogues' collective life.

The Dura-Europos Synagogue's Western Wall: Torah Niche Surrounded by Frescos

Source: Goodenough, E. R., *Jewish Symbols in the Greco-Roman Period*. Copyright © 1988 by Princeton University Press. Reprinted/reproduced by permission of Princeton University Press.

**The Dura-Europos Synagogue's Western Wall:
Pharaoh's Daughter Rescuing Moses**

Source: Goodenough, E. R., *Jewish Symbols in the Greco-Roman Period*. Copyright
© 1988 by Princeton University Press. Reprinted/reproduced by permission of
Princeton University Press.

They were general community institutions representing the needs and tastes
of local Jewish populations. Though Sages served the Patriarch and Exilarch
as public administrators, they did not build and decorate synagogues or preside over their activities.

These activities were initiated and overseen at the local level by whoever had the funds, the initiative, and the communal respect. Rabbinic authorities and their disciples surely visited and taught in such synagogues.
From the fourth century and onward, they seem also to have frequently
prayed in them (and argued with other worshippers about how the service

should be conducted). But, in the main, they appear to have accepted conditions they were temporarily unable to alter.[13]

Many archeologists have noted another striking discrepancy between rabbinic norms and the reality of the synagogue. Rabbinic law, especially by the end of our period, explicitly exempted women from the public performance of synagogue rites. Further, it required that men and women sit in separate areas of the synagogue divided by a partition (recall Philo's Therapeutae, page 147). The seating plans of surviving synagogues, however—where they can be reconstructed—show little indication of separate seating arrangements. Moreover, numerous inscriptions from throughout the Greek-speaking Jewish world testify that women were frequent visitors to synagogues, providing as well donations for their construction and decoration. Such evidence suggests that women were integrated with men in many synagogue environments beyond explicitly rabbinic communities.

The question of their participation in its rituals is more difficult to answer. Even rabbinic sources acknowledge that women could be called to read from the Torah, although the Sages discouraged the practice on a variety of grounds (Tosefta Meg: 3:11–12). Could women lead prayers? Here the evidence of diaspora tomb inscriptions may yield a clue. These reveal that some diaspora women bore prestigious titles of office, such as *archisynogogos* (Head of the Synagogue) or *presbyteros* (Elder). Because the honor of leading prayers would be offered to a community officer, it is at least possible that women might indeed have served in this way in some diaspora communities. But until firmer evidence emerges, we cannot clarify the question any further.[14]

Despite disagreements between rabbinic Sages and other Jews about propriety in synagogue decoration and seating plans, most Jews seem to have shared at least one common perception of the synagogue. Many remains of the Byzantine period contain inscriptions referring to the synagogue as a holy place (Greek: *hagios topos*; Aramaic: *atra kadisha*). Similarly, rabbinic Sages, citing an obscure reference in the book of Ezekiel 11:16, commonly called the synagogue a *mikdash me'at*, a Temple in miniature. Rabbinic and nonrabbinic Jews alike viewed the synagogue as a space that, wherever it was geographically, brought its congregants into a relationship with that center of the world represented by the Temple. Within the ritual space of the synagogue, the heavenly Temple continued to shape the way Jews experienced the subtle intersections of the mundane world and the heavenly order.

Ritual Activities

By the fourth century, there is little doubt that transitions between these two orders of reality were most often enacted through the rituals of public scriptural readings and communal prayer. The rabbinic literature of the Byzantine period takes for granted that Jews used the synagogue, the *bet haknesset*

Rufina, the Head of the Synagogue (Archisynagogos)

This inscription, from second-century CE Smyrna in Turkey, is one of a number that suggest that wealthy women might serve as leaders of diaspora Jewish communities. Whether Rufina's title, "Head of the Synagogue," implies a purely civic function or one of greater involvement in religious leadership is not clear. The original inscription was carved on a marble plate that adorned a tomb.

> Rufina, a Jewess, head of the synagogue, built this tomb for her freed slaves and the slaves raised in her house. No one else has the right to bury anyone here. If someone should dare to do so, he or she will pay 1500 denars to the sacred treasury and 1000 denars to the Jewish people. A copy of this inscription has been placed in the archives.

Source: B. Brooten, *Women Leaders of the Ancient Synagogue* (Scholars Press, 1982), p. 5.

(meeting-place) in rabbinic terminology, for both the public declamation of the Torah and the celebration of communal prayer. Rabbinic halakhah neither justifies nor criticizes the practice. It simply organizes both activities in accord with rabbinic conceptions of order and propriety.[15]

Thus, on the one hand, the Mishnah provides lists of passages from the Torah, Nevi'im, and Ketuvim that should be read on various Sabbaths, weekdays, holidays, public fast days, and so on (Meg. 1:1, 3:4–6). On the other, it proposes ritual roles for prayer leaders and worshippers (Meg. 4:1–10; Taanit 2:1–5) and establishes broad guidelines for the wording of the prayers themselves (Ber. 4:1–5:5; Tos. Ber. 3:1–26). Most important, rabbinic traditions assume that the public reading of the scriptures was an act of worship, surrounded with its own benedictions that could be integrated into the overall communal celebration.

THE PUBLIC RECITATION OF SCRIPTURE

Despite rabbinic assumptions, there is good reason to doubt that prayer and Torah study had always been linked into a single ritual performance. Most probably, public scriptural readings and communal prayer emerged as independant rituals, originating in separate spheres of Jewish ritual life. The oldest literary reports concerning public Jewish prayer, we have already noted (see page 176), do not specifically associate it with synagogues. Corre-

---

An Early Rabbinic List of Scriptural Readings
for Festivals (Mishnah Megillah 4:5)

On Passover (*pesah*) they read from the section of the Torah concerning Festivals, as found in the Guide for Priests (Lv. 23:4 ff.)

On the Feast of Pentecost (*atzeret*)—the section "Seven Weeks" (Dt. 16:9 ff.)

On the New Year (*rosh hashanah*)—the section "On the Seventh Month, on the First Day of the Month" (Lv. 23:23 ff.)

On the Day of Absolution (*yom hakippurim*)—the section "After the Death" (Lv. 16:1 ff.)

On the first Festival Day of Tabernacles (*hag*) they read from the section of the Torah concerning Festivals as found in the Guide for Priests (Lv. 23:4 ff.)

And on the rest of the days of Tabernacles they read concerning the sacrifices of Tabernacles (Nu. 29:17 ff.)

---

spondingly, the earliest specific references to the synagogue describe it primarily as a setting for Torah study. Although it is not yet possible to trace with certainty the independent histories of scriptural recitation and communal prayer prior to their Byzantine synthesis, a few observations can be offered.

Public Torah recitation had surely played a role in at least some Temple celebrations during the Persian period. The depiction of Ezra's reading of the Torah before the entire restored community of Yehud (Neh. 8–9) assumes as much. But the practice of gathering outside the Temple on fixed days of the week and year to proclaim the Torah text in public gatherings is a different matter than occasional proclamations in the course of Temple celebrations. When the Torah was read in the course of the Temple service, it was a secondary element in a grander ritual spectacle, the sacrificial *avodah*. The regular reading of the Torah and Nevi'im throughout the year in a specific communal setting, however, established the scripture text as a unique center of attention, independent of the sacrificial order.

The impact of this development was profound. Removed from the overpowering setting of the Temple, the Torah reading came into its own as an activity that could transform the place in which it was read. A common room or building, because of the texts it sheltered, became a center of holiness. Though independent of the sacrificial center, it was nevertheless a space in which different orders of reality could intersect. Its walls framed a repeated encounter with sacred utterances, the words given to Moses and other prophets, and offered unique access to the world from which those words originally had been imparted. The act of public declamation was more than the transmission of useful or interesting information. It was a setting for reestablishing the original moment of Israel's formation at Sinai, when the Torah was first heard "in public."

By the late first century CE, the Gospel writers could assume that the public recitation and exposition of sacred scriptures was the essence of Jewish communal activity (e.g., Luke 4:16–22). Their contemporary Josephus shared this view, ascribing the practice to ancient Mosaic legislation (Against Apion 2:17). Similarly, a Greek inscription from first-century BCE Jerusalem records the proud declaration of one Theodotus, "priest and head of the synagogue," to have built a "synagogue for purposes of reciting the Torah [Greek: *nomos*, "law"] and studying the commandments, and as a hotel with chambers and water installations to provide for the needs of itinerants from abroad. . . ."[16] Here, as elsewhere in the first century, prayer goes unmentioned among the list of services offered in the synagogue.

Yet we know that the synagogue ultimately became the preferred site for communal prayer as well. It became a place to address God as well as to hear him speak through the voices of those who read his words. Precisely how this happened, and from which areas of life public prayer emerged, is difficult to say. Clearly enough, as Joshua ben Sira reported, the Temple itself included among its rituals acts of public prayer in which those gathered prostrated themselves and uttered praises or petitions to God. These included the utterance of priestly benedictions over the community and communal responses. Scriptural texts, such as Psalms or the Ten Commandments, may have been publicly recited. But, as with the public Torah readings, such acts were adornments to the sacrificial offerings, not the substance of worship.

COMMUNAL PRAYER

Archeological evidence for the existence of prayer as a communal activity outside the Temple first emerges with the *proseuchai* of third-century BCE Egypt. Historians, however, do not know what kinds of prayers were uttered in them. Nor are there any descriptions of associated ritual actions such as bowing, prostrations, or other common expressions of worshipful attitudes.

The Egyptian situation receives a bit more illumination from the second century BCE onward. The Letter of Aristeas, for example, assumes that "all Jews" wash their hands in a body of water as a prelude to prayers.[17] Philo, we saw, claims that communal prayer among the first-century CE Egyptian Therapeutae involved the antiphonal singing of hymns on Sabbaths or holy days. He also describes daily prayers at dawn and sunset, but it is unclear whether this was a private devotion or a communal liturgy.[18] But we cannot project his description of a self-consciously intentional community onto the blank screen of larger Egyptian-Jewish society.

The earliest actual texts of Jewish communal prayers, outside the canonical boundaries of the book of Psalms, are Palestinian. These are the psalm-like hymns preserved primarily in the Thanksgiving Scroll and the Songs for the Sabbath Sacrifice discovered among the Qumran writings. These, stemming from the first century BCE, were probably sung in the worship groups of the Yakhad. The Songs for the Sabbath, in particular, offer rich evocations of the heavenly Temple, with God's Throne surrounded by adoring angelic celebrants. They offer an important insight into the way the Yakhad understood its ritual space as a setting for invoking the heavenly order. The songs shed no particular light, however, on the rituals associated with the singing of the hymns.

Another source of insight into kinds of prayers offered by Jews outside rabbinic circles comes from a surprising source in fourth-century CE Syria. These are the daily, Sabbath, and Festival prayers collected in a Christian liturgical document called the Apostolic Constitution. Among the many Christian prayers in this collection are at least seven that share a peculiar feature: scattered and ill-fitting references to Christian ideas. When these are deleted from the texts, the remaining prayers seem to reflect the sentiments of a Greek-speaking, highly philosophical Judaism of the second to third centuries CE. Presumably, the prayers of a Jewish community had been carried, with appropriate editorial modifications, into the life of a Syrian Christian community. Such texts show how profoundly Judaism's prayer traditions affected those of Byzantine Christianity. But here, as at Qumran, the ritual setting of the prayers in their original Jewish context is unclear.[19]

Communal prayer, therefore, seems to have developed independent of the rabbinic Sages in a variety of different Jewish settings in Palestine and the Diaspora. Its presence in the synagogue was a given for the Sages. Their own rules of communal worship, to a degree, depended upon these earlier developments even as they shaped them in the patterns distinctive to rabbinic preference. But the Sages' indisputable contribution was to make explicit the connections between the synagogue's communal prayers and the public recitation of the Torah and other scriptures. They did so by linking the Sinaitic memories stirred by the Torah reading to longings for the vanished Temple service. Israel's great past and anticipated future were knotted together in the rabbinic worship service.

The Rabbinic Service. This service linked the community to heaven as well. As a dominant tradition of rabbinic masters conceived of it, communal prayers were a kind of sacrificial service that substituted for and, indeed, continued the ancient priestly sacrifices at the altar. The term commonly applied to prayer, *avodah* (service), is the one used in scripture to describe the Temple service. The point is explicitly drawn by a common interpretation of

---

A Sabbath Hymn from Qumran (4Q405)

The Book of Ezekiel's opening vision of the divine Throne-Chariot (*merkavah*) inspired much speculation in early Judaism. In liturgical texts from Qumran, it is clear that the worshipping community understood its prayers to correspond to the heavenly adoration of God's celestial *merkavah* by cherubim, or angelic attendants. Below is a sample of such prayer from a collection commonly called "Songs for the Sabbath Sacrifice." The square brackets and ellipses represent the translator's effort to fill in or identify gaps in the preserved manuscript.

[Praise the God of . . . w]onder, and exalt him . . . of glory in the te[nt of the God of] knowledge. The [cheru]bim prostrate themselves before him and bless. As they rise, a whispered divine voice [is heard], and there is a roar of praise. When they drop their wings, there is a [whispere]d divine voice. The cherubim bless the image of the throne-chariot above the firmament, [and] they praise [the majes]ty of the luminous firmanent beneath his seat of glory.

Source: G. Vermes, *The Dead Sea Scrolls in English*, 3rd ed. (Penguin, 1987), p. 228.

---

the custom of offering prayers in the early morning and the late afternoon. Many Sages argued that these times were selected in order to correspond to the biblical schedule for the Tamid Offering. In this view, the cosmic effects of priestly sacrifices and public prayer recitations were the same. Just as the priestly offering of the Tamid had brought the blessing of heaven into the world through the altar, so, too, the communal prayer of Jewish commoners turned the synagogue into a conduit for life-sustaining energies.

This conception of communal prayer ultimately governed the principles by which the Torah recitation was integrated into the worship setting. In the Temple service, the Torah reading served as a minor adjunct to the sacrificial service. In the rabbinic construction, the reading of scriptural passages on Sabbaths or other special occasions became a focal part of the sacrificial prayer service. Sinaitic pronouncements could blend with sacrificial offerings in a single "service of the lips" that opened the heavens to the petitions of Israel.

This conjunction of symbolic meanings can be seen from the daily prayer service assumed by the Mishnah and related early rabbinic texts. The service was relatively simple. In order to constitute a genuinely communal offering, it required the presence of ten adult males who served as a deputation of the community of the town or village as a whole. The main sacrificial

A Sabbath Prayer from the Apostolic
Constitution (7.36)

The ease with which Jewish adoration of God might express Christian attitudes toward Christ is exemplified in the following Greek prayer-text.
In its present form, the prayer is clearly designed for Christian worship,
yet much of it consists of passages that seem drawn from non-Christian
Jewish sources. The latter are italicized in the present translation.

*Lord, almighty, you created the world through Christ and set apart the
Sabbath to remember this—because on it you rested from (your) works—*
for meditation on your laws, *and you ordained feasts for the gladden-
ing of our souls, so that we may be reminded of the Wisdom created by
you:*
   How he submitted to birth by a woman on account of us, he appeared in life manifesting himself in (his) baptism, how the one
who appeared is God and man, by your consent he suffered on
our behalf and died and arose by your power. Wherefore also we
celebrate the resurrection festival on the Lord's Day and rejoice
because of the one who not only conquered death but brought to
light life and incorruption. For through him you brought the gentiles to yourself for a special people, the true Israel, the beloved of
God, the one who sees God.
   *For you, Lord, led our fathers out of Egypt and saved (them) from the
iron furnace and from the clay and the making of bricks. You redeemed
them from the hands of Pharoah and those under him, and you brought
them through the sea as through dry land, and you endured their character in the wilderness with all sorts of good things.*
   *You gave them the Law of ten oracles clearly expressed by your voice
and written by your hand. You commanded (them) to keep the Sabbath,*
not giving a pretext for idleness but an opportunity for piety, *for
the knowledge of your power, for prevention of evil. Therefore you confined (them) in the sacred precinct for the sake of teaching, for exultation
in the number seven. On account of this (there are) one seven and seven
sevens and a seventh month and a seventh year and according to this cycle the fiftieth year is for remission.*
   *(This is) so that men may have no excuse to plead ignorance. On ac-
count of this you entrusted (them) to keep every Sabbath that no one may
desire to send forth a word from his mouth in anger on the day of the Sabbath.* For the Sabbath is rest from creation, the complement of the
world, the seeking of laws, thankful praise to God for (those
things) which were given to men.

All of which the Lord's day surpasses, pointing to the Mediator himself, the Administrator, the Lawgiver, the Cause of resurrection, the Firstborn of all creation, God the Word and a man born of Mary, the only one begotten without a man, the one who lives a holy life; who was crucified under Pontius Pilate and died and rose from the dead. The Lord's day was commanded by you, Master, to offer thanks for all (these) things.

For your grace alone by its magnitude has obscured every (other) benefit.

Source: D. Fiensy, *Prayers Alleged to Be Jewish* (Providence, R.I.: Scholars Press for Brown Judaic Studies, 1985), pp. 75–79.

offering was a series of blessings, petitions, and praises of God, collectively known as the Prayer (*hatefillah*), or the Eighteen Benedictions (*sh'moneh esreh*). Recited in a posture of attention, they eventually came to be called the Standing Prayer (*amidah*). There was no official prayer-book. Such written aids to memory emerged only in the eighth or ninth centuries CE. Rather, early rabbinic literature assumes that the texts of these benedictions were fluid. Sages of the third and fourth centuries concentrated on establishing the prevailing theme of each benediction and fixing the words with which each began and concluded. Within this structure, individual worshippers were free to amplify according to local custom.

In general, the opening series of benedictions praised God's loyalty to Israel's ancestors, his creative and redemptive power, and his absolute holiness. These opening benedictions surrounded the central benedictions, which changed depending upon the occasion. On common weekdays, worshippers recited a series of benedictions that petitioned God for personal well-being and health, forgiveness of sins, as well as such collective Jewish concerns as the rebuilding of Jerusalem, the gathering of the exiles, and the restoration of the Davidic dynasty. On Sabbaths, Festivals, and New Moons, a single, longer benediction appropriate to the theme of the day replaced the central weekday petitions. On all days, the series of benedictions concluded with a prayer of thanksgiving and a plea for God to establish peace in the heavenly and earthly realms.

On weekdays, Sabbaths, and Festivals, the manner of offering the Prayer was the same. Worshippers stood at attention, their faces toward Jerusalem. Before them stood a *hazzan* (supervisor) who took his place before the Ark containing the Torah scroll, with his back toward the community. The leader would announce a call to prayer once uttered by priests in the Temple: "Bless now the Blessed LORD!" The community responded as the Temple witnesses had once responded: "Blessed is the Blessed LORD, for all eternity!" Then the entire community would whisper its benedictions in uni-

Opening and Closing Benedictions
of the Rabbinic Amidah

In rabbinic liturgical tradition, these six benedictions were recited three times daily every day of the year. The break between them was filled in with other benedictions depending on whether the prayer is offered on a weekday, a Sabbath, or a Festival. The text below represents the version used by contemporary Jews who follow the medieval German tradition. No complete texts of these benedictions survive from premedieval times. The name "Adonai" is a euphemism used in rabbinic tradition to avoid pronouncing the actual letters of the Divine Name.

Blessed are you, Adonai, our God and God of our fathers, God of Abraham, God of Isaac, God of Jacob. The great, mighty and awesome God, the Supernal God, who bestows profound kindness, creates all and recalls the righteous acts of the fathers, and shall bring a redeemer to their children's children in love, for the sake of His name—King, Helper, Redeemer and Shield. Blessed are you, Adonai, Shield of Abraham.

You are eternally mighty, Adonai—reviving the dead. You redeem magnificently, sending round the winds and bringing down the rains. He sustains life with kindness, revives the dead in profound mercy, supports the fallen, heals the sick, frees the imprisoned and keeps his trust with those who sleep in the dust. Who is like you, Marvel Worker, and who is comparable to you? A King who kills and gives life, who brings forth redemption—you are certain to revive the dead. Blessed are you, Adonai, who revives the dead.

You are holy and your name is holy, and the Holy Ones praise you each day! Blessed are you, Adonai, the holy God.

* * *

Adonai our God, accept your people Israel and their prayer. And restore the sacrificial service to the sanctuary of your house. And accept with love their prayer, and may the service of Israel your people be always acceptable to you. And may our eyes witness your compassionate return to Zion. Blessed are you, Adonai, who restores his presence to Zion.

We thank you! For you are Adonai—our God and the God of our fathers for ever and ever. Foundation of our life, shield of our salvation—this you are in all generations! We are grateful to you and recount your praises for our lives which are in your hands, and for our souls which are entrusted to you, and for your miracles which support us every day, and for your wonders, and your kindnesses which we receive each moment—evening, morning and noon. You are a source of goodness whose mercy never fails, a source of mercy whose kindness is never exhausted. Eternally do we place our hope in you. And for all this by your name, our king, be blessed and exalted forever. And all life is grateful to you and praises your name in truth—the God of our salvation and our help. Blessed are you, Adonai—your name is good and to you is all thanks due.

Grant peace, plenty, blessing, grace, kindness and compassion to us and all your people Israel. Bless all of us as one, our father, with the presence of your face. For through the presence of your face have you given us, Adonai our God, a Torah of life, and loving mercy, and righteousness, and blessing and compassion, and life and peace. And you deem it good to bless your people Israel at every moment and hour with your peace. Blessed are you, Adonai, Blesser of his people Israel with peace.

son from memory. The recitation was punctuated by prostrations at appropriate intervals, expressing submission to the kingship of God. Aside from these movements, the worshippers were not even permitted to shift their feet out of reverence for the divine King before whom they now stood.

At the conclusion of the collective act of prayer, the leader repeated the blessings in a loud chant on behalf of those whose memorization or recitation of their own blessings had been defective. He acted as a messenger, gathering the prayers of individuals into a single perfected, collective offering to Heaven. His recitation of the third benediction in particular—called the *kedushah* (sanctification)—was the high point of the service. Composed of quotations from chapter six of the book of Isaiah, in which the prophet is overcome by a vision of God seated on his heavenly Throne, the kedushah was offered in the form of a call and response by the leader and the community.

The rabbinic form of the benediction recalls the far richer hymns known from Qumran's Songs of the Sabbath Sacrifices. The Qumranian versions offer detailed descriptions of the angelic choir singing its praises to God in Heaven, as the human community offered its praises on earth. It is likely that the rabbinic appropriation of this kedushah served a similar purpose. At the moment of its performance, the barrier between the world of the

The Rabbinic Kedushah

The kedushah is known in many versions within rabbinic liturgical tradition. The following translation represents the text used by contemporary Jews who follow the medieval German tradition. The paragraphs are recited antiphonally by the congregation and the prayer leader, in imitation of the angelic choir's song.

> *Let us sanctify your Name in the world, just as they sanctify it in the heights of heaven, as it is written by your prophet:*
> *"And they called each to the other, saying: Holy, holy, holy is Adonai of Hosts, his Glory fills all the world!"*
> *Each opposite the other proclaims, "Blessed":*
> *"Blessed is the Glory of Adonai from his Place!"*
> *And in your holy writings it is written, saying:*
> *"May Adonai reign for eternity, your God, O Zion, for all generations, halleluyah!"*
> *In every generation we shall expound your greatness, and for all eternity we shall sanctify your holiness; and your praises, our God, shall never cease from our lips, for you are God, the great and holy King. Blessed are you, Adonai, the holy God.*

everyday and that of heaven was penetrated. The mortal worshippers became part of the immortal community of heaven.

On Sabbaths and Festivals, as well as on the market days of Monday and Thursday, rabbinic custom called for the public reading of the Torah as the capstone of the morning worship service. This was performed immediately following the Prayer, while the kedushah's powerful evocation of heaven remained fresh. The procedure for this reading was carefully plotted to enable the assembly to stage for itself the original opening of heaven, when Israel first heard the Torah from God through the prophet Moses.

The Torah scroll was removed from its ornamental Ark with great ceremony, carefully unwrapped from its decorative coverings, and unrolled on a reading table in the center of the synagogue. On Monday and Thursday, three members of the community—first a priest, then a Levite, and then a commoner—would be honored with an "ascent" (Hebrew: *aliyah*) to the Torah to read selected passages aloud. On Sabbaths there were seven such ascenders. These readers served as communal representatives. Through them, the entire people Israel ascended to Sinai to receive the Torah. Each would precede and conclude his reading with a benediction praising God for bestowing his gift of the Torah upon his special people Israel.

As each read, a specially designated interpreter (Aramaic: *meturgeman*) rendered the Hebrew passage into Aramaic so that all would understand the holy utterance. In addition to the practical matter of helping Aramaic speakers grasp the Hebrew text, this procedure enhanced the ability of the audience to recapture the original revelatory moment. It duplicated the revelation process as understood in rabbinic tradition: God spoke and Moses interpreted. At the conclusion of the series of prescribed readings, the Torah scroll was rewrapped and returned to its Ark. With the holy text returned to its place, the service was concluded, but for a summary recitation of hymns from the Psalms.

Summary

Let us draw together some of our observations about prayer in the synagogues of the Byzantine period. Although we cannot assume the universality of rabbinic descriptions of the Jewish worship, we can feel confident about certain basic assumptions. The first is that Torah recitation and communal prayer were seen by many Jews as natural elements of the larger worship offered in the synagogue. Second, the basic form of communal prayer was the utterance of benedictions of praise, petition, and thanksgiving that established a sense of genuine communication between the earthly community and the heavenly order. Human prayer in the synagogue was an earthly form of divine service that imitated an angelic celebration in the heavenly Temple. Finally, although the imagery of the Temple permeated the synagogue setting and the community's prayers, the synagogue ritual had a profound impact upon the ways in which Jews experienced the heavenly prototype of their own earthly community.

The priesthood, after all, was absent as officiants in the rabbinic prayer service in particular. Priestly and levitical families of the Byzantine period (as today) maintained proud memories of their descent from those who served in the Temple's celebrations. Many were treated with great social deference. But there seem to have been few official synagogue functions they alone could perform. They *might* lead prayer services, if their recitation was fluent. But any male Jew with a pious heart, a good memory, and a pleasant voice might just as well call the community to its prayers as priests had once inaugurated the sacrificial service.

We recall that deference was given to priests and Levites in the order of calling men to read from the Torah scroll. But as the Mishnah put it, this was a measure only to protect the honor of a group deprived of its former lofty functions (Git. 5:8). Whereas the High Priest had once read the Torah to the people in the Temple, now the people read it themselves without priestly supervision; the interpreter rendered its meaning and implications free of priestly guidance. Similarly, on regular occasions, priests were called before the community to confer upon it the ancient priestly blessings, as the High

Priest had done in the Temple. But even here, their recitation of the blessing was directed not by a priest, but by a common leader who could be trusted to have memorized the blessings and its associated scriptural text.

So the world of the heavenly Temple was persistently evoked in the synagogue's prayer service, but the earthly space of its evocation was utterly different from the Jerusalem Temple. The cosmic symbolism of that Temple survived, but in a transformed physical setting. Priesthood and sacrificial pageantry played no role in drawing heaven and earth together. Rather, a congregation of commoners led by one of their own number lifted up holy words to heaven in Torah recitations and in communal chants. Most of the officiants of this new "sacrifice of the lips" could claim no holiness from priestly birth. They claimed only the holiness of their commitment to the Torah of Moses. Delivered to them in an ancient revelation, its physical embodiment in a leather scroll now sanctified the space of their common worship. Spoken to it and through it, their words continued the ancient sacrificial labor of linking God and Israel, heaven and earth.

The Home as a Ritual Center

The Temple and synagogue did not exhaust opportunities for creating ritual openings to the heavenly realm in early Judaism. Even before the destruction of the Temple and the emergence of the synagogue as a site of communal worship, domestic space had provided the setting for numerous rituals. By the end of the first Judaic millenium, under the impact of rabbinic halakhic norms, it would become a prime ritual center in its own right. We shall describe some characteristic domestic rituals shortly. For the moment, however, we must understand the way in which the home was marked out as an effective ritual setting.

The Ritual Space

The Doorpost Amulet. As in the synagogue, a piece of scriptural writing proved crucial. A common marker of a Jewish dwelling in antiquity was the *mezuzah*, an amulet of wood, leather, or metal containing a parchment on which were written certain verses from the Torah of Moses. Usually, such amulets were affixed to the righthand entrance of the front door. In later rabbinic custom, *mezuzot* (plural) adorned the doorway of every room within the house (outhouses, bathhouses, and other undignified places were not adorned with holy words).

The word mezuzah itself means "doorpost," as in the following passage from Deuteronomy 6:9: "inscribe [these words] on the doorposts of your house and upon your gates." We will see momentarily that the Bible itself is not clear which words are to be posted in fulfillment of this commandment.

This ambiguity is reflected in the various passages that ancient Jews actually inscribed on the mezuzah's scroll.

The mezuzah is already mentioned in the Letter of Aristeas (158–159).[20] The earliest known examples of mezuzah scrolls, however, are included among the other texts from Qumran. One of these, similar to Samaritan mezuzot, contains the text of the Ten Commandments found in Exodus 20. A commonly found passage is Deuteronomy 6:4–9, the core of a text that rabbinic tradition knows as the Sh'ma, after the first Hebrew word of the passage. Some Qumran texts also include a second passage, Deuteronomy 11:13–21, which is mandated as well in rabbinic tradition.

Together, these two passages from Deuteronomy consititute a forceful summary of the Torah's understanding of the covenant:

Hear (*sh'ma*), O Israel: The LORD is our God, the LORD alone. You shall love the LORD your God with all your heart, with all your soul, and with all your might. Keep these words that I am commanding you today in your heart. Recite them to your children and talk about them when you are at home and when you are away, when you lie down and when you rise. Bind them as a sign on your hand, fix them as an emblem on your forehead, and write them on the doorposts of your house and on your gates.

If you will only heed his every commandment that I am commanding you today—loving the LORD your God, and serving him with all your heart and all your soul—then he will give the rain for your land in its season, the early rain and the later rain, and you will gather in your grain, your wine, and your oil; and he will give grass in your fields for your livestock, and you will eat your fill. Take care, or you will be seduced into turning away, serving other gods and worshipping them, for then the anger of the LORD will be kindled against you and he will shut up the heavens, so that there will be no rain and the land will yield no fruit; then you will perish quickly off the good land that the LORD is giving you. You shall put these words of mine in your heart and soul, and you shall bind them as a sign on your hand, and fix them as an emblem on your forehead. Teach them to your children, talking about them when you are at home, and when you are away, when you lie down and when you rise. Write them on the doorposts of your house and on your gates, so that your days and the days of your children may be multiplied in the land that the LORD swore to your ancestors to give them, as long as the heavens are above the earth.

The focus of the passages, quite clearly, is on a total, loving obedience to God as expressed in scrupulous regard for his commandments. But what explains their presence upon a parchment placed on doorposts?

The explanation comes from the passages themselves. Each requires Israel to place "these words" on its doorposts and gates. But it is unclear precisely which of "these words" are to be inscribed. The archeological evidence suggests that Jews made various choices within their understanding of the spirit of the commandment. The rabbinic understanding is only one among others. Whatever differences they had about the precise content of the mezuzah scroll, however, Jews agreed upon the theme of its text and the necessity of placing it at the entryway to the home.

Interpreting the Mezuzah. How did they understand the significance of this object that so clearly marked off their homes as Jewish dwellings? The biblical texts we have looked at suggest both an educational and a protective function. The words on the doorpost were to serve as a reminder of Israel's covenantal obligations to God. Those who took the reminder to heart would enjoy blessings, but those who did not would suffer other consequences. The theme of protection seems to have ultimately won out.

The first-century CE historian Josephus explained that the mezuzah was not a crude good-luck charm, but a sign of gratitude for all the benefits received from God (Antiquities 4:213).[21] That he had to make this point suggests that, in fact, many Jews did regard the mezuzah as a protective charm. The Palestinian Talmud, for its part, records a story about Rabbi Judah the Patriarch. In gratitude for the gift of a pearl, the compiler of the Mishnah sent a mezuzah. Rebuked that his gift was hardly equivalent in value to the precious pearl, Rabbi is said to have replied: "What you sent me I must guard, what I sent you will guard you!" (Peah 1:1, 15d).

In Rabbi's view, "these words" of the Torah did not simply decorate a parchment. Rather, unread and wrapped in their case, they nevertheless conveyed the attention of God to the home. This perhaps helps to explain how the mezuzah helped to create a particular sort of ritual space. From their encasement in the doorpost amulet, the words of the Torah presided over a point of passage between two very different sorts of space. Beyond the door of the home lay "the world" at large, shared alike by Jew and non-Jew. It was a place of commonness, disorder, and impurity. But the domestic space, even though it served the commonest of needs, could be evocative of the heavenly world from which the Torah originally came.

What the presence of the Torah scroll did for the synagogue, transforming a mere meeting room into a place filled with the potential to host the divine Presence, the mezuzah did for the home. It marked off a space in which the name of God could be evoked in due regard for its holiness. Indeed, the mezuzah enabled the home to serve as a new hub of holiness. Sacred words from the Torah formed a barrier, keeping the common world outside the home, where it belonged. At the same time, the mezuzah transformed the home into a space in which it was possible, as in the Temple or synagogue, to communicate between the world of the everyday and that relatively inaccessible world of the heavens.

The Protective Incantation. It is clear, however, that many Jews of late antiquity, from Palestine to Babylonia, were of the opinion that the simple mezuzah was not alone sufficient to protect the home. Nor did it open communication with the entire range of beings who might populate the heavenly and earthly domains. Judaic worlds, you'll recall, included nonhuman personal beings—angels and demons—whose ability to affect the human order was no less real than that of God. Since the latter part of the nineteenth century and throughout the twentieth, archeologists have discovered rich evidence of how Jews established (or avoided) relations with such visitors. This evidence is found in the remains of amulets and shards of pottery containing incantations designed to ward off demonic beings or, in many cases, to enlist their aid in enhancing the wealth, health, or romantic success of the amulet's owner.[22]

Here we can discuss only one form of "homeowner's insurance," that found in what archeologists have called the Aramaic "incantation" or "magic" bowls. Many of these were discovered in 1913 in an archeological site at the Iraqi city of Nippur, within the ancient Sasanian Empire. Dating from the sixth to eighth centuries CE, they reveal the degree to which the rabbinic concern with angelic and demonic powers, noted in Chapter Three, reflects a widespread concern of ancient Babylonians, Jews, and non-Jews alike. It appears that bowls were inscribed with various prayers. After the utterance of the prayer, the text was built into the foundations of homes or placed in other appropriate places, such as thresholds. These had the effect of protecting the household and its members from the demonic visitors who might otherwise meddle in the family's affairs.

Note how the following example interweaves the text of the Sh'ma, found on the mezuzah, with other scriptural passages as a kind of introduction to its real concern—to protect the writer of the incantation and his wife from the curses of the demoness, Lilith:

> Hear, O Israel, the LORD is our God, the LORD alone (Deut. 6:4). According to the command of the LORD they would encamp, and according to the command of the LORD they would travel. The observance of the Mighty One they kept according to the Command of the LORD through Moses (Num. 9:23). And the LORD said to Satan: May the LORD rebuke you, Satan, may the LORD who chose Jerusalem rebuke you. Is not this a firebrand snatched from the fire? (Zech. 3:2)
>
> Again, bound and seized are you, evil spirit and powerful Lilith, so that you may not appear to Brikhyah Beyah bar Mami and this Ispandarmed bat Hotedora either during the day or during the night, during

any evening or morning, during any hour, during any time. But depart from their presence and take your divorce and your separation and your letter of dismissal. I have written against you as demons write divorces for their wives and, furthermore, they do not return to them.[23]

As the text's conclusion makes clear, it was viewed by its owner as a symbolic divorce document. Demons themselves honored the institution of divorce, and so Lilith could be adjured to honor a human's desire to end all further relations with them.

The combined evidence of the mezuzah and the magical bowls shows the degree to which Jews of antiquity sought to transform the home into a refuge from dangers lurking beyond the threshold of the domestic space. People ate, slept, worked, raised children, and routinely died in this space. The home was no less common than the street, and therefore just as subject to the incursion of worldly and otherworldly forces. Accordingly, the home required protection, on the one hand, and a positive source of blessing, on the other. The bowl built into the foundation warded off otherworldly dangers, but the mezuzah made the home permeable to the world of holiness and blessing. The words of the Torah, formerly intoned by priests in the Temple and regularly read by synagogue readers on Sabbaths and Festivals, functioned even silently and unread to draw divine blessing upon those who held fast to them.

Ritual Activities

The guardianship of texts enabled the home, like the synagogue, to serve as a center of ritual performance. Rabbinic literature, our richest source for studying domestic rituals in early Judaism, can help us appreciate the ritual life that took place there. Here we focus upon two of the many ritual observances that, from the early centuries CE, were commonly celebrated in rabbinic domestic settings.

First, we discuss a ritualized act of Torah study, the recitation of the Sh'ma. It played a particularly central role in the lives of Jewish men. Then we move to a discussion of a series of ritual procedures in which a woman's participation was crucial—the baking and eating of bread. The most common act of domestic life, preparing and eating a meal, was transformed by rabbinic custom into an opportunity to recall and evoke, in the humblest home, the holiness once concentrated on the Temple's altar.

THE RECITATION OF THE SH'MA

The core text of the Sh'ma, we have seen, had already been singled out during the second century BCE as a particularly significant passage of the Torah. We do not know, however, whether Deuteronomy 6:4–9 was itself routinely uttered in the course of some kind of ritual performance. Both Josephus (Antiquities 4:212) and the Mishnah (Yoma 4:1–2) assume that some portion of the Sh'ma was repeated by Temple priests in the course of their daily activities. But rabbinic tradition alone seems to hold that a ritually defined recitation of the Sh'ma is an obligation incumbent upon all Jewish males.

As described in the Mishnah (Ber. 1:1–3:3), it was fundamentally conceived as a ritual of covenant submission. Appropriately enough, the central performance was an act of Torah study. This may explain why, in addition to Deuteronomy 6:4–9 and 11:13–21, the rabbinic tradition included a third biblical passage, Numbers 15:37–41, in the recitation:

> The LORD said to Moses as follows: Speak to the Israelite people and instruct them to make for themselves fringes on the corners of their garments throughout the ages; let them attach a cord of blue to the fringe at each corner. That shall be your fringe; look at it and recall all the commandments of the LORD and observe them, so that you do not follow your heart and eyes in your lustful urge. Thus you shall be reminded to observe all my commandments and to be holy to your God. I the LORD am your God, who brought you out of the land of Egypt to be your God; I, the LORD am your God.

This text stresses the need for constant awareness of the covenant and documents the constant danger of distraction from covenant awareness.

As a reminder of covenantal obligation, the passage mandates the donning of fringed garments. Such fringes (Hebrew: *tzitzit*) were not unique to rabbinic Jews. They have been found at some archeological sites and are depicted in the paintings at Dura-Europos. We observe here that in the context of the earlier two paragraphs of the Sh'ma, the theme of the passage links obedience to God to enjoyment of his redemptive power as expressed in the liberation from Egypt.

By the time of the seventh-century Islamic invasions, the recitation of the Sh'ma had become integrated into rabbinic communal worship as a preamble to the Prayer. But it was imagined in the earliest rabbinic traditions as a domestic ritual for men. They were obliged to recite it at nightfall and dawn, in fulfillment of Deuteronomy 6:4–9's mandate to recite holy words "when you lie down and when you rise." The ritual recitation of the Sh'ma included more than the biblical text. It was preceded and followed by supplementary benedictions that drew out the implications of its meaning and linked it to the creative and redemptive power of the God of Israel.

In the morning, the first of these benedictions praised God as creator of light; the second expressed gratitude for God's selection of Israel as his covenant nation. This second benediction introduced the three paragraphs of the Sh'ma itself. These were followed by a benediction expressing confidence in God's redemptive promise. The evening benedictions began with praise of

---

The Final Benediction Following the Evening Sh'ma

The following text accords with the liturgical tradition followed by many contemporary communities of Hasidic Jews. It incorporates elements of medieval German, Spanish, and Eastern European liturgies. As with other rabbinic prayer texts, there are no surviving texts from the premedieval rabbinic literature.

> Our Father, let us lie down in peace, and raise us up, our King, to a life rich in peace. And perfect us before you with good counsel, and redeem us speedily for the sake of your Name, and defend us, and remove from us enemies, disease, war, famine and anguish; and remove Satan from before and behind us, and shelter us in the shade of your wings, and protect our comings and goings for a life rich in peace, now and forever, for you, God, are our preserver and protector. Blessed are you, Adonai, protector of his people, Israel, forever.

God for bringing evening and rest upon the universe, continued as in the morning ritual, and concluded with a fourth benediction that praised God for permitting his people to lie down to their rest in security and confidence.

As the themes of the Sh'ma's benedictions and its content suggest, the ritual recitation fostered an intensely private engagement with the entire world evoked within the symbolic vocabulary of Judaism. Within the space of a few minutes—the time it took to utter the benedictions and recite the brief texts—a man linked his own waking and rest to the cosmic dimensions of God's creativity as well as to the covenantal history and future of his community. His own existence, as that of his people and the entire cosmos, was linked to submission to the commandments of the Torah, the expression of God's creative and redemptive powers.

At dawn, moreover, the recitation was associated as well with another ritual activity required of males, the strapping to bicep and forehead of leather amulets (Hebrew: *tefillin*; Greek: *phylakteria*). In rabbinic versions, these contain the first two paragraphs of the Sh'ma and of Exodus 13:1–10, 11–16. The latter passage repeats the Sh'ma's admonition to regard the liberation from Egypt "as a sign upon your hand and as a symbol on your forehead" (Ex. 13:16). His body thus transformed into a covenantal symbol, a man began his day by reciting out loud the words that transformed his doorway into a sacred passage. These words now sanctified his body as well for a new day of covenantal life. Correspondingly, his last act before going to bed was to confirm, in his recitation of the Sh'ma, that his life had indeed conformed to covenantal norms.

THE RITUAL TRANSFORMATION OF BREAD

In the ritual of the Sh'ma, the covenantal symbol of Torah dominated. The Temple played no symbolic role at all. In other domestic rituals, however, the Temple reasserted itself as a dominant image of holiness and sanctification. We can see this most clearly in the ritual performances that structured one of the most common acts performed in the home—the taking of meals.

Ironically, the inevitable presence of women in the domestic setting made them crucial participants in a ritual act that most vividly evoked the Temple's exclusively male priestly activities. This is because the centerpiece of the meal was a loaf of bread, and women, in their role as housewives, were assumed to be the principal bakers of bread. We can best appreciate the priestly resonances of the act of eating by following the trail of that loaf from the time the dough was formed in the kneading trough until its consumption at the table.

The transformation of bread into a ritual object began with the kneading of the dough. In the halakhic form of the ritual, the kneader (whether the housewife or a professional baker) was required to remove a measure of dough, called *hallah*, from each batch and set it aside before the baking of the bread. The removal of this lump of dough was accompanied by a benediction linking the act to a divine commandment: "Blessed are you, LORD our God, King of the universe, who sanctified us by his commandments and commanded us to remove the hallah."

The rabbinic ritual is based upon a scriptural injunction: "When you enter the land to which I am taking you and you eat of the bread of the land, you shall set some aside as a gift to the LORD: as the first yield of your kneading you shall set aside a loaf [*hallah*] as a gift. . . ." (Num. 15:17–20). The sense of the passage suggests the offering of baked loaves rather than dough. Indeed, nonrabbinic authorities, such as Josephus and Philo, speak matter-of-factly of bread routinely offered to priests in fulfillment of scriptural rules.[24]

It is unclear exactly when and why the removal of raw dough came to substitute for baked loaves. The substitution is probably associated with the destruction of the Temple and the dissolution of the priesthood as a functioning institution. In light of the new situation, rabbinic halakhah transformed a customary tax of bread for the priests into a ritual of Temple commemoration. The hallah offering ceased to feed priestly families in the Temple compound. Instead, because there was no Temple in which priests might eat the sanctified bread, a symbolic portion of dough was burned in the oven until black and inedible. All the remaining bread made from that batch of dough became permissible as food through the surrender of the hal-lah. Centuries after the Temple's destruction, each loaf of bread baked in a rabbinic household was an occasion for recalling the Temple of the past and anticipating the messianic future time when priests would once again be fed from the Land's bounty.

The capacity of bread to invoke the symbolic presence of the Temple did not cease with its preparation and baking. Indeed, as we saw in Chapter Two, rabbinic tradition had inherited from Pharisaism a tendency to see the domestic table as more than a place to take a meal. If rabbinic Sages came to view the synagogue as a "Temple in miniature," they viewed the domestic table as a substitute for the Temple's altar. All who dined at that table could, in principle, transform their act of nourishment into one that nourished the world with the blessings of the divine Presence.

This was accomplished by surrounding the eating of bread with actions that called to mind priestly activities in the Temple. Here, Jewish men and women alike took upon themselves priestly roles. Just as priests had washed their hands from a laver prior to their conduct of the sacrificial service, rab-binic custom required common men and women to rinse their hands prior to eating bread. Just as priestly sacrifices had been accompanied with offerings of salt, so too rabbinic custom required bread to be eaten with salt. After the utterance of a benediction praising God "who brings forth bread from the earth," the loaf was broken, dipped in salt, and distributed to the diners.

In breaking and consuming their bread, then, diners enacted at the do-mestic table a small commemoration of the Temple's sacrificial service. Only after partaking of the sacrificial bread could they then begin to eat the other foods that had been prepared for the meal. Moreover, having blessed the bread, diners were released from the obligation to recite benedictions over the other foods served in the meal. The benediction over the bread served to consecrate the entire meal as an act that ensured that God's plentiful bless-ings would continue.

As the meal began with a benediction, so was it concluded. Neither men nor women could take leave of the table-altar without first formally ac-knowledging the Presence that had graced the gathering. The common rab-binic ritual of leavetaking, the "benediction over food" (Hebrew: *birkat hamazon*), mandated a series of blessings of praise and thanksgiving. The theme of these benedictions is instructive. They focus on God's graciousness in providing food to the world, praise him for giving Israel a holy Land rich in agricultural produce, and petition him to rebuild Jerusalem, the heart of the Land.

The meal, then, began with acts that recalled the Temple ritual and con-cluded with reminders of the centrality of Jerusalem in God's restorative plan for Israel. As we have seen throughout our discussion of ancient Ju-daism's ritual life, whatever came under the control of ritual was made to point to a rather limited framework of meanings. In the rabbinic world, these

---

The Third Benediction of the Birkat Hamazon

The third of four benedictions recited after every meal in which bread is eaten, this benediction draws special attention to Jerusalem and the Temple.

> Have compassion, Adonai our God, upon Israel your people, and upon Jerusalem your city, and upon Zion the dwelling place of your Glory, and upon the dynasty of David your Messiah, and upon the great and holy House over which your Name is invoked. Our God, our Father, our Shepherd, our Provider, our Rescuer—rescue us, Adonai our God, speedily from all our troubles. Do not make us needful, Adonai our God, of human gifts or loans. Rather, may we depend only upon your generous, open, holy and broad hand, that we may never be shamed or humiliated. And build Jerusalem your holy city speedily in our days. Blessed are you, Adonai, who builds Jerusalem in compassion, Amen.

---

are simple: the vanished-but-still-present Temple, the eternal Torah, and the Land of Israel, awaiting the return of its exiled people.

Conclusions

We have seen that the ritual spaces of ancient Judaism can be understood metaphorically as a series of wheels—hubs and spokes. The synagogue and the home derived their power as centers of holiness from the central hub of the earthly (and heavenly) Temple. As such, they were spokes emanating from the Temple as the center. But they also served as hubs in their own right, sacred centers or privileged spaces in which ritual evocations of the most sublime dimensions of reality could routinely take place.

Indeed, as the Temple receded into the past and became a purely heavenly reality, the synagogue and the home seem to have come into their own as ritual spaces. This development coincided, we have suggested, with the increasing dominance of the Torah scroll as a source of holiness in the ritual space and as a symbol of connection between heaven and earth, God and Israel. Both synagogue and home were marked off as ritual spaces by the sacred words of the Torah, the entire scroll or a selection of texts that summarized its essential covenantal focus. Within these spaces, a variety of deeds from the public to the private—communal prayer to eating—could be transformed into means for traversing the normal barriers between worlds.

If ancient Jews had an untroubled confidence in the interpenetration of heavenly and earthly worlds, this was because their daily experience of ritual performance nurtured it.

Notes

1. For further reading on the way the concept "ritual" is interpreted by historians of religion, see the following: Robert S. Ellwood, *Introducing Religion: From Inside and Outside*, 3rd ed. (Englewood Cliffs, NJ: Prentice Hall, 1993), pp. 80–89; James C. Livingston, *Anatomy of the Sacred: An Introduction to Religion*, 2nd ed. (New York: Macmillan Publishing Company, 1993), pp. 104–135; William E. Paden, *Religious Worlds: A Comparative Study of Religion* (Boston: Beacon Press, 1988), pp. 93–120.

2. Up-to-date discussions of Herod's Temple, rich in the results of archeological research, may be consulted in Carol Meyers, "Temple, Jerusalem," in David Noel Freedman, ed., *The Anchor Bible Dictionary, Vol. VI* (New York: Doubleday, 1992), pp. 364–365, and, more expansively, in E.P. Sanders, *Judaism: Practice and Belief, 63 BCE–66 CE* (London and Philadelphia: SCM Press and Trinity Press International, 1992), pp. 47–76. Archeologists tend to present their measurements in biblical cubits or in metric language. I have done my best to approximate these measurements in terms of feet and yards (1 cubit = ca. 18 inches).

3. See his discussions in H. St. J. Thackeray, tr., *Josephus: The Jewish War, Books IV–VII* (Cambridge, MA, and London: Harvard University Press, 1928), pp. 265–267.

4. See Sanders, *Judaism*, p. 61.

5. The Torah, primarily in Leviticus 12–16, prescribes a number of sources of bodily pollution that prevent the person suffering them from entering the camp or Tent of Meeting. These were all regarded as applicable to the Temple as well.

6. See Sanders, *Judaism*, pp. 103–118, for an overview of the sacrificial offerings.

7. Reports about this institution are found in later biblical works, the Dead Sea scrolls, Josephus, rabbinic traditions, and in inscriptional remains discovered by archeologists. For an attempt to cover all the various types of evidence, see E. Schuerer, *The History of the Jewish People in the Age of Jesus Christ, Vol. II*, rev. and ed. by G. Vermes, F. Millar, and M. Black (Edinburgh: T&T Clark, 1979), pp. 245–250.

8. Reliable and up-to-date discussions of the origins and early history of the synagogue can be consulted in Lee I. Levine, ed., *Ancient Synagogues Revealed* (Detroit: Wayne State University, 1982), Lee I. Levine, ed., *The Synagogue in Late Antiquity* (Philadelphia: American Society for Oriental Research, 1987). Most conveniently, consult Eric M. Meyers, "Synagogue," in *Anchor Bible Dictionary, Vol. VI*, pp. 251–260, and A.T. Kraabel, "Diaspora Synagogues," pp. 260–263 of the same volume.

9. The great pioneer in the interpretation of Jewish artistic images in the Greco-Roman world is E.R. Goodenough, upon whose work I have drawn for my interpretations here and in the following discussion of the synagogue at Dura-Europos. His multivolume study of Jewish symbols in antiquity is now in a conveniently abridged edition of great use to newcomers to the field. See Er-

win R. Goodenough, *Jewish Symbols in the Greco-Roman Period,* Abridged Edition. Ed. Jacob Neusner (Princton, N.J.: Princeton University Press, 1988).

10. Spectacular reproductions of the Dura paintings are available in the color plates at the back of Carl H. Kraeling, augmented ed., *The Synagogue: The Excavations at Dura-Europos* (New York: KTAV, 1979). For an excellent interpretation of their religious meaning, see the recent essay of Jonathan A. Goldstein, "The Judaism of the Synagogues (Focusing on the Synagogue of Dura-Europos)," in Jacob Neusner, ed., *Judaism in Late Antiquity. Part 2: Historical Syntheses* (Leiden, The Netherlands: E.J. Brill, 1995), pp. 109–155.

11. For discussion of these and other sources, see Lee I. Levine, "The Sages and the Synagogue in Late Antiquity," in Lee I. Levine, ed., *The Galilee in Late Antiquity* (New York and Jerusalem: Jewish Theological Seminary of America, 1993), pp. 201–222.

12. A remarkable reflection upon the meaning of nudity in the Dura paintings has recently been offered by Warren G. Moon, "Nudity and Narrative: Observations on the Frescoes from the Dura Synagogue," *Journal of the American Academy of Religion* 60 (1992), pp. 587–658.

13. For specifics, see the discussion in Levine, *The Galilee in Late Antiquity,* pp. 207–219.

14. A useful overview of the evidence for women's participation in the ancient synagogue is offered by Hannah Safrai, "Women and the Ancient Synagogue," in Susan Grossman and Rivka Haut, eds., *Daughters of the King: Women and the Synagogue* (Philadelphia: Jewish Publication Society, 1992), pp. 39–49. The pioneering scholarly study in this field is that of Bernadette J. Brooten, *Women Leaders in the Ancient Synagogue* (Chico, CA: Scholars Press, 1982).

15. There are two essential works on the development of prayer in Judaism. The first is by Ismar Elbogen, *Jewish Liturgy: A Comprehensive History,* tr., Raymond P. Scheindlin (New York: Jewish Theological Seminary, and Philadelphia: Jewish Publication Society, 1993). This is an encyclopedic discussion of all aspects of the worship that became normative in Judaism from rabbinic antiquity into the early twentieth century. The second is by Stefan C. Reif, *Judaism and Hebrew Prayer: New Perspectives on Jewish Liturgical History* (Cambridge: Cambridge University Press, 1993). It provides a marvelous synthesis of all the textual and archeological evidence relevant to the development of Judaic prayer traditions from the Temple period through modern times.

16. Cited in Eric M. Meyers, *Anchor Bible Dictionary, Vol. VI,* p. 252.

17. See R.J.H. Shutt's translation in James H. Charlesworth, ed., *The Old Testament Pseudepigrapha, Vol. Two* (Garden City, NY: Doubleday & Company, 1983), p. 33.

18. See his Contemplative Life, 27, translated by F.H. Colson, *Philo IX* (Cambridge: Harvard University Press, and London: Heinemann, 1967), pp. 127–129.

19. These prayers may be consulted in D.R. Darnell's translation in Charlesworth, *Old Testament Pseudepigrapha, 2,* pp. 677–697. D.A. Fiensy's introduction to the translation (pp. 671–676) helps to explain how to distinguish the Christian from the Jewish elements of the prayers.

20. See the translation of Shutt, p. 23. For further details of ancient mezuzot, you can consult the article, "Mezuzah," *Encyclopaedia Judaica* (1972), 11, pp. 1474–1477.

21. See H. St. J. Thackeray, *Josephus: Jewish Antiquities, Books I–IV* (Cambridge: Harvard University Press, and London: Heinemann, 1930), p. 577.

22. Many of these can be consulted in English translation in Charles D. Isbell, *Corpus of the Aramiac Incantation Bowls* (Missoula, MT: Scholars Press, 1975); Joseph Naveh and Shaul Shaked, *Amulets and Magic Bowls: Aramaic Incantations of Late Antiquity* (Leiden, The Netherlands: E.J. Brill, and Jerusalem: Magnes Press, 1985); and Lawrence H. Schiffman and Michael D. Swartz, *Hebrew and Aramaic Incantation Texts from the Cairo Genizah* (Sheffield: JSOT Press, 1992).

23. Isbell, *Corpus*, pp. 89–90.

24. See Philo, *The Special Laws* I:132 (Colson, p. 175) and Josephus, *Antiquities* IV: 4 (Thackeray, p. 511).

Six

Transformative Knowledge

Introduction

The Judaic worlds of antiquity all assumed that common humans, after appropriate preparation, had the capacity to penetrate worlds beyond that of ordinary experience. The Jerusalem Temple, the synagogue, and the home all served as settings for traversing at least for a moment the boundary between this world of mortality and the eternal world of God and his angels. In worlds so permeable to the heavenly order and its awesome beings, it should not surprise us to find specialists who cultivated otherworldly knowledge, teachers who could guide efforts to experience the wonders that lay at the boundaries of the ordinary. We shall look at some of these efforts presently.

The Jews, of course, were hardly alone among Hellenistic peoples in their preservation of otherworldly knowledge. Rather, knowledge of a heavenly "mystery" (Greek: *mysterion*) was a common feature of many Hellenistic religious worlds. People knew *about* such mysteries, just as many of us know *about* (but hardly understand) certain concepts of nuclear physics. But only the few truly claimed to possess such knowledge (Greek: *gnosis*). To have it was a sign of inclusion in an elect spiritual fellowship. Its collective knowledge was withheld from outsiders who had not undergone some initiatory induction into the group.

Such esoteric or hidden knowledge flowed through various channels. From ancient Greece, Hellenistic culture inherited and further developed many secret societies devoted to experiential knowledge. Some of these societies transmitted the teachings of sublime teachers, such as Pythagoras, or claimed to preserve knowledge granted to ancient Egyptian or Babylonian priesthoods. Others imparted their knowledge in the initiatory mysteries of various gods (Dionysius, Mithras) and goddesses (Isis, Cybele). Yet other groups, often referred to derisively by early Christian polemicists as Gnostics (Knowers), claimed knowledge revealed by a God greater than the one known to Jewish tradition as the Creator of the World.[1]

Possession of these traditions of knowledge was more than an intellectual achievement. To truly *know* was, in a sense, to become a tranformed person or, commonly, to be translated into a different sort of being altogether. This experiential dimension of knowledge was, indeed, the essential value of these traditions. Knowledge of the immortal world, experienced in one's psychological depths rather than simply as a subject for learned discourse, ushered a person into the companionship of the immortals. As a quasi-celestial being, one might enjoy the fruits of that companionship even during one's transitional period of embodied, earthly life.

In this chapter, we examine some particularly Judaic versions of transformative knowledge. We saw in Chapter Four how intentional Judaic communities could provide a context for the pursuit of special experiences. In the last century of the Temple's existence, the Therapeutics, the Yakhad, and, most probably, the earliest Jewish followers of Messiah Jesus all cultivated forms of transformative knowledge. They associated such knowledge with conversion to a new communal life. Now, however, we focus on groups emerging after the Temple's destruction, apparently in at least loose association with the developing rabbinic communities of the second through seventh centuries.

We begin with some observations about the nature of rabbinic knowledge. In early rabbinic communities, the process of becoming a disciple was an initiation into a body of transformative knowledge. We have to ask, however, whether such knowledge was indeed "esoteric" in the rabbinic setting. The question is important in light of the remainder of our chapter, which explores knowledge that was restricted to small groups. Though such knowledge was usually quite compatible with rabbinic conceptions of the world, it was also seen—by those possessing it, at least—to be more profound.

The Transformative Knowledge of the Rabbinic Sage

In the first century CE, pharisaic teachers claimed to possess ancestral traditions that were fundamental to the proper maintenance of Israel's covenantal obligations. Second-century rabbinic Sages made similar claims, going so far as to designate some of their customs "halakhah stemming from Moses on Sinai" (e.g., Mishnah Yadayim 4:3). By the third century, discipleship to rabbinic Sages involved the complete transformation of behavior in accordance with the master's conception of this traditional Torah. The Torah Sage, it was believed, had been transformed by his own master's Torah, and his master before him, in a chain of transformative relationships that had begun with Moses' relation to God: "Moses was sanctified in the Cloud so as to receive Torah from Sinai" (Avot d'Rabbi Nathan A, 1:1).

The Communal Setting of Knowledge. Scrupulous behavior in accordance with the norms of the Sage's Torah was, of course, the outer sign of a disciple's transformation into a Sage. To be a Sage was not a professional choice. Rather, it was to enjoy a certain status. A Sage earned his living as a farmer, artisan, or merchant, as did other Jews. But he transformed these tasks into forms of divine service by virtue of his particular absorption of revelation. Whatever he did was interpreted by his disciples as an embodiment of Torah in human form. Moreover, the Sage made it clear to all disciples that his behavior was a reflection of knowledge that he had mastered in a most particular way. His personal transformation into a model of Torah had been made possible by his diligent memorization of words of Torah, both those written in Israel's national Scripture and those preserved in the oral teachings of earlier Sages. In rabbinic culture, the training of a disciple's memory was the key to his moral transformation as a person worthy of covenant partnership with God.

The rabbinic learning community (*bet midrash*, House of Study) was the social setting of this transformation of memory and character. Like the school (Latin: *schola*) of Greco-Roman philosophers and other teachers of redemptive truths, the rabbinic schools were organized as communities of disciples supervised by a Sage, who was both a teacher of traditional knowledge and a role model of wisdom. These were not endowed institutions like our contemporary universities, but much more like extended families embarking in common on a distinctive way of life. Within them, the traditions of the Sage were mastered and elaborated as disciples and their immediate households undertook to live in accordance with norms embodied by their teachers.[2]

In rabbinic culture, accordingly, the bet midrash was the central religious institution, of greater importance than the synagogue itself. Prayer was important, and the synagogue as the house of prayer was respected. But, as we saw earlier (pages 185–188), the synagogue was a public institution that the Sages could try to influence but not always control. Their power there would depend upon the degree to which those attending the synagogue knew or respected rabbinic traditions of piety. What the Sages could control, however, was the disciple circle, where their own traditions reigned supreme and they were the unquestioned authorities. The community of the bet midrash forged

Centers of Rabbinic Learning

A bet midrash existed wherever disciples gathered around a rabbinic Sage to absorb the traditions of Oral Torah. Rabbinic literature mentions as well the existence of a number of major centers of learning (Hebrew: *yeshivot*) that attracted large numbers of disciples. This map locates those that loom largest in later rabbinic memory. The Palestinian academy of Sepphoris is usually regarded as the site at which Rabbi presided over the editing of the Mishnah. The Babylonian academies of Sura and Pumbedita served as the setting for the compilation of much of the Babylonian Talmud.

Source: Based on *Encyclopedia Judaica*, Vol. 2. (Jerusalem: Keter Publishing House), pp. 203–204.

the characters of those who would fan out into the larger Jewish community to make the rabbinic tradition the common tradition of Israel.

The Innovation of Rabbi's Mishnah. From the third century onward, we have already observed (page 48), the Mishnah of Rabbi Judah the Patriarch became the primary focus of study in the bet midrash, the most prestigious representation of rabbinic Torah. Prior to Rabbi's work, it is likely that learned traditions were organized for transmission (if they were organized at all) as lists of teachings under the names of a particular Sage. These were cultivated and preserved within the bet midrash of that Sage and, perhaps, shared with the disciples of other Sages. But until the ascension of Rabbi to the Patriarchate in the late second century, no one Sage had commanded enough authority throughout rabbinic communities to transform the diverse traditions of the rabbis into a *single* tradition.

This was the primary achievement of Rabbi's editorial efforts in his Mishnah. He supervised the reshaping of the received traditions of various masters into coherent tractates or weavings (*masekhtot*; sing., *masekhet*) on specific legal topics. Eventually, sixty-two such tractates came to be included in the mishnaic canon. They were organized in six divisions of thematically related tractates. These divisions or orders (*sedarim*) covered agricultural practices (Seeds, *zera'im*), the celebration of festivals (Times, *mo'ed*), various elements of family law pertaining to women in particular (Women, *nashim*), civil and criminal law (Damages, *nezikin*), the conduct of the sacrificial system in the Temple (Sanctified Things, *kedoshim*), and, finally, forms of pollution and modes of purification from them (Purities, *tohorot*). The result was a comprehensive compendium of legal tradition on all topics relevant to rabbinic communities.

The main innovation of these tractates was in the way they presented the teachings of past Sages. Students were discouraged from learning lists of statements by their own masters alone. With only a few exceptions, tractates were organized thematically rather than in terms of the names of specific teachers. When a teacher's name appeared, it was invariably attached to a specific opinion on a given question and normally juxtaposed with the position of another Sage on the same matter. It was now possible to determine each Sage's place in the development of a coherent body of halakhic principles and cases.

This synthesis of the teachings of diverse first- and second-century masters into a coherent system was more than a teaching innovation. It also clarified the role of the Sage in the larger stream of halakhic tradition. As Rabbi conceived it, Sages were bearers of universal principles of Torah. Their authority was rooted in the mastery of those principles and the ability to apply them. Students of Rabbi's Mishnah, accordingly, were encouraged to see themselves as heirs to a tradition in which their own masters were contributors to an ancient knowledge that transcended the opinions of any one of them. Moreover, the topical organization of tractates highlighted the rational, logical character of the tradition. It helped students to see how apparently unrelated principles intersected, yielding contradictions or resolutions. Mastering the principles through the cases, students were then in a position to discern how the opinions of diverse masters drew upon and employed them.[3]

Perhaps a brief look at a famous mishnaic text will help to illustrate the economy of Rabbi's method. Here is the first paragraph of the Mishnah, the beginning of Tractate Berakhot (Blessings) in the Order of Seeds. The problem is to define the moment in the evening at which a man becomes obliged to recite the Sh'ma. We have divided the paragraph into four sections so that the flow of its topics is clearer:

1. From when do they recite the Sh'ma in the evenings?
From the time the priests enter to eat their priestly offerings.
Until the first watch—the words of Rabbi Eliezer.
But Sages say—until midnight.
Rabban Gamaliel says—Until the morning star rises.
2. A case: His sons once came from a wedding feast.
They said to him—we haven't yet recited the Sh'ma. He said to them—if the morning star hasn't risen, you are obliged to recite.
3. And not only this did previous teachers say, but
also: Whenever Sages said a commandment could be filled until midnight, it is obligatory until the rise of the morning star.
The burning of sacrificial fat and limbs is obligatory until the rise of the morning star.
And every sacrifice that must be eaten within a single day may be eaten until the rise of the morning star.
4. If so, why did Sages say until midnight?
To remove a person from transgression.

This compact paragraph begins in a simple question, but the answer engulfs the student in a mire of unexpected details. Let's move through each of the four units to see exactly how the Mishnah involves its student in its own distinctive picture of the world.

The Mishnah's answer to the question of when to recite the evening Sh'ma has, first of all, to be decoded. It assumes you know that when the Temple stood, priests would eat their holy offerings shortly after sundown, after the priests had been purified from whatever sources of uncleanness might prevent them from touching sanctified food. The evening Sh'ma, we now learn, is recited so as to coincide with a moment in the Temple's rhythm of purification.

The allusion to the Temple is carried forward in the three opinions that round out unit 1. Rabbi Eliezer, the majority of Sages, and Rabban Gamaliel are all assigned opinions regarding the *latest* moment it is possible to recite the evening Sh'ma. That is, when does "evening" end? Briefly, Rabbi Eliezer's opinion would correspond to bedtime, the Sages' to the middle of the night, and Rabban Gamaliel's to shortly before dawn. What they are disputing, of course, is whether evening ends when people go to sleep or when some celestial event occurs.

We might put it this way: is evening determined by social conventions or by natural occurrences? Practically speaking, if you followed Rabbi Eliezer's society-oriented view, you'd have to recite the Sh'ma by the conventional bedtime of your community, even if you stayed up later. Sages, who want to divide the night into two equal halves between sunset and sunrise, give you a bit more latitude. You can go to bed, get up before the night is half over, and still satisfy your obligation to recite the evening Sh'ma. But Rabban Gamaliel insists that you have the entire period until the dawn of a new day. The case at unit 2 illustrates Rabban Gamaliel's view and, by implication, suggests that his is the one to be followed. You can party all night, or rise before dawn, and still satisfy your obligation.

The interesting contribution, however, comes at unit 3. It shows, first of all, that the opinions of Sages and Rabban Gamaliel amount to the same thing. Those parts of the sacrificial service that had to be completed by midnight could, in fact, be delayed until dawn without spoiling the procedure. These last illustrations, of course, reinforce unit 1's view that the recitation of the Sh'ma continues in some sense the liturgical life of the Temple, for the principles that governed the Temple's sacrificial rites govern those of the Sh'ma's performance as well.

Unit 4 asks the natural question: if the Sages agreed with Rabban Gamaliel in principle, why didn't they say so? The answer is to the point: Sages didn't want people to get lax in meeting their duties. So they stipulated an earlier time for the performance of certain commandments even though, technically speaking, they could be satisfied many hours later.

You will appreciate how the Mishnah orients its student to the outlines of a specific world. At one level, this world is evoked through the terms used by the Mishnah. It doesn't speak simply of "twilight," for example, but does so only indirectly by reference to an obscure moment in the priestly regimen. Moreover, when individual teachers offer opinions, their grounds are taken for granted rather than explained. You are expected to infer for yourself that underlying their dispute is an issue of whether social convention or celestial realities govern the time for the Sh'ma's performance. Similarly, you are expected to understand that the Sages' choice of terms allude to the details of sacrificial procedures last performed by priests well over a century before the Mishnah's compilation. Finally, you are shown how two opinions in particular—those of Sages and of Rabban Gamaliel—agree in substance despite the apparently dramatic difference in their language.

The compact language of Rabbi's Mishnah, then, communicates a subtle intellectual exercise in a kind of technical code. Mastery of the Mishnah entails more than memorizing its terse diction. What is required, rather, is a prior knowledge of the code its language supposes. But whereas the Mishnah speaks in the code, it nowhere supplies the student with a decoding key. It assumes that the key to the code will be supplied by the oral teaching of the Sage. In this way, knowledge of the Mishnah's mere text is not knowledge of the Mishnah at all. Textual knowledge can become personal knowledge only when the words are enlivened in the face-to-face relationship with a rabbinic master.

Rabbi's Mishnah, then, preserved the centrality of the Sage as a transmitter of Torah even as it provided a body of knowledge that transcended the teaching of any particular Sage. As with most major innovations in education, Rabbi's edition of Repeated Teaching may have met some initial resistance. Nevertheless, within a century the Mishnah became the universal text of rabbinic discipleship training. It inspired at least one supplementary compilation of traditions, the Tosefta, and ultimately became the basis of the Talmuds of Palestine and Babylonia. Wherever rabbinic communities spread, they brought Rabbi's Mishnah with them and used it as the foundation of their efforts to teach Jews to think like Sages. Mastering their knowledge was the first step on a journey that would transform a disciple into the kind of person the Sage was—an embodiment of Torah.

The Orality of Oral Torah.   The transformative project represented by disciplined study of the Mishnah is best understood by pointing to the way the Mishnah was taught. According to the evidence of the rabbinic literature, it is clear that the Mishnah was memorized by students who listened to teachers repeating it as a kind of song or chant; and they analyzed the Mishnah in the process of their own recitations before teachers. Though there is good reason to believe that the compilation of the Mishnah required the tool of writing, its life in the setting of rabbinic instruction was almost entirely oral.[4]

The manner of this oral teaching, as well as its larger meaning in the religious world of the Sages, is described in a famous passage from the Babylonian Talmud (Eruv. 54b):

> Our rabbis taught: How was oral teaching conducted?
>
> Moses learned from the mouth of the Almighty. Then Aaron entered and Moses repeated his portion for him. Aaron stepped aside and sat at the left of Moses. Aaron's sons entered and Moses repeated their portion for them. They stepped aside, Elazar sitting to the right of Moses and Itamar to the left of Aaron. . . . The elders entered, and Moses repeated their portion for them. They stepped aside. All the people entered, and Moses repeated their portion for them.
>
> Thus Aaron heard it four times, his sons three times, the elders twice, and all the people once.
>
> Then Moses stepped aside and Aaron repeated his portion with them. Then Aaron stepped aside and his sons repeated their portion with them. Then his sons stepped aside and the elders repeated their portion with them. It turns out, then, that everyone heard it a total of four times.
>
> On this basis, said Rabbi Eliezer: A man is obliged to repeat for his disciples four times. . . .
>
> Rabbi Aqiva says: How do we know that a man is obliged to repeat

for his disciples until he teaches them? For it is said in Scripture: "Teach it to the children of Israel" (Deut. 31:19).

And how do we know that he does so until it is mastered orally? For it is said in Scripture: "Place it their mouths (Deut. 31:19)."

The passage links rabbinic methods of instruction to the original imparting of Torah to Moses by God. The relation of Sage and disciple imitates that of God to Moses and of Moses to his original associates. Clearly, as the comments of Rabbis Eliezer and Aqiva make clear, interest in Moses' teaching method was generated by the need to explain the origins of the pedagogical techniques developed by the Sages.

The method of teaching rabbinic tradition reinforced the conviction that with the Mishnah and its associated halakhic traditions, the disciple was absorbing more than mere knowledge; he was absorbing the oral tradition of Mosaic revelation, the Oral Torah. Indeed, by the third and fourth centuries, many Sages formally prohibited study of Oral Torah from a written manuscript. The only way to gain knowledge of this Torah was to learn it from a Sage as a disciple. This requirement helps us to appreciate the degree to which the authority of the Sages and that of the Oral Torah were mutually intertwined.

In the first place, preservation of mishnaic studies in oral form preserved the Sages as the authoritative interpreters of the tradition. Masters of a text committed to memory, they alone could transmit it. Sole mediators of the text imparted to their students, they were able to control and direct its range of interpretation. As the passage of tractate Berakhot (page 218) has shown, Oral Torah could not be readily grasped without the help of an expert. Someone who could read only a copy of the Mishnah would remain in the dark about its meaning without the Sage's oral instruction.

Second, oral transmission of the Mishnah ensured that the text would be mastered only as part of a personal relationship between master and disciple. In this way, the student learned not only the code of the text and its intellectual substance, but also a way of being human in imitation of the Sage. The Sage was the trustee of Oral Torah until all Israel could be taught its ways, until all Israel could be transformed into a bet midrash humming with the recitation of Oral Torah.

The Mishnah as Mystery. Clearly, knowledge of Oral Torah was treasured in rabbinic communities as knowledge that truly changed the knower. Possession of the knowledge in one's memory, as demonstrated in one's oral performance of the Mishnah, made one a different sort of Jew than one had been before and continued to distinguish the knower from other Jews. Moreover, the content of this knowledge was difficult and required devoted efforts of understanding. Was such knowledge, then, esoteric in the sense we discussed at the beginning of this chapter?

At least one passage in the classical rabbinic midrashic literature, with a clear anti-Christian bias, might yield that impression (Midrash Tanhuma, Ki-Tissa 34):

Said Rabbi Judah ben Rabbi Shalom: Moses wanted the Repeated Tradition (*mishnah*) to be written. But the Blessed Holy One foresaw that the other nations would translate the Torah and read it in Greek. And they would say: "The Jews are not Israel (for we have the Torah as well)!"

Said the Blessed Holy One to Moses: O Moses! The other nations will say: "We are Israel! We are the sons of the All Present!" And Israel, too, will say: "We are the sons of the All Present!". . .

Said the Blessed Holy One to the other nations: You claim to be my sons, but I recognize him alone who holds my mystery (*mistoryn*) in his hands. He alone is my son!

They said: What is this mystery of yours?

He said to them: It is the Repeated Tradition!

The passage clearly identifies rabbinic Oral Torah as a "mystery" of God, employing a Hebraized form of the Greek term *mysterion*, which others used to denote heavenly secrets. Does this passage, then, suggest that we should consider the Mishnah and its related traditions part of an ancient rabbinic *gnosis*?

Probably not. The polemical nature of the passage makes its meaning clear: at issue is whether Jews or Christians are the true people of God. Just as Christian theologians routinely accused Jews of misunderstanding their own Scripture's hidden references to Christ's redemptive power, rabbinic Sages repaid the compliment, arguing that the true meaning of Scripture lay well beyond the comprehension of Christians. Only one who knew the Oral Torah knew what God wanted of his covenant partner. And here is the point: the Mishnah is not the possession of the rabbis alone, but of all Israel. *All* Jews, not simply Sages and their disciples, are God's covenant partners.

Surely, knowledge of Oral Torah did distinguish its possessors as a special social group, and the knowledge was arcane. Although it was carefully preserved within the Sages' communities of memory, it was guarded in order to be spread. Oral Torah had been given by God to Moses on behalf of all Israel. It came from heaven but was now on earth, the possession of humans who developed and expanded that knowledge through their own intellectual labors. Moses' descendants, the Sages, were only the trustees of the knowledge and its preservers. The entire point was to transform all Israel as the Sages' disciples had been transformed. The discipleship was rigorous, but it was a discipleship open to all Jewish men and, through them, to their wives and children. As the Sages' vigorous missionary activity among Jews demonstrated, they hoped their tradition could transform Israel into what it had originally committed itself to becoming—loyal covenant partners of God.

Transformative Visions of God's Glory

For all its obscure language and arduous process of memorization, then, knowledge of the Mishnah and its associated traditions was public knowledge open to all who would accept rabbinic discipline. But this body of knowledge hardly exhausted the range of knowledge cultivated by rabbinic Sages or other Jews who shared many aspects of the Sages' religious world. At least some Jews both within and beyond the communities of the bet midrash cultivated types of knowledge that were reserved for a small, select group.

The major texts of rabbinic tradition, beginning with the Mishnah (Hagigah 2:1), alluded to it indirectly as knowledge of the Heavenly Throne-Chariot (*merkavah*) of God. Sages believed that this Throne-Chariot, and the divine beings surrounding it, had been seen in its totality in ancient times by the prophet Ezekiel, who described such a vision in the first chapter of his scriptural book. The Mishnah counsels caution in expounding this chapter of prophetic teaching in public. Many Jews—and at least some Sages were certainly among them—believed that even now a person with proper preparation and guidance could still make the journey.[5]

The Puzzle of the Hekhalot Literature

Rabbinic tradition alludes episodically to those who travel to the Merkavah, but the most explicit discussion of this transformative journey comes from outside the officially transmitted rabbinic literature of antiquity. It is found in a collection of obscure, loosely edited texts called the literature of the *hekhalot* (Heavenly Halls). Most of these texts are early medieval compilations of prayers, instructions, and narratives. Most historians, however, believe them to have been transmitted as a kind of esoteric knowledge for many centuries prior to their compilation into specific literary documents. Thus, their traditions were formulated during the time of rabbinic Judaism's spread throughout Byzantine Palestine and Sasanian Babylonia.[6]

The identities of those who transmitted the original traditions, as well as the later editors, remain unknown. Certain famous mishnaic Sages, however, such as Rabbi Akiva and Rabbi Ishmael, figure prominently in the hekhalot texts. Those who transmitted these traditions seem to have been in some communication with the major rabbinic schools. At the least, they assumed that rabbinic heroes were important enough to be depicted as transmitters of this hidden knowledge. Nevertheless, few historians believe that the traditions recorded in these texts stem from the same groups responsible for the widely studied literature gathered into the Talmuds. These texts re-

The Mystery of Ezekiel's Vision
of the Divine Throne-Chariot

The rabbinic traditions recorded in the Mishnah and its major talmudic interpretations are highly suspicious of those who cultivate speculations on the experience described in Ezekiel 1:1–28 (cf. 10:1–22). The Mishnah's tractate Hagigah (2:1) summarizes such speculation under the title "Dynamics of the Throne-Chariot" (Hebrew: *maaseh merkavah*). It limits instruction in the matter to a single disciple, under the condition that "he already understands it on his own." The Babylonian Talmud (Hagigah 13a) expresses its reservations with the following story about one who came too close to grasping Ezekiel's mysterious reference to *hashmal* (Ez. 1:27), a gleaming substance that conceals a human-like figure sitting on a Throne.

Our Masters transmitted an oral tradition: There was the case of a child who was reading from the Book of Ezekiel in his Teacher's house and penetrated the mystery of the hashmal. Immediately a tongue of fire spat forth from the hashmal and consumed him. Accordingly, the Sages sought to suppress public access to the Book of Ezekiel.

mind us that beyond the tight circles of the bet midrash, elements of rabbinic culture spread in diverse forms, often beyond the control of established rabbinic masters.

What is clear is that some of the knowledge offered in the hekhalot literature had circulated among Jews since the early centuries BCE. In Chapter Three, we read Palestinian texts from the Hasmonean period and earlier that describe the heavenly visions of ancient prophets such as Enoch and Ezra. We know that speculation about the angelic beings surrounding God's Throne in the heavenly Temple attracted the attention of the Yakhad as well and figured prominently in their Sabbath hymns. We may even have seen a picture of the Merkavah on the synagogue floor at Bet Alpha (page 184). The hekhalot texts drew deeply upon these earlier traditions of esoteric knowledge.

They differed, however, in a number of crucial respects. The earlier apocalyptic literature described the experiences of ancient biblical heroes and seemed to serve readers as food for intellectual nourishment or inspiration to hold on a little longer for the ultimate redemption of Israel. The Qumran hymns were primarily concerned with descriptions of the angelic adoration of God. The newer traditions, by contrast, placed such descriptions in the mouths relatively recent of rabbinic figures of the mishnaic generation. More important, the texts containing these traditions seem designed to serve as a kind of guidebook for one who would experience what Sages had seen. In further contrast to the apocalyptic literature, the messianic end is not a fundamental focus. Rather, the immediate goal is to confront the fullness of the divine Presence here and now, in one's personal experience.

Some of these texts insist that the preparation for a journey to the Merkavah involved complete self-purgation. Note the disqualifying character traits, for example, named in Hekhalot Rabbati (Chapters of the Heavenly Halls, 15:2 [par. 199]):[7]

> What is it like to have the ability to descend to the Merkavah? It is like having a ladder in one's house. Any person who would descend to the Merkavah must be purged and cleansed of idolatry, sexual excess, bloodshed, slander, vain oaths, profanation of the Name of God, haughtiness, and arbitrary hatred. And he must observe every positive and negative commandment.

These vices are commonly criticized in rabbinic writings, and the division of the Torah into positive and negative commandments is unique to rabbinic legal thought. This text seems to assume, therefore, that only a person who already embodies rabbinic Torah is suitable for the ultimate transformation awaiting those who have a heavenly ladder in their homes.

This insistence upon complete immersion in rabbinic halakhic norms is characteristic of only some of these texts. In most, however, the would-be traveler was at least expected to engage in extended prayer and fasting prior to the journey. Indeed, the journey was often portrayed as being the culminating point of prayer. We saw in the last chapter how the public recitation of the kedushah in the later rabbinic synagogue liturgy explicitly sought to make the earthly worship service an opportunity to share in the angelic adoration of God in heaven. In some hekhalot texts, the kedushah seems to serve as the immediate setting for the worshipper's journey to the Merkavah. Others, however, offer private prayers as meditative hymns that either aid the traveler's efforts to penetrate the divine realm or serve as exultant signs of his safe arrival.

The Realm of the Merkavah

Common to most of the texts is the detailed description of seven stages of heavenly journey. A series of ascents through the seven hekhalot, or heavenly halls, culminate in a final descent to the chamber of the Merkavah itself. Each stage of ascent and descent has its own character, which the traveling teacher describes to his disciples. The following example is from Maasei Merkavah (The Dynamics of the Merkavah, par. 556), which depicts angelic recitations of the kedushah and other portions of the rabbinic liturgy. In this translation, the letters YH, YHWH, and YY represent the unpronounced name of God:[8]

Rabbi Akiva said: Who can contemplate the seven Hekhalot, and gaze at the highest heavens, and see the inner chambers, and say, "I have seen the chambers of YH? . . . In the first Hekhal, Merkavot of fire say, "Holy, holy, holy is YHWH of Hosts, the whole earth is full of His Glory" (Is. 6:3) and their flames spread out and gather together to the second Hekhal, and say, "Holy, holy, holy." In the second Hekhal, Merkavot of fire say, "Holy, holy, holy"; and their flames gather to- gether and spread out to the third Hekhal and say, "Holy, holy, holy." In the third Hekhal, Merkavot of fire say: "Blessed is the name of His Majesty's Glory forever and ever from the place of His Presence"; and their flames gather together and spread out to the fourth Hekhal and say, "Blessed is the name of His Majesty's Glory for ever and ever." In the fourth Hekhal, Merkavot of fire say, "Blessed is YY, living and en- during forever and ever, magnificent over all the Merkavah"; and their flames gather together and spread out to the fifth Hekhal and say, "Blessed is YHWH, living and enduring forever and ever." In the fifth Hekhal, Merkavot of fire say, "Blessed is the Holiness of His Majesty from the place of His Presence"; and their flames gather together and spread out to the sixth Hekhal and say, "Blessed is the Holiness of His Majesty from the place of His Presence." In the sixth Hekhal, Merkavot of fire say, "Blessed is YHWH, Lord of all power, Who creates power, and Ruler over all the Merkavah"; and their flames gather together and spread out to the seventh Hekhal and say, "Blessed is YHWH, Lord of all might, and Ruler over all the Merkavah. In the seventh Hekhal, Merkavot of fire say: "Blessed be the King of Kings, YY, Lord of all power. Who is like God, great and enduring? His praise is in the heav- ens' heaven, the holiness of His majesty is in the highest chambers. . . .

In other accounts, the basic knowledge required of the traveler is mastery of specific incantations or bits of hidden wisdom. At each of the seven stages of the journey, these can be recited in order to appease the various angelic be- ings, with unpronounceable names, who seek to protect heaven from inva- sions by mortals. The following example, from Hekhalot Rabbati 21:3–22:1 [par. 233–235], reveals its rabbinic milieu as the traveler enters the sixth hall. The capital letters indicate elements of secret divine names:

At the gate to the sixth hall, Dumiel the Prince, who guards the thresh- old of the gate to the right of the sixth hall, sits on a bench of pure ivory which radiates heavenly luminescence as at the Creation of the world. 'RST'N W'RZ' 'RST'R WBNPYNN SMNSH 'RGH YHWH, Lord of Israel, and Dumiel the prince receive him with gladness and set him on a bench of pure ivory and sit beside him to his right.
    Dumiel says to the traveler: "Of two things must I testify and warn before you: No one descends to the Merkavah unless he possesses the

following two virtues. He must be able to study the Torah, the Prophets, and the Writings, and he must have mastered Repeated Tradition, halakhic and aggadic interpretation, and the resolution of legal decisions regarding the permissible and forbidden. Also, he must have fulfilled all that is written in the Torah in its entirety, observing all the warnings, the statutes, the judgments, and the teachings which were given to Moses on Sinai."

And if he says to Dumiel the Prince, "I have one of these virtues," immediately Dumiel the Prince takes counsel with Gabriel the Scribe, who writes on parchment with permanent ink on behalf of that man, saying, "This is the Torah learning of this particular person and those are his deeds, and he requests to enter before the Throne of Glory."

The recommendation of Dumiel and Gabriel, however, is not entirely sufficient to safeguard the traveler. First, he must pass two final tests (HR 26:1–2 [par. 258–259]):

"I saw one like the lightning" (Ezek. 1:27) who would interrogate the descender to determine if he was worthy to descend to the Merkavah or not. If one was worthy to descend to the Merkavah, when they say to him "Enter," he does not enter. They repeat to him, "Enter," and he enters immediately. . . . But if he was not worthy to descend to the Merkavah, when they say to him, "Do not enter," he enters immediately. They then throw thousands of iron bars on him.

Then the guards of the gate of the sixth palace throw upon him a million waves of water, but there is not any water there, not even a drop. And if he says: "What kind of water is this?" they immediately pursue him for stoning. They say: "Numbskull! Perhaps you are the offspring of those who kissed the Golden Calf! You are not worthy to see the King and his Throne of Glory." They do not move from there until they throw a million bars of iron on him.

One wonders about the consequence of failure. What is the experiential equivalent of being buried under thousands of iron bars? Are millions of them a harsher punishment?

At any rate, the text is more concerned with success. One who overcomes the deceptions of the angelic protectors of the Throne is ushered into the goal of his journies at last (HR, 22:2 [par. 236]), attaining his personal experience of the vision of Ezekiel:

They then present him before the Throne of Glory, parading before him all types of music and song, and they proceed to sing until they raise him and seat him near the Cherubim, near the Ofanim, and near the holy Creatures (cf. Ezek. 1:10–21). He sees wonders and powers, majesty and greatness, holiness and purity, terror and humility and righteousness at the same time.

Having experienced this vision, the traveler returns to earth. His experience has forever distinguished him among the earthbound, enabling him to have a ladder in his house that he can ascend at his pleasure. Other Jews may imagine the heavenly world in prayer; he has visited it, matched wits with heavenly beings, and penetrated their gates to gaze upon the unseeable and the indescribable. For most people, one supposes, this would be sufficient.

Enoch's Transformation

At least one text, however, usually known as the Third Book of Enoch, reports that the first heavenly traveler, the biblical Enoch, had been transformed into a heavenly being. He had become none other than Metatron, the angelic Prince of the Divine Presence (*sar hapanim*). The question remains whether the account of Enoch's heavenly transformation is to dissuade others from seeking such angelic transformation or to encourage them to hope for it. In any event, the account, as reported in the name of Rabbi Ishmael, is remarkable (III Enoch 9):[9]

> Rabbi Ishmael said: Metatron, Prince of the Divine Presence, said to me: In addition to all these qualities, the Blessed Holy One laid his hand on me and blessed me with 1,365,000 blessings. I was enlarged and increased in size till I matched the world in length and breadth. He made to grow on me seventy-two wings, thirty-six on one side and thirty-six on the other, and each single wing covered the entire world. He fixed in me 365,000 eyes and each eye was like the Great Light. There was no splendor, brilliance, brightness, or beauty in the luminaries of the world that he failed to fix in me.

The transformation of Enoch-Metatron's body beyond all human proportions prepares him to be placed by God on a special Throne (in Greek, Metatron means "behind the throne") signifying his rulership of the entire heavenly domain beneath God. At that point, his physical transformation completed, he receives at last the transformative knowledge that distinguishes the immortal celestial beings from their mortal, earthbound inferiors (III Enoch 11):[10]

> The Blessed Holy One revealed to me from that time onward all the mysteries of wisdom, all the depths of the perfect Torah and all the thoughts of men's hearts. All the mysteries of the world and all the orders of nature stand revealed before me as they stand revealed before the Creator. From that time onward I looked and beheld deep secrets and wonderful mysteries. Before a man thinks in secret, I see his

thought; before he acts, I see his act. There is nothing in heaven above or deep within the earth concealed from me.

Such a tranformed being, of course, need never leave heaven for earth. His home is now with God and the angels.

The Merkavah and Rabbinic Knowledge. Clearly, those who journied to the Merkavah sought an esoteric, experiential knowledge that had little to do with rabbinic halakhic interest in the precise performance of divine commandments. For this reason, as we have seen (pages 223–225), recent scholars have argued that the Merkavah literature originated in groups at the edges of the rabbinic culture of the bet midrash. This may be so. But by the early Middle Ages, descriptions of Merkavah journies came to be copied and studied within rabbinic communities. Viewed as part of ancient esoteric lore, they were deemed compatible with the public knowledge transmitted in rabbinic schools.

From the perspective of our study of Judaic worlds, it appears that the tradition of the bet midrash and that of the hekhalot literature offer complementary, not opposed, bodies of knowledge. Knowledge of Oral Torah transformed a man into a proper Jew, the kind of human being God had created him to be. But knowledge of the Merkavah made him into a kind of angel. It helped him to exceed the possibilities inherent in his creation.

This, of course, had been the aspiration of the first human couple as well, leading to their eating from the forbidden tree of knowledge. But thanks to the new knowledge of the Merkavah, some men could become like heavenly beings without violating the divine will. Indeed, they would be helped along by heavenly associates. Even a rabbinic Sage might be tempted to overcome the constraints of mortality with divine help.

Preparing to Meet the Prince of the Torah

Not all Jews sought transformative experience in a journey to heaven. Some portions of the hekhalot literature seem to describe attempts to evoke the presence on earth of an angel known as the Prince of the Torah (*sar haTorah*). As his name suggests, he was conceived as the angelic guardian of all knowledge of the Torah. When properly appealed to, he could disclose in a flash the esoteric knowledge that others traveled to heaven to discover.

Some texts suggest, moreover, that his aid was particularly useful for enhancing the mental faculty of greatest use to rabbinic disciples—the memory. The angelic Prince could enhance the disciples' ability to memorize the traditions of Oral Torah and help to strengthen the memory against forgetfulness. But we cannot be overly hasty in locating these traditions firmly within the central schools of the rabbinic movement.

Invoking the Sar HaTorah. Attempts to achieve an earthly audience with the Prince of the Torah seem to have drawn on techniques similar to those used by the navigators of the heavenly halls. Both heavenly travelers and invokers of the Prince felt it important to know the unpronounceable names of countless heavenly beings and the spells that pacify them. Both seekers of transformative experience, similarly, made extensive use of prayer and ritual to trigger the desired transformation or to show a sign of having attained it.

An interesting example of the Prince of the Torah invocation is found in a document we examined earlier, the Maasei Merkavah. In the midst of its descriptions of the heavenly journeys of Rabbis Akiva and Ishmael, the text breaks off to report upon a quite different exercise (Maasei Merkavah II, 560):[11]

> Rabbi Ishmael said: I was thirteen years old and my mind was occupied every day I was engaged in fasting. When Rabbi Nehuniah ben HaQannah revealed to me the Prince of the Torah, Suriel, the Prince of the Presence was revealed to me. He said to me: The name of the Prince of the Torah is Yofiel, and every one who seeks him . . . must sit for forty days in fast, eat his bread with salt, and must not eat any kind of defilement; he must perform twenty-four immersions, and not look at any kind of colored garments; his eyes must be cast to the ground. And he must pray with all his strength, direct his heart to his prayer, and seal himself with his own seal, and pronounce twelve utterances.

The text describes a sustained period of bodily self-affliction and purification as a preparation for a visionary experience of the Prince. This is similar, of course, to the practices used by Merkavah travelers. But the goal is different. Now the idea is to bring the Prince, with the aid of the Prince of the Presence, down to the seeker of Torah.

In order to do so, the initiate must make himself as much as physically possible into an inhabitant of the heavenly realm. The first step is to utter a series of prayers that surround his body with diverse divine names. The various unpronounceable names in these prayers (signified in the following in capital letters) serve as "seals." Their purpose seems to be to attract like to like; by surrounding the human with divine names, they encourage the descent of the angelic figure from the divine world. Thus (Maasei Merkavah II, 562):[12]

> In purity I pronounce Your name, You Who are One over all creatures. SBR DR'Y 'DYR DRY'S WHPS DRSYN, a seal for his body. . . . , 'P M'WPP' YHW, holy and blessed be His name; a seal above my head; secrets, secret above all secrets: HGGBWB YH YHW, may You be blessed; in Your name: may evil demons be silent in fear of the majesty of Your Dignity; let there be a seal on my limbs. . . . I have pronounced the name of SQDHWZYH Your servant so that there may be miracles,

wonders, many marvels, signs and many great and wondrous portents for me, in the chambers of wisdom and the orders of understanding. . . .

A later portion of the text suggests, in fact, that the "seals" of the seeker's body were physical objects as well as verbal utterances (II, 566):[13]

By the seven seals that Rabbi Ishmael sealed on his heart: 'WRYS SSTYY on my feet; 'BG BGG on my heart; 'RYM TYP' on my right arm; 'WRYS TSY Y'H on my left arm; 'BYT TL BG 'R YYW DYW'L on my neck . . .

And so on. The text seems to describe amulets that were bound upon various limbs, a kind of esoteric version of the phylacteries that Jewish males would have worn while reciting the Sh'ma. Here, they serve to garb the seeker in a "camouflage suit," enabling him to inhabit the same space as an angelic presence.

His body surrounded by such seals, the seeker is then prepared for the actual act of invocation (II, 562):[14]

He must raise his eyes to heaven so that he does not die; he must stand and recite a name and give praise so that the name be engraved on all his limbs and wisdom and the search for understanding be in his heart; and he should call upon His name, and he should pray in His name. He should make a circle for himself and stand in it, so that the demons will not come and liken him to the angels and kill him.

Before us is a clear description of the ritual used to prepare the way for an audience with the Prince of the Torah. The seeker is psychologically prepared through fasting and prayerful meditation, which alter normal consciousness. His body, deprived through fasting of material sources of strength, is adorned by a new source of power, the utterances and amulets containing sacred words. Finally, the space surrounding the seeker is marked off as a pure space into which demons may not enter. Here is the ritual arena within which a human being prepares for his confrontation with a being from the world of heaven.

Our text, unfortunately, is reticent about describing the actual encounter with the Prince of the Torah. Nor do others describe details about the "interview" with the Prince. But we may surmise from other texts of this type the results of the meeting. The final chapter of Hekhalot Rabbati (par. 300–303) describes a ritual similar in its basic outlines to the one we have just discussed. After a period of fasting, purification and self-isolation, the seeker of an audience with the Prince is advised to "recite the midrash (i.e., invocation) of the Prince of the Torah regularly in his prayer three times every day after the Prayer (i.e., the Amidah)" for a period of twelve days.

The expected results are made clear in this text: "At the end of twelve days, he [i.e., the disciple] may proceed to any aspect of Torah he requests: whether to Scripture, to Repeated Tradition (*mishnah*), to dialectic argument (*talmud*), or gazing at the Merkavah." In other words, whatever body of knowledge a disciple would master—from Written Torah, to the genres of Oral Torah, to the hidden mysteries of the heaven—all can be acquired in a flash and retained perfectly in the memory.[15]

Who Met the Sar HaTorah? It would seem that in a community of disciples competing with one another for mastery of Torah and the approval of their masters, the Prince of the Torah offers the "competitive edge." We can, however, imagine other possible communal settings of such writings. It is frequently observed, for example, that aspects of the purification practices described in these texts are not wholly compatible with the legal traditions found in the canonical rabbinical traditions. The continuation of the preceding text, moreover, is difficult to imagine in a rabbinic setting: "For we have in hand a teaching, a decree of the forebears and a tradition of the ancients, who wrote it down and left it for the generations, so that the humble could make use of it. Whoever is worthy is answered by them."

This is one of many allusions in the hekhalot literature and elsewhere to secret writings known to only a few. Why would the chief proponents of Oral Torah claim to preserve a *written* tradition beyond Scripture that enables one to master Oral Torah? We cannot solve the puzzle of the social origins of the hekhalot and the Prince of the Torah traditions here. Obviously, the transmitters of these texts had at least a superficial knowledge of rabbinic learning and viewed rabbinic Sages as models of authoritative teaching. But, just as obviously, they cultivated types of written traditions that would seem to be foreign to the dominant rabbinic schools.

Perhaps, as some scholars have suggested, the "humble" referred to in this passage were Jews excluded from formal rabbinic studies, yet who nevertheless aspired to the social prestige increasingly accorded to rabbinic disciples. Among such Jews, it became possible to enlist heavenly aid in learning all that the Sages knew, and more.[16]

Sharing the Power of Divine Speech

The traditions of heavenly travel and of the Prince of the Torah imagined personal transformation to involve an absorption of mysterious information. But there were Jews in the last centuries of antiquity with other perspectives. In addition to viewing the Torah as a body of information awaiting their understanding, many Jews had for centuries conceived it as a creative cosmic power. The Israelite wisdom tradition, as reflected in Proverbs 8, had long ago identified Wisdom as a primordial creation of God. In the Hellenistic era, many Jews—from Joshua ben Sira to Philo—viewed the Torah as this cosmi-cally creative Wisdom. Rabbinic midrashists inherited and elaborated this view, describing the Torah as an architectural plan for the structure of the cosmos (see page 115).

As the first Judaic millennium drew to a close, however, a new devel-opment of this tradition seems to have occurred. It bore obvious similarities with theories, stemming from Hellenistic Pythagorean philosophy, about the creative role of number as a structuring principle of the cosmos.[17] Whereas non-Jews might speculate about the role of triads (groups of three), septads (groups of seven), and decads (groups of ten) in ordering worlds visible and invisible, the Judaic form of this theorizing took a distinctive and predictable twist. Among some Jews, the basic elements of the Torah—the letters in which the record of divine wisdom was recorded—were ascribed creative powers. The principle of number, in this view, was an expression of these more basic cosmic forces.

Thus, again, an aspect of an encompassing non-Judaic conception of re-ality was absorbed into a distinctively Judaic world picture. In light of the covenantal images of Judaic worlds, we should not be surprised that Jews absorbed numerological thinking in a way that placed them at the center of the cosmic process. The forces represented in the Hebrew letters could be mastered only by those humans who were, in all creation, closest to the Cre-ator—the Jews. Some Jews sought to use the letters of the Hebrew alphabet as God was said to have done, as a Creator of worlds. They attempted, so to speak, an exercise in self-transformation that would allow them to share di-rectly in the most distinctive of divine prerogatives.

The Origins of Sefer Yetzirah

The most explicit theory of how the power of creation could be harnessed in the Hebrew alphabet was offered in a text called Sefer Yetzirah, the Book of Formation. As with the hekhalot literature discussed earlier, it is difficult to identify the originators of Sefer Yetzirah's traditions, those who compiled them into a literary work, or even the precise time or place in which they did their work. Historians have suggested dates from 300 to 900 CE as plausible settings for its composition. Is this a product of a specifically rabbinic esoteric tradition? Perhaps, for the Talmud does occasionally refer to certain Sages who could create animals or quasi-human creatures. But if this is a rabbinic work, it fails to employ one of the most common elements of rabbinic literary style. That is, Sefer Yetzirah ascribes none of its teachings to any rabbinic Sages.[18]

On the contrary, it follows a literary convention common in nonrab-binic Jewish circles but largely ignored by the editors of rabbinic traditions. It appeals for its authority to an ancient biblical hero. Some versions of the text identify Abraham, the first Jew, as the source of its knowledge. The de-scription of Abraham's achievement is worth reporting (SY 6:4):[19]

The Sage as a Creator

Rabbinic traditions recorded in the Babylonian Talmud and elsewhere assert that at least some Sages had the ability to create living beings. The techniques under their control are not specified, but the following passage alludes to a control of the Hebrew alphabet such as we find in Sefer Yetzirah. The introduction modifies the magical elements of the two stories by linking the Sages' powers to their righteousness. The passage is from tractate Sanhedrin of the Babylonian Talmud 65b:

> *Said Rava: If they so desired, the righteous could create the world, for it is said: "Nothing but your sins distinguish you from your God" (Is. 59:2)*
>
> *Rabbah once created a man. He sent him to serve before Rabbi Zeira. The latter tried to speak to him, but he hadn't the ability to reply. Rabbi Zeira said to him: You must have come from my colleagues! Return to your dust!*
>
> *Rav Hanina and Rav Oshayah spent an entire Sabbath Eve immersed in Sefer Yetzirah. They created a three-year-old calf and ate it.*

When Father Abraham came, he gazed, saw, delved, grasped, engraved, carved out, and succeeded at Creation. The Lord of All was revealed to him, and He placed him at His bosom, and He kissed him upon his head, and He called him His beloved, and made him His son, and He cut a covenant with him and with his offspring forever, "And Abraham believed in the LORD and it was accounted as his righteousness" (Gen. 15:6). . . , and He cut a covenant with him between the ten toes of his feet, and that is the flesh of the circumcision, and between the ten fingers of his hands, and that is the tongue, and He tied the twenty-two letters upon his tongue, and the Holy One revealed to him a secret . . .

The mysterious powers of creation given to Abraham are covenantal gifts, a reward for Abraham's devotion to God. By implication, they are accessible as well to later members of the covenant community, true disciples of Abraham, his "offspring forever." Men are prepared for this knowledge by the covenant sealed in their bodies by circumcision. Their initiation into the covenantal knowledge is expressed in their mouths through creative mastery of the letter powers of the Torah. With the secrets of Abraham in his possession, any worthy Jew could be transformed from a creature of God into a co-creator, a former of worlds.

Though Sefer Yetzirah alludes to the methods for such creative efforts, it is impossible to fully reconstruct what was involved. The book's second chapter prescribes a contemplative exercise in which the mind is trained to focus upon and then manipulate various combinations of letters. Because each letter is both a graphic image and a creative force in its own right, the visual combination of the letters achieves results that are at once both psychological and external to the mind. A "word" created in the mind is translated into a creative event, a "thing" in the world.

Sefer Yetzirah's real interest is theoretical rather than practical. That is, you would be disappointed if you opened its pages looking for just that combination of letters that might create a freezer full of steaks or a suitcase filled with dollars. Rather, its brief chapters offer an exposition of how disparate dimensions of existence—primarily space, time, and the moral order—are woven into a single web of reality through the creative and formative forces sealed in the letters of the Hebrew alphabet. Here is how it works.

The Letter Powers and Cosmic Structures

The twenty-two letters of the Hebrew alphabet are divided into three basic categories. First are the Three Mothers: the letters Aleph (which has no sound), Mem (sounded "mmmmm"), and Shin (sounded "shhhhhh"). They are seen as the basic linguistic sounds and, therefore, correspond to basic cosmic forces: "Their foundation is the scale of merit and the scale of guilt, but the tongue decisively tips the balance between them. . . . Mem stands still, Shin hisses, Aleph is Air which tips the balance between them." (SY 2:1). At the foundation of existence stand moral categories, actualized in reality through speech.

Sefer Yetzirah is interested in how this delicate linguistic balance of sounds is connected to the balance of cosmic forces (SY 3:3–4):

> There are Three Mothers—Aleph, Mem, Shin—in the universe: Air, Water, and Fire. The heavens were created first from Fire, and earth was created from Water, and the ether was created from Air, and tips the balance between them.
> There are three Mothers—Aleph, Mem, Shin—in the year: Air, Water, and Fire. Heat was created from Fire, Cold was created from Water, and Moderation was created from Air, and tips the balance between them.
> There are three Mothers—Aleph, Mem, Shin—in the body. The head was created from Fire, the belly was created from Water, and the torso was created from Air, and tips the balance beween them.

Here cosmic space, seasonal patterns, and the bodily sites associated with human thought and passion are viewed as various transformations of three elemental powers—Air, Water, and Fire as represented in the Three Mothers. These divine speech elements are the basic stuff from which all things are compounded. Existing things are modifications of these elements held in an es-

	NAME	SYMBOL	LATIN SIGN	SOUND
I. Three Mothers	Aleph	א	ʾ	silent
	Mem	מ	M	Mmmm
	Shin	ש	Š	Shhh
II. Seven Doubles	Bet	ב,ב	B	Ba, Bha
	Gimel	ג,ג	G	Ga, Gha
	Dalet	ד,ד	D	Da, Dha
	Kaf	כ,כ	K	Ka, Kha
	Peh	פ,פ	P	Pa, Pha
	Resh	ר,ר	R	Ra, Rha
	Tav	ת,ת	T	Ta, Tha
III. Twelve Simple	Heh	ה	H	Ha
	Vav	ו	V	Va
	Zayin	ז	Z	Za
	Khet	ח	Ḥ	Kha
	Tet	ט	Ṭ	Ta
	Yod	י	Y	Ya
	Lamed	ל	L	La
	Nun	נ	N	Na
	Samekh	ס	S	Sa
	Ayin	ע	ʿ	Silent
	Tzadi	צ	Ṣ	Tza
	Qof	ק	Q	Qa

Sefer Yetzirah's Alphabetic System

sential balance. Specially directed speech governs all the creative modifications.

This theory is expanded by discussion of the second category of creative letters. The seven letters of the Hebrew alphabet, in Sefer Yetzirah's view, have a dual pronunciation. For example, the letter Bet can be pronounced as a hard *b* (*beged*, clothing) or as a soft *v* (*kavod*, glory). At the simplest level, each of these letters corresponds to a certain kind of destiny that can be hard or soft. Thus (SY 4:1):

Seven Double Letters: Bet Gimel Dalet, Kaf, Peh, Resh, and Tav. Their foundations are: Life, Peace, Wisdom, Wealth, Fertility, Beauty, and Dominion. And they are activated through two sounds which are transformations of dualities: Bet/Vet, Gimel/Ghimel, Dalet/Dhalet, Kaf/Khaf, Peh/Feh, Resh/Rhesh, Tav/Thav—corresponding to hard and soft, modeled upon power and weakness. And these are their transformations: the transformation of Life is Death, that of Peace is Evil, that of Wisdom is Foolishness, that of Wealth is Poverty, that of Fertility is Devastation, that of Beauty is Ugliness, that of Dominion is Subjugation.

On this scheme, the vagaries of human experience—long life versus early death, comfort versus misery—are not normally subject to human planning. Rather, destiny is a product of lawful processes governed by elemental structures of reality. Knowing this, of course, one can control these forces, the Seven Doubles, rather than be manipulated by them.

The Seven Doubles are primarily viewed as extending the structuring powers of the Three Mothers. This structuring role is described in two complementary ways. On the one hand, they structure the extremities of space—the four compass points, the two directions above and below. Linking these six directional points into a unified structure of cosmic space is "the Holy Temple [which] is set in the middle and supports them all" (SY 4:2). Here, the ancient priestly motif of the Heavenly Temple as the center of the cosmos receives yet another expression. As an expression of the letter Tav, the Temple itself is conceived as a function of a primordial letter of the Torah.

But Sefer Yetzirah gives most of its attention to another formulation of the structural role of the Seven Doubles. At the moment of Creation, God (SY 4:3–4, 5:5–6):

> . . . engraved them, carved them out, combined them, weighed them, established their transformations, and formed through them: Stars in the cosmos, Days in the year, Gates in the body—seven of each . . .
>
> And these are the seven Stars in the cosmos: Sun, Venus, Mercury, Moon, Saturn, Jupiter, Mars. And these are the seven Days in the year: the seven Days of Creation. And these are the seven Gates in the body: two eyes, two ears, the two nostrils and the mouth. . . .
>
> He first established the reign of Bet and bound it for his Crown, and combined them each with the other, and formed from this Saturn in the cosmos, the Sabbath in the year, and the mouth in the body.
>
> He next established the reign of Gimel and bound it for his Crown, and combined them with each other, and formed from this Jupiter in the cosmos, Sunday in the year, and the right eye in the body . . .

The text goes on to describe how the remaining Seven Doubles were fused in various combinations. Each such combination enabled a single letter to govern dual possibilities of experience for all the elements of the cosmos, the year, and the head created under its dominion.

The completion of the cosmic system is assigned to the remaining twelve letters of the alphabet. These are the Simple Letters: Heh, Vav, Zayin, Khet, Tet, Yod, Lamed, Nun, Samekh, Ayin, Tzadi, and Qof. They are simple because each represents only a single sound. As powers, they correspond to the various states of being characteristic of the senses and the physical and emotional life: "Their foundation is sight, hearing, smell, speech, taste, sexuality, work, process, anger, laughter, thought, sleep" (SY 5:1).

Though the Seven Doubles correspond to six spatial dimensions and the dynamic power that holds them in a stable relationship, the Twelve Simples expand the borders of space diagonally in twelve directions (SY 5:1). But, as with the Doubles, this spatial function is secondary to their penetration of various aspects of the cosmos, time, and the human body: the twelve constellations of the heavens, the twelve months of the year, and twelve bodily organs (SY 5:2, 6:4):

> These are the twelve Constellations in the heavens: the Ram (Aries), the Bull (Taurus), the Twins (Gemini), the Crab (Cancer), the Lion (Leo), the Virgin (Virgo), the Scales (Libra), the Scorpion (Scorpio), the Archer (Sagittarius), the Goat (Capricorn), the Waterer (Aquarius), and the Fish (Pisces).
>
> These are the twelve Months in the year: Nisan (March-April), Iyar (April-May), Sivan (May-June), Tammuz (June-July), Av (July-August), Elul (August-September), Tishrei (September-October), Kheshvan (October-November), Kislev (November-December), Tevet (December-January), Shevat (January-February), Adar (February-March).
>
> These are the twelve Organs in the body: two hands, two feet, two kidneys, liver, gall, spleen, large intestines, small intestines, and stomach, . . .
>
> He first established the reign of Heh and bound it for His crown, and combined them with each other, and formed from this the Ram in the cosmos, Nisan in the year, and the liver in the body. . . .

The Simples complement the creative powers of the Seven Doubles. As the latter govern the moving planets, the former govern the fixed constellations; as the latter govern the rhythms of the seven weekly circuits of the sun, the former govern the cycle of months, established in Judaic reckoning by the moon. Finally, as the Doubles govern the apertures of the head, the Twelve Simples govern organs distributed throughout the body.

Who Is "The Creator"?

As interesting as these speculations might be, we must at this point wonder how these descriptions of what God did to create the world count as "transformative knowledge." Why do we not regard Sefer Yetzirah as an example of abstruse philosophical speculation? Note the description of Abraham (page 234) that concludes Sefer Yetzirah. It claims that God transmitted his world-creating knowledge to Abraham as a kind of covenantal gift. Just as this gift enabled Abraham to "grasp, explore, engrave, carve out and succeed at Creation," so, too, are such powers available to Abraham's descendants.

The first chapter of Sefer Yetzirah, in fact, explains how this is so and what the consequences are. This chapter introduces Sefer Yetzirah with the claim that in addition to the twenty-two letters of the alphabet, God used ten creative forces called *sefirot* to form the world. In Sefer Yetzirah, sefirot probably should be rendered as "defining powers." Together with the twenty two letters, the sefirot constitute "thirty-two wonderful paths of wisdom" by which God "engraved" the world (SY 1:1).

Much of the chapter offers various metaphors by which the creative powers of the sefirot in particular may be understood. The chapter settles on no single metaphor as the right one; rather, it presents each model on its own terms. One is particularly important for our discussion (SY 1:3–4):

> Ten Intangible Sefirot: the number of ten fingers, five opposite five. And in the center is set the covenant of the Only One, with the circumcision of the tongue and mouth, and with the circumcision of the sexual organ.
> Ten Intangible Sefirot: ten and not nine, ten and not eleven. Understand with wisdom, and be wise with understanding. Test them and explore them. Know, count, and form. Give it a firm foundation and restore the Creator upon His place. Their attributes are ten and infinite.

The striking thing about the first paragraph is that the sefirot are imagined as two sets of hands emanating from a covenantal being. This is precisely the image ascribed earlier to Abraham. This being's covenantal powers are located in his power of speech and in his sexual organ—the centers of intellectual and biological expression and creativity.

Apparently, the divine creative powers are here imagined as having penetrated the Jew who would employ them. Emanating from a body sealed in covenantal signs, his hands "form" reality in a way comparable to God's own sefirotic fingers. The second paragraph complements this picture. The wielder of this creative power is now advised to explore and test his powers thoroughly. He will find, if he reaches the utter extremities of his knowledge, that his powers are none other than God's. He "restores the Creator upon his place."

But which Creator and which place? The language is ambiguous. We might think that the man utilizing the tools of creation discovers his indebtedness to God for these powers. On this interpretation, our text conforms neatly to general Judaic conceptions of the absolute difference between humans and God. By restoring the Creator to his place, the man underscores his inferiority to God and recognizes himself only as a borrower of divine powers.

It is possible, however, to interpret the phrase differently. Why, after all, should God be restored to his place? Can he have left it? Perhaps, then, is it the *man* using the sefirotic tools who is now restored to *his* proper place as Creator? If so, Sefer Yetzirah constitutes a radical claim indeed: humans can acquire a power appropriate only to God! If Enoch, a descendant of Noah, became the angel Metatron, might not a Jew born of Abraham anticipate an even more remarkable transformation? The possibility is a tantalizing one, but Sefer Yetzirah does not enable us to give a decisive interpretation.

Conclusions

Our survey of transformative knowledge in the closing centuries of the first Judaic millennium forces a question upon us: do these journeys move through distinctly different Judaic worlds or do they describe alternate paths through a single world? Do rabbinic disciples, merkavah travelers, seekers of the Prince, and manipulators of letter powers share one comprehensive view of reality, or must we view these various pursuits as evidence of many different worlds of Judaism? On balance, it seems that we have traveled through the same world, seeing it from a variety of vantage points.

Surely, all the texts we have examined recognized a similar organization of cosmic and terrestrial space—angelic figures attending the divine Throne populated the heaven of Mishnah memorizers just as surely as they confronted those who struggled for a glimpse of the Merkavah. What differs is a judgment about the *relevance* of the angels to one's transformative goals.

Moreover, as we have seen, the focus on Torah in all these texts reveals broadly shared conceptions of Israel's covenantal responsibility and uniqueness within the larger human community. Torah, in all the texts we have examined, is the absolute value, a unique gift of God to his special community of Israel. Where the texts differ is in their estimate of the inner nature of Torah and the implications of possessing knowledge of that inner nature.

The editors of the rabbinic literature were disciples of masters of Repeated Tradition. Accordingly, they found in the Sage's embodiment of Oral Torah a unique transformative project that they sought to emulate. Matters of heavenly transport seemed of lesser moment than the ability, through the master's teaching, to experience the ancient Sinaitic revelation in their own study circles on a routine basis. *Their transformative quest, in other words, was focused upon efforts to reinhabit in the present a specific moment in the distant past—the perfect submission to covenantal laws manifested by Israel at Sinai.* They wanted to reexperience Moses' sanctification in the Cloud again and again as they mastered in ever greater detail the traditions of learning that constituted a living link to God's original self-disclosure to Israel.

Merkavah explorers and those calling upon the Prince of the Torah, by contrast, sought transformative revelation in a different direction. For them, the transformative possibilities of mastering rabbinic tradition were genuine.

Yet, surer, more immediate, and more profound opportunities were made possible by the assimilation of heavenly secrets. *The task was not to bridge the gap between the sacred past and the mundane present, but to bridge that equally yawning gulf between the heights of heaven and the depths of earth.* The cloud of historical Sinai was not the goal; it was a far more distant site beyond the seventh heavenly hall. There, in the seventh hall or in an appropriate ritual re-creation of it on earth, one might master in a flash all the Torah disclosed at Sinai as well as matters never heard by earthbound ears.

The transformative possibilities of Torah are, of course, at the heart of the tradition represented by Sefer Yetzirah. But the gap that must be bridged is not between past and present or between heaven and earth. *Rather, it is the gap between human createdness and the cosmic source of creation.* For Sefer Yetzirah, therefore, the transformative value of Torah is not in any specific message. It is in the syllables that convey the message, for these are the tools of God's work of creation. One needn't travel to heaven, therefore, to learn a mystery from an angel or apprentice oneself for years to a master of Oral Torah. Better to master the discipline employed by the Creator at the moment he formed the world. One might "restore the Creator upon his place" and, thereby, become his earthly associate and colleague. A master of God's creative power was surely the equal of any created angel and the superior of any Sage.

Notes

1. For an overview of such currents in the Hellenistic world, see Luther H. Martin, *Hellenistic Religions* (Oxford: Oxford University, 1987), pp. 58–155. Marvin W. Meyer, ed., *The Ancient Mysteries: A Sourcebook* (San Francisco: Harper & Row, 1987), offers a fine selection of translated original sources.

2. The fullest effort to reconstruct the institutional life of the rabbinic-disciple communities focuses upon the Babylonian communities of the third to sixth centuries. See David M. Goodblatt, *Rabbinic Instruction in Sasanian Babylonia* (Leiden, The Netherlands: E.J. Brill, 1975). For a discussion of the Sages of third- to fourth-century Palestine, see Lee I. Levine, *The Rabbinic Class of Roman Palestine* (Jerusalem: Yad Izhak Ben-Zvi and Jewish Theological Seminary of America, 1989), pp. 98–133.

3. Questions regarding the nature and goals of Rabbi's compilation of the Mishnah are hotly debated by contemporary scholars. For two different views, see Dov Zlotnick, *Iron Pillar Mishnah: Redaction, Form and Intent* (Jerusalem: Bialik Institute, 1988) and Jacob Neusner, *The Mishnah: An Introduction* (Northvale, NJ: Jason Aronson, 1989). My own views generally follow those of Neusner.

4. The richest source of examples is provided in Birger Gerhardsson, *Memory and Manuscript: Oral Tradition and Written Transmission in Rabbinic Judaism and Early Christianity,* tr. Eric J. Sharpe (Lund and Copenhagen: Gleerup and Munksgaard, 1961). For a careful analysis of how the Mishnah's forms of expression aid memorization, see Jacob Neusner, *Oral Tradition in Judaism: The Case of the Mishnah* (New York and London: Garland Publishing, Inc., 1987). On the question of the relation of rabbinic oral tradition to written sources, see Hermann L.

Strack and Guenter Stemberger, *An Introduction to Talmud and Midrash* (Edinburgh: T & T Clark, 1991), pp. 35–49.

5. The pioneering discussion of the relation of the Merkavah traditions to those of early rabbinic Judaism is that of Gershom Scholem, *Major Trends in Jewish Mysticism* (New York: Schocken Books, 1961), pp. 40–79. A comprehensive recent study of what rabbinic Sages and disciples knew and did not know about the journey to the Merkavah is that of David J. Halperin, *The Merkabah in Rabbinic Literature* (New Haven: The American Oriental Society, 1980). His is the most careful account of the main rabbinic sources on the Merkavah: Tosefta Hagigah 2:1–7, PT Hagigah 77a-d and BT Hagigah llb–16a.

6. For an up-to-date account of the various hekhalot texts and their major ideas, see Peter Schaefer, *The Hidden and Manifest God: Some Major Themes in Early Jewish Mysticism,* tr. A. Pomerance (Albany: SUNY Press, 1992).

7. A convenient translation of a large section of this material, and a commentary upon it, is offered by David Blumenthal, *Understanding Jewish Mysticism: A Source Reader* (New York: KTAV, 1978), pp. 53–91. My own translations are based upon the texts presented in Peter Schaefer, ed., *Synopse zur Hekhalot-Literatur* (Tuebingen, Germany: J.C.B. Mohr [Paul Siebeck], 1981). For convenience of citation, I use both the traditional chapter numbers (e.g., 15:2) and the paragraph numbers of Schaefer's edition (e.g., par. 199).

8. For an explanation of the relationship of "ascent" to "descent," see Elliot R. Wolfson, *Through a Speculum That Shines: Vision and Imagination in Medieval Jewish Imagination* (Princeton: Princeton University Press, 1994), pp. 82–85. All translations of Maasei Merkavah are based upon the translation found in Michael D. Swartz, *Mystical Prayer in Ancient Judaism: An Analysis of Ma'aseh Merkavah* (Tuebingen, Germany: J.C.B. Mohr [Paul Siebeck], 1992), pp. 224–251.

9. The translation follows that of P. Alexander, in James H. Charlesworth, ed., *The Old Testament Pseudepigrapha, Vol. 1* (Garden City, NY: Doubleday & Company, 1983), p. 263.

10. Ibid., p. 264.

11. Translated following Swartz, *Mystical Prayer,* p. 235.

12. Ibid., p. 236.

13. Ibid., p. 238.

14. Ibid., p. 236.

15. My interpretation of this ritual is dependent upon that of Michael D. Swartz, "Like the Ministering Angels: Ritual and Purity in Early Jewish Mysticism and Magic," *AJS Review* 19 (1994), pp. 135–168. Swartz discusses this and other rituals of the merkavah tradition in great detail in *Scholastic Magic: Ritual and Revelation in Early Jewish Mysticism* (Princeton: Princeton University Press, 1996).

16. David M. Halperin, *The Faces of the Chariot: Early Jewish Responses to Ezekiel's Vision* (Tuebingen, Germany: J.C.B. Mohr [Paul Siebeck], 1988) offers the fullest argument that most of this literature stems from Jews relatively ignorant of rabbinic tradition who felt at a disadvantage in relation to the powerful Sages. His view remains a minority one among specialists in this field.

17. A wonderful introduction to the numerological systems of world religions is that of Annemarie Schimmel, *The Mystery of Numbers* (Oxford: Oxford University Press, 1993). Her discussion of Pythagoreanism is on pp. 11–16.

18. Steven M. Wasserstrom, "Sefer Yesira and Early Islam: A Reappraisal," *Journal of Jewish Thought and Philosophy,* 3 (1993), pp. 1–30, offers a strong argument that the literary style of Sefer Yetzirah—"gnostic encyclopedism"—originates in the

ninth-century milieu of Shi'ite Islam. This would place the editing of Sefer Yetzirah, like the hekhalot literature, after our period.

    As with the hekhalot literature, however, it is likely that much of the tradition
behind the text originated in the latter centuries of the first Judaic millennium.
The Babylonian Talmud, for example, assumes that a Sefer Yetzira contains secrets regarding creation.

19. This translation follows the text published by Ithamar Gruenwald, "A Prelimi-
    nary Critical Edition of Sefer Yezira," in Israel Oriental Studies I (Tel Aviv: Tel
    Aviv University, 1971). A useful translation of all of Sefer Yetzirah, which I have
    also consulted, is that of Blumenthal, *Understanding Jewish Mysticism*, pp. 15–44.
    My enumeration of chapters and verses follows Gruenwald's text.

Concluding
Observations

The portrait of early Judaism drawn in the previous chapters is just that—a portrait rather than the thing itself. A painter produces the impression of a living person by exaggerating certain features and neglecting others. Similarly, this book provides an impression of the religious worlds of Judaism's first millennium by selecting certain features for emphasis and permitting others to remain obscure. Different artists will represent the same person differently; so, too, different historians, asking different sorts of questions, have produced (and will produce) portraits of early Judaism quite different from the present one. This is as it should be. Each portrait of early Judaism that is attentive to the evidence discloses an aspect of its subject that other portraits might neglect. Each contributes to the efforts of other historians to understand early Judaism better by understanding it afresh.

The particular portrait drawn here differs from others in many details of emphasis and interpretation. But there is one crucial distinction that this book shares with relatively few others. By emphasizing the conception of early Judaism as a collection of related, but distinct, religious worlds, it insists that any portrait of early Judaism must be a group portrait. As we argue, early Judaism is *misunderstood* by viewing it as a single body of doctrine and practice originating pure and whole in a flash of revelation.

Thus, we reject the possibility of talking about biblical Judaism as if there had ever been a coherent religious world incorporating all of ancient Israel into its borders. Similarly, we avoid viewing our entire millennium as moving in a straight evolutionary line culminating inevitably in a victorious rabbinic Judaism. To the contrary, we take the earliest form of early Judaism in Persian Yehud and its ultimate form in Sasanian Babylonia as parentheses—limiting cases—within which the patterns of diverse Judaic worlds in between can be examined. What we find between these parentheses is a barely coherent record of human groups struggling to embody more or less articulate visions of what it means to be Israel in a world created and governed by the God of Israel.

The portrait we draw will not in all respects prove attractive to those who live within the contemporary religious worlds of Judaism and Christianity. This is as it should be. The study of early Judaism, happily, has progressed beyond the need to defend modern Jews from the slanders of anti-Semites, secular or Christian. It is no longer necessary, then, to counter hostile caricatures of "pharisaic legalism" with flattering portraits of early Judaism as a religion in tune with the sensibilities of modern styles of religious life and belief.

This book reflects this new freedom from apologetics. It is finally possible, at the close of the twentieth century and the beginning of the twenty-first, to examine early Judaism in a spirit of curiosity about religion rather than out of the need to defend the right of Jews to practice their own Judaism. Freed from an obligation to create a usable past for the modern descendants of rabbinic Judaism, scholars can pay much more attention to the vanished forms of early Judaism as autonomous and legitimate expressions of the possibilities of Judaic religious imagination. Instead of a portrait stressing a harmonious bridge between Judaism "then" and Judaism "now," therefore, this book emphasizes patterns of disharmony and points of intellectual and social stress, a picture of flux and experiment, rather than one of continuity and broadly recognized authority.

Thus, we begin by painting the early history of the scriptural canon as the sum of a millennium of conflict over the nature and meaning of Israel's past and future (Chapter Two). The Bible, in this view, became by the end of our period a principle of Judaic unity. But for most of a millennium it had been a sounding board for every unharmonious chord. These unharmonious chords, in fact, catch our attention repeatedly.

Moreover, rather than stressing Judaic monotheism as a principle of intellectual and moral unity among Jews, we show how the symbolic vocabulary of Judaic monotheism developed in and through dispute about the meanings and implications of serving Israel's God (Chapter Three). The theme of divine unity, it turned out, made for a multiplicity of pictures of reality and Israel's place within the cosmic order.

Our survey of early Judaism's diverse patterns of communal life discloses broad agreement on certain basic traits of identity (Chapter Four). But of far greater importance throughout the millennium were the vigorous disagreements about how best to embody that identity in coherent, and mutually incompatible, ways of living.

On the crucial matter of rituals of worship, our millennium is cut in two by barely congruous patterns of ritual life—those associated before 70 CE with the Temple sacrifices and those associated in subsequent centuries with prayer in the synagogue and home (Chapter Five). Such continuity and uniformity that existed depended not upon shared ritual acts, but upon the Temple-oriented metaphors that governed the understanding of prayer. Finally, even at the end of its first millennium, early Judaism offered no universal conception of the highest goals of religious transformation toward which Jews might aspire (Chapter Six). Different ritual paths led people into significantly independent types of personal knowledge.

In sum, this book uses the interpretive methods of the modern humanities to firmly root our picture of early Judaism in the cultural structures of its own time and place. We encounter the arcane concerns of ancient peoples. Our connection to them has been grounded solely in our common humanity. Like those who lived in early Judaic worlds, we, too, must live in a world. By exploring the manner in which early Judaism constructed its own worlds, it is possible to have clearer insight into the constructed character of our own worlds. By reflecting upon the ways Jews found, or failed to find, nourishing connections to the foundations of the universe, we become ever more aware of the nature of our own gropings toward those connections.

But no world constructed by contemporary people can be equivalent to any of the worlds of early Judaism. And no contemporary scholarly portrait of the worlds of early Judaism can be identical to those actual worlds. Only with difficulty can any aspect of early Judaism be selectively appropriated by the modern faithful as a foundation of their own attempts to dwell in a religious world. Pulling one thread from the weave of early Judaism will unravel the whole cloth; yet it will produce no new garment.

This book, therefore—unlike more than a few others—makes no claim to interpret the religious truth of Judaism as contemporary ears might wish to hear it. Its sole goal is to ensure that the study of Judaism in the context of the contemporary university continues to find its home where it ought to be—in programs and departments devoted to the critical study of humanity's religious traditions from a comparative and historical perspective. This is, in other words, an "academic" book for those learning how to think with the critical and interpretive tools of the humanities.

The future of Judaism outside the life of the humanities—that is, in the living worlds of Jews—will not be secured by books such as this one. The future of Judaism cannot be found in the excavated remains of early Judaism. Rather, that future lies, as it has lain for well over two millennia, in the hands of those who seek God's living Presence in the Torah and who attempt to draw that Presence into the lives of their communities. They will have little need for this book. For, as the Sages often remarked in their discussions of the past: *mai d'hava hava*, "what was—was!"

Index